THE GREAT THE LATE
(ALMOST)
UNITED STATES
OF
AMERICA!

THE GREAT THE LATE
(ALMOST)
UNITED STATES
OF
AMERICA!

LELAND M. STENEHJEM, JR.

XULON PRESS

Liberty Hill Press
2301 Lucien Way #415
Maitland, FL 32751
407.339.4217
www.libertyhillpublishing.com

Printed in the United States of America.

Paperback ISBN-13: 978-1-6312-9527-0
Hardcover ISBN-13: 978-1-6312-9528-7
Ebook ISBN-13: 978-1-6312-9529-4

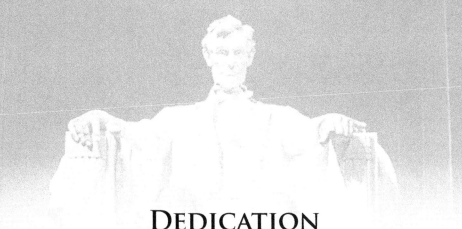

DEDICATION

This book is dedicated to my wife, Sue, who has always been my best friend and biggest supporter, through the good times and the not-so-good times. She has been my rock. I strive to be the same for her every day

This book is also dedicated to our grandchildren and to our nieces and nephews and to their children who follow them. It is also dedicated to all the children of the United States and to children everywhere of every gender, race, and national origin. They are the ones that will be the beneficiaries of the greatness of this country if it can be maintained, or the victims of its decline if the generation(s) before them do not take them into account in enacting the policies that determine the fate of the country. It is the author's hope that this book will help people understand the conservative philosophy and how important it is to the survival of this great country.

INTRODUCTION

This book was supposed to be completed before the 2016 election between Hillary Clinton and Donald Trump. The polls indicated that Mrs. Clinton would be the victor. If Mrs. Clinton had won and if the Democrats would have won the Congress, it was the author's belief that the future of the United States would be in doubt. The tax-and-spend precedent, heavy regulation, increase in entitlements, and failure in foreign affairs policies would have continued. That would lead to economic disaster and the continuing diminishment of the United States' reputation around the world. The Democrats would have continued to add people to the rolls in entitlement programs, which would have given them more voters, solidifying their power going forward to continue policies that do not work.

Hence the title "The Great The Late (A*lmost*) United States of America."

With the election of President Trump, and the control of the House of Representatives and the Senate in Republican hands, the Republicans showed the electorate the difference between Democrat control and Republican control. In the mid-term election of 2018 the Democrats gained a majority in the House of Representatives while the Republicans maintained control of the Senate. The Democrats are doing everything they can to discredit President Trump while not talking about his tremendous accomplishments in turning the economy around and making the

United States once again respected in the world. The Democrats in the House will not pass any legislation for fear that they would give President Trump a victory. They care more about defeating President Trump than about what is in the country's best interest. They hate President Trump more than they love their country! Under this scenario, and if they succeed, the "Almost" will need to be removed for we will then truly be "The Great, The Late, United States Of America!

CONTENTS

1

CONSTITUTIONAL BLESSINGS

"We the people of the United States, in Order to form a more perfect Union, establish Justice, insure domestic Tranquility, provide for the common defence, promote the general Welfare, and secure the Blessings of Liberty to ourselves and our Posterity, do ordain and establish this Constitution for the United States of America."

So begins the Preamble of our Constitution.

This country has been blessed. It has been blessed by geography. Being separated from the other continents by considerable spans of water has helped protect us from some of the wars and disputes that would have embroiled us had we not been separated by so much water. More recently, the oceans have become less important, but they are still a formidable force in keeping us at a distance from those who would do us harm. We have also been blessed by our location on a continent with friendly neighbors to the north and the south. The one exception is Cuba, which has not, with the exception of a period in the early '60s, been a major threat

1

to us. While we are having border difficulties with Mexico, at least we have not had to worry about military attacks from them.

We have been blessed by productive soil, abundant natural resources, and weather that enabled the hard-working immigrants to produce food, shelter, and power to provide for the growth of the country. They ventured into the vast wildernesses of this country, often at great personal peril from other people or animals that would do them harm, from weather (floods, drought, blizzards, tornadoes), from geography (deserts, mountains), or from the myriad other dangers that the frontier people endured.

Immigrants came from all over the world. Those immigrants wanted to become a part of the United States of America, with an emphasis on the word *United*. They came from all parts of the world with their own languages and customs. Over time they learned our language and our customs, subordinating their own language and customs to those in their new land. Because of this we became a "melting pot" where all the different languages and customs came together under one United States. This has enabled us to remain *United*.

Founding Fathers

We have been blessed because the founding fathers understood the evils of the government that had ruled them and were determined to have a completely different form of government. The founding fathers gathered in 1776 to draft the documents that gave direction to—and the framework of—our system of government. They used their experience, having lived under a tyrannical government, to design a new government to be run on a set of principles that were based on individual liberty and limited federal power. They drafted and signed the Declaration of Independence, the Constitution, and the Bill of Rights that created a limited federal government and that recognized the powers of the states. They created a federal government with legislative, executive, and judicial branches. Throughout most of our history, the branches have recognized and appreciated the authority of the others.

Limited Federal Government

The founders of this nation realized the importance of decisions being made at the lowest possible level in the Declaration of Independence and in the United States Constitution. They had been operating under a tyrannical central government and did not want the citizens of this country to be subject to the same type of system.

The Constitution is the supreme law of the United States. It is the framework for the organization of the United States government, for the relationship of the federal government to the states, and for the relationship of the federal government to all of the people in the United States. It was adopted on September 17, 1787, by the Constitutional Convention in Philadelphia and ratified by Conventions in each state. Amended twenty-seven times, the first ten amendments of the Constitution are known as the Bill of Rights. Eleven of the thirteen states ratified it, and the government began to operate in New York City on March 4, 1789. It is the second oldest Constitution still in use by any nation in the world after the 1600 Statutes of San Marino.

The Tenth Amendment to the United States Constitution declares: "The powers not delegated to the United States by the Constitution, nor prohibited by it to the States, are reserved to the States respectively, or to the people." The federal government had no power. Thus, the founders gave some powers to the federal government but they did not give the states all of the other powers— they were *reserved* to the states—thus recognizing that the states had them already. The Constitution recognizes that the people were bestowing certain powers on the federal government—not the other way around. It established a government based on the delineation of power between the national and state governments and "We the People." This states the Constitution's principle of federalism by providing that powers not granted to the federal government, nor prohibited to the states by the Constitution, are reserved to the states or to the people.

Thomas Jefferson said that: "Congress has not unlimited powers to provide for the general welfare but only those specifically enumerated." And James Madison said: "The powers of the federal government are enumerated; it can only operate in certain cases; it has legislative powers on defined and limited objects, beyond which it cannot extend its jurisdiction."[1]

President Ronald Reagan, the fortieth president of the United States, described the relationship between the levels of government in his first Inaugural Address:

> So as we begin, let us take inventory. We are a nation that has a government, not the other way around. And this makes us special among the nations of the Earth. Our government has no power except that granted to it by the people. It is time to check and reverse the growth of government, which shows signs of having grown beyond the consent of the governed.
>
> It is my intention to curb the size and the influence of the Federal establishment and to demand recognition of the distinction between the powers granted to the Federal Government and those reserved to the States or to the people. All of us need to be reminded that the Federal Government did not create the states; the States created the Federal Government.

Now so there will be no misunderstanding, it's not my intention to do away with government. It is rather to make it work—work with us, not over us; to stand by our side, not ride on our back. Government can and must provide opportunity, not smother it; foster productivity, not stifle it.

If we look to the answer as to why for so many years we achieved so much, prospered as no other people on Earth, it was because here in this land we unleashed the energy and individual genius of man to a greater extent than has ever been done before. Freedom and the dignity of the individual genius of man to a greater extent than has ever been done before. Freedom and the dignity of the individual have been more available and assured here than in any other place on Earth. The price for this freedom at times has been high, but we have never been unwilling to pay that price.

A conservative believes that the mandate of the Constitution limiting the power of the federal government should be followed and that the less regulation there is from the federal level, the better. To a liberal, the more regulation there is from the federal level, the better. Liberals believe the Constitution is an outdated document. They believe that it should be interpreted in view of the political or moral feelings of society at the time. Their choice would be to have activist judges.

Conservatives believe that the Constitution is as valid today as it was when adopted more than two hundred years ago. Laws should be interpreted according to the wording of the Constitution and its background when it was adopted. Conservatives would have traditional judges who would take the literal wording of the

Constitution in deciding cases. If something is not prohibited or permitted by the wording of the Constitution, justices should not legislate what their beliefs are, or the beliefs of the political party to which they belonged at the time. That is why one of the most important powers of the president is to appoint judges to the Supreme Court and other federal courts. One of the most important powers of the United States Senate is to approve or disapprove of the President's choice(s).

A Constitution does not have the same force and effect as a law passed by Congress and signed by the President. *It is a higher authority.* If the judges on the Supreme Court do not believe in interpreting the Constitution as it is written, but instead they are swayed by what the justices believe is the political tide, or their political beliefs, they are not a Supreme Court. They are another branch of the legislature—a *super legislature*—over the House and the Senate and the president.

Thomas Jefferson also said, with regard to the Supreme Court: "The purpose of a written constitution is to bind up the several branches of government by certain laws, which, when they transgress, their acts shall become nullities; to render unnecessary an appeal to the people, or in other words a rebellion, on every infraction of their rights, on the peril that their acquiescence shall be construed into an intention to surrender those rights." He also said "...the opinion which gives to the judges the right to decide what laws are constitutional and what not, not only for themselves in their own sphere of action but for the Legislature and Executive also in their spheres, would make the Judiciary a despotic branch."[2]

Rather than having activist judges, the proper course of action, if the states and the people want to have a provision amended or added to the Constitution, is to follow the process mandated therein and have the Constitution amended (as it has many times throughout its history).

The Constitution does not have to be rewritten. It needs to be reread.

Decisions Should Be Made At The Lowest Possible Level

A conservative believes that decisions should be made at the lowest possible political level. That could be at the township, borough, city, county, parish, or whatever other level exists that has the power to make decisions for the community. The basis for this belief is that no one knows the local area, local problems, local economy, and local people better than those who live there. They are the ones who know better the quality of the schools and the teachers, what family or individual needs help, the state of the economy, or the condition of the local infrastructure, than those who do not live there.

At the local level, especially in the smaller communities, people serving the community in elected positions often do so for little or no money, believing that their service can be beneficial to the area. They may have contact with their constituents on a daily or weekly basis, and they may know most of their constituents and those who work in the area, whether in farming, construction, service, business, a profession, or at the local school(s). They know firsthand what is happening in their community.

State governments are at the next level, farther removed from the people than the layers of government below them, but still closer to the people than those serving at the federal level. The farther that you take decision-making from those who know the conditions the best, the less likely that help is going to be given to those who need it or that needed work gets done in the best and most efficient manner. Moreover, the farther you get from the area being affected, the more people and the larger the bureaucracy that is needed to administer whatever the program happens to be.

Individual Freedoms

The American Revolutionary War, also known as the American War of Independence, began as a conflict between Great Britain and its thirteen colonies that had declared independence as the United States of America. It lasted from April 19, 1775, to September 3, 1783. [3] It was a war for independence, not only for the colonies, but for the citizens of those colonies. The American people were strongly independent. They wanted to do things for themselves. As a result the founding fathers had a passion for freedom for all individuals. They had lived under a repressive government and saw what happened to freedom under such a system. Great Britain was a long way across an ocean. The American people did not want people an ocean away regulating them, taxing them, and telling them how to live their lives.

When the Constitution was approved and sent to the states for ratification, some states disapproved because of a lack of a specific statement of rights and some demanded that a Bill of Rights be added to the Constitution. Some states ratified the Constitution only conditionally, i.e., that they would approve the Constitution only if certain rights were included.

The Bill of Rights was added to the Constitution as the first ten amendments two years after the new government began. Five freedoms and five rights make up the Bill of Rights. They are the Freedom of Religion, the Freedom of Speech, the Freedom of the Press, the Freedom of Assembly, the Freedom of Petition, the Right to Bear Arms, the Non-Quartering Right (the right not to have a soldier in a time of peace to be quartered in any house), the Right to Equal Justice, The Right to Own Private Property, and the right to enjoy many other freedoms. The last one, the Ninth Amendment, states that the list of rights contained in the Bill of Rights is not complete so there are many other rights that Americans enjoy, e.g., the freedom to freely live and travel anywhere, to work at any job for which they can qualify, and to marry and raise a family.[4]

President Ronald Reagan, the 40th President of the United States, said: "Freedom is never more than one generation away from extinction. We didn't pass it to our children in the bloodstream. It must be fought for, protected, and handed on for them to do the same, or one day we will spend our sunset years telling our children what it was once like in the United States where men were free." He also said: "Man is not free unless government is limited."[5]

Individual Responsibility

When the United States was founded, part of that moral base was the requirement that people take care of themselves and their family. "Individual freedom demands individual responsibility."[6]

If they needed something that they could not provide for themselves, they got together and traded with neighbors. If a neighbor needed help because of illness, injury, or death, or if they lost a crop or something to fire, or if for any other reason they required assistance, the other neighbors pitched in to help and provide whatever the family needed. If someone needed help building a house or a barn or some other structure, the neighbors would pitch in. Men, women and children would all participate. As the population in an area grew, neighbors would get together to build a home, a church, a school or another community building.

In farm country today there are examples every year of farmers coming to the aid of other farmers that for some reason—health issues, death or absence as examples—are unable to plant, care for, or harvest their crops. There are also examples daily on ways that people in larger areas come together to help other people in need. With the devastation caused by floods, hurricanes, and tornadoes in recent years, more examples of people putting aside their concerns and going to the aid of those affected by weather issues have occurred. We have all been heartened by scenes of people boating or wading through water to save people and to help them remove damaged property from homes. People have opened up their homes to others and donated property or money to individuals or to charities to help those in need.

To succeed, democracy requires individual responsibility. Only with individual freedoms, individual responsibility, and limited federal power could the new government, or any government, survive and prosper for any length of time. Everyone needs to have a goal of taking care of themselves and their family. Starting at a young age, kids must be encouraged to do their best and given moral support to do their best. Whether they try hard and fail, or do well, they must be congratulated and encouraged to continue to try to do their best.

Mothers and fathers are responsible for at least their children. They are responsible for teaching their children values that will help them throughout their lives. Some of these values are honesty, integrity, character, proper treatment of others, the value of education, the value of hard work, and the value of a religious base. Parents, relatives, teachers, school administrators, coaches, and other role models must preach the message of individual responsibility—not individual dependence—and a message of hope.

Freedom Of Religion

This nation was founded upon the principle of God-given rights. Conservatives believe in the importance of religion in their daily lives. Faith was important to the Founding Fathers of the new country and the importance of a strong faith was recognized by them in the founding documents of the United States of America. The First Amendment to the Constitution of the United States demands that "Congress shall make no law respecting an establishment of religion, or prohibiting the free exercise thereof."

The United States was founded on the principle that God, not government, is the source of our fundamental rights. Our founders stated this principle in the Declaration of Independence:

> We hold these truths to be self-evident, that all men are created equal, that they are endowed by their Creator with certain unalienable rights, that among these are life, liberty and the pursuit of happiness. That to secure these rights, governments are instituted among men.

In his farewell address in 1796, after serving as our first president, President George Washington advised:

> Of all the dispositions and habits, which lead to political prosperity, Religion and Morality are indispensable supports. In vain would that man claim the tribute of Patriotism, who should labor to subvert these great pillars of human happiness, these firmest props of the duties of Men and Citizens. The mere politician, equally with the pious man, ought to respect and to cherish them. A volume could not trace all connections with private and public felicity. Let it simply be asked: Where is the security for property, for reputation, for life, if the sense of religious obligation desert the oaths which are the instruments of investigation in courts of justice? And let us with caution indulge the supposition that morality can be maintained without religion. Whatever may be conceded to the influence of refined education on minds of peculiar structure, reason and experience both forbid us to expect that

national morality can prevail in exclusion of religious principle.[7]

A few years later, President John Adams, agreed with President
Washington: "Our Constitution was made only for a religious
and moral people. It is wholly inadequate for the government of
any other."[8]

Liberals do not believe in freedom of religion, at least for
Christians and Jews. They have seen to it that Christians have not
been able to practice their religious principles in a number of ways.
For example, bakeries, bed and breakfast inns, photography shops,
and florists have all been forced to serve same-sex couples; a church
has lost its New Jersey tax-exempt status for its refusal to rent a part
of its facilities for a same-sex civil union ceremony; and in Illinois,
the state government refused to renew contracts with Catholic
Charities and other faith-based adoption agencies because they
would place children only with heterosexual married couples. In
addition, the Internal Revenue Service has engaged in harassment
of numerous conservative groups and a post-graduate counseling
student in Michigan was expelled from the program for asking if
she could refer a homosexual client to another counselor. If she
could not properly represent that person, or any other person with
whom she disagreed (such as one side of a domestic dispute) that
alone is enough of a reason to decline representation. She should
not have been expelled for acting ethically.

In all of the instances mentioned above, there were other options
for the supposedly aggrieved persons from other businesses or persons. However, that was not enough for the liberals. They wanted to
eliminate the right of Christians to practice their religious beliefs
and they succeeded. They wanted to make a point to continue the
elimination of the right to exercise one's religious beliefs as guaranteed by the United States Constitution.

Evangelical colleges, Christian societies, Evangelical churches, a Jewish university, and a Baptist-affiliated organization have all lost the right to practice their religious beliefs. The Chief of Atlanta's Fire Department was fired for exercising his religious beliefs.

There are other examples of liberals' actions against Christians. Because owners of a business had expressed religious beliefs at some time in the past, they are trying to take away the businesses' right to exist. Liberals have urged that Home Depot be boycotted. They have also attempted to boycott and to prevent Chick-fil-A from opening new franchises in Boston and Chicago. After the attempted boycott of Chick-fil-A, their sales rose 12 per cent.

This type of intimidation has only one goal—to eliminate freedom of religion and the practice of religious beliefs, at least by Christians, in the United States. Big government programs like the Obamacare mandate which forced the Little Sisters of the Poor to purchase contraception, including abortion-producing abortion drugs, and sterilization coverage for their employees, is one example of the government trying to force people of faith to engage in behavior that is in violation of their religious beliefs. [9]

However, the liberals have no problem with whatever Muslims want to do.

Over the years, the liberals have done everything they could to take religion out of our everyday lives.

A federal judge threatened participants in a high school graduation ceremony, including the valedictorian, with jail time if there was a prayer offered at the ceremony. [10]

This is a statement that was read over the PA system at the football game at Roane County High School, Kingston, Tennessee by school Principal Jody McLoud, on September 1, 2000.

It has always been the custom at Roane County High School football games to say a prayer and play the National Anthem to honor God and Country.

Due to a recent ruling by the Supreme Court, I am told that saying a prayer is a violation of Federal Case Law.

As I understand the law at this time, I can use this public facility to approve of sexual perversion and call it an alternate lifestyle, and if someone is offended, that's OK.

I can use it to condone sexual promiscuity by dispensing condoms and calling it safe sex. If someone is offended, that's OK.

I can even use this public facility to present the merits of killing an unborn baby as a viable means of birth control. If someone is offended, it's no problem.

I can designate a school day as earth day and involve students in activities to religiously worship and praise the goddess, mother earth, and call it ecology.

I can use literature, videos and presentations in the classroom that depict people with strong, traditional, Christian convictions as simple minded and ignorant and call it enlightenment.

However, if anyone uses this facility to honor God and ask Him to bless this event with safety and good sportsmanship, Federal Case Law is violated.

This appears to be inconsistent at best, and at worst, diabolical.

Apparently, we are to be tolerant of everything and anyone except God and His Commandments.

Nevertheless, as a school principal, I frequently ask staff and students to abide by rules that they do not necessarily agree. For me to do otherwise would be inconsistent at best, and at worst, hypocritical. I suffer from that affliction enough unintentionally. I certainly do not need to add an intentional transgression.

For this reason, I shall render unto Caesar that which is Caesar's and refrain from praying at this time. However, if you feel inspired to honor, praise and thank God, and ask Him in the name of Jesus to bless this event, please feel free to do so. As far as I know, that's not against the law—yet.

AND ... one by one, the people in the stands bowed their heads, held hands with one another, and began to pray. They prayed in the stands. They prayed in the team huddles. They prayed at the concession stand. And they prayed in the announcer's box. The only place they didn't pray was in the Supreme Court of the United States of America—the seat of "justice" in the one nation under God.

Somehow, Kingston, Tennessee, remembered what so many have forgotten ... we are given the Freedom OF Religion, not the Freedom FROM Religion.

Praise God that His remnant remains![11]

Alexis de Tocqueville was a French diplomat, political scientist, and historian. One of his best known works is "Democracy in America." He analyzed the improved living standards and social conditions of individuals in western societies.[12] "He noted Liberty cannot be established without morality, nor morality without faith." "Society is endangered not by the great profligacy of a few, but by the laxity of morals amongst all." [13]

Monsieur de Tocqueville also said:

> I sought for the greatness and genius of America in her commodious harbors and her ample rivers—and it was not there...in her fertile fields and boundless forests and it was not there . . . in her rich mines and her vast world commerce—and it was not there . . . in her democratic Congress and her matchless Constitution—and it was not there. Not until I went into the churches of America and heard her pulpits aflame with righteousness did I understand the secret of her genius and power. America is great because she is good, and if America ever ceases to be good, she will cease to be great.[14]

General Douglas MacArthur, one of the greatest Army generals in United States history, had this to say about religion:

> The issues which today confront the nation are clearly defined and so fundamental as to directly involve the very survival of the Republic. Are we going to preserve the religious base of our origin, our growth and our progress, or yield to the devious assaults of atheistic or other anti-religion forces? Are we going to maintain our present course toward State Socialism with Communism just beyond or

reverse the present trend and regain our hold upon our heritage and freedom? I am concerned for the security of our great Nation; not so much because of any threat from without, but because of the insidious forces working from within.

Are we going to continue to yield personal liberties and community autonomy to the steady inexplicable centralization all (sic) political power or restore the Republic to Constitutional direction, regain our personal liberties and reassume the individual state's primary responsibility and authority in the conduct of local affairs? Are we going to permit a continuing decline in public and private morality or re-establish high ethical standards as the means of regaining a diminishing faith in the integrity of our public and private institutions? [15]

Dr. Benjamin Carson, a black man who journeyed from humble beginnings to become a gifted neurosurgeon, is now the United States Secretary of Housing and Urban Development. He had this to say about religion at the National Prayer Breakfast on May 20, 2014.

. . . we don't want to go down the pathway as so many pinnacle nations that have preceded us. I think particularly about ancient Rome. Very powerful. Nobody could even challenge them militarily, but what happened to them? They destroyed themselves from within. Moral decay, fiscal irresponsibility. They destroyed themselves. If you don't think that can happen in America, you get out your books and you start reading, but you know, we can fix it.

Dr. Carson, has also said we should:

> ". . . resist this war on God, the forced cleansing
> of religious and moral principles from public life.
> He views this as an "absolutely absurd" assault on
> freedom of speech and religion. "Let's everybody
> believe what they want to believe,' he countered.
> "And that means, P.C. police, don't you be coming
> down on people who believe in God and who
> believe in Jesus." [16]

What better foundation for a new country than religion—than a belief in God—of a Higher Being. Religion provides a strong moral base for its believers. Without a strong moral base, people are free to do whatever they want—whatever feels good at the time.

Clayton Christensen, Professor at the Harvard Business School, posted the following on YouTube. It is transcribed here:

> Some time ago I had a conversation with a Marxist
> economist from China. He was coming to the end
> of a Fulbright Fellowship here in Boston and I asked
> him if he had learned anything that was surprising
> or unexpected. Without any hesitation he said yeah.
> I had no idea how critical religion is to the func-
> tioning of democracy. The reason why democracy
> works, he said, is not because the government was
> designed to oversee what everybody does but rather
> democracy works because most people most of the
> time voluntarily choose to obey the law. In her past
> most Americans attended a church or a synagogue
> every week and they were taught there by people
> who they respected. My friend went on to say that
> Americans followed these rules because they had

come to believe that they weren't just accountable to society, they were accountable to God. My Chinese friend heightened a vague but nagging concern at Harvard inside that as religion loses its influence over the lives of Americans, what will happen to our democracy? Where are the institutions that are going to teach the next generation of Americans that they too need to voluntarily choose to obey the laws? Because, if you take away religion, you can't hire enough police.[17]

People wonder why we have so much violence in the country and the world. It comes at a time when the liberals have been gradually eroding the presence of religion in the schools and in our communities. "Let's "resist this war on God, the forced cleansing of religious and moral principles from public life.[18]

There is an erosion in the moral base of our society. As Clayton Christensen said above: "Where are the institutions that are going to teach the next generation of Americans that they too need to voluntarily choose to obey the laws? Because, if you take away religion, you can't hire enough police."

A country without a strong moral base will ultimately collapse from within. "If we ever forget that we are One Nation Under God, then we will be a nation gone under." [19]

Freedom of the Press and Freedom of Speech

The First Amendment to the Constitution of the United States orders: "Congress shall make no law . . . abridging the freedom of speech, or of the press"

Freedom of the Press

In totalitarian countries, i.e. Russia, China, North Korea, Iran, and others, there is no free media, the news being controlled by the government. The citizens in those countries hear what the government wants them to hear and only what the government wants them to hear. The growth of social media has changed this to some extent and people may be able to get news from alternative sources.

The United States Constitution guaranties that we will have free speech and a free press. The practice of democracy requires free speech and a free press.

To work properly a democracy requires an unbiased media, not a biased media. For democracy to work, the citizens—the voters—must be educated on all sides of an issue so that their collective education, backgrounds, experience, and common sense leads to decisions that are in the best interests of the country. After schooling most of the education comes from the media, whether it be by print, audio and/or video. An unbiased media may well be impossible to achieve. If it is not possible, what are the chances of the country surviving? In the absence of that, it requires that all sides of an issue be presented to a broad audience.

The mainstream media is not unbiased. It leans heavily to the left—in favor of liberals. Bias in the mainstream media—the "drive-by media" to some—is responsible for the growth of conservative talk radio shows. The desire for the truth by conservatives—and others—led to this growth. They knew that they were not getting it from the everyday media. Bias in the mainstream media is also responsible for the growth of the Fox News Channel. Conservative talk radio is as popular as ever, and Fox News Channel is one of the—if not the—most watched cable television channel. Commentators such as Rush Limbaugh, Sean Hannity, Mark Levin, Laura Ingraham, Michelle Malkin, Judge Jeanine Piro, the late Charles Krauthammer, and others have led the way.

Without conservative radio and television and other media, the liberals would have a free run in politics. A news media that is biased and presenting the news to only support one side of an issue is not allowing the collective wisdom of the people to prevail. The people cannot be spoon-fed only one side of an issue. People presenting the other side of an issue should not be outshouted or simply ignored so that their message is not heard.

If you doubt that the media is biased, just watch the nightly television news. The networks will have a few reports favorable to the liberals and a few reports that are negative to conservatives. Or, watch CNN and MSNBC and shows like *The View* on ABC. Their new call signs should be "ATN, the Anti-Trump Network." Print media, as exemplified by the New York Times and the Washington Post, also have a heavy bias toward the liberals.

For fun, watch the coverage of NBC, CBS, and ABC on the night of the 2016 election as Donald Trump was winning the election against Hillary Clinton despite opinion polls to the contrary. You would have thought the anchors and the reporters were attending the funeral of a close relative, a clear indication of their bias. Maybe there was a funeral—of Hillary Clinton's political career.

As a more recent example of the bias of NBC, CBS and ABC consider the coverage of the hearings held by the Democrats in the House Intelligence and Judiciary Committees involving the impeachment inquiry of President Trump. The hearings of both committees were covered each day from gavel to gavel. When Michael Horowitz, the inspector general of the Justice Department, released his report on the investigation into the Russian influence on the 2016 election a hearing was scheduled two days later in the Senate to hear his testimony. His report was critical of the actions of the Obama Administration's FBI and Justice Department. When the hearing was held none of the three networks carried live coverage. Fox News Channel had gavel to gavel coverage as it had during the House Intelligence and Judiciary Committees hearings.

The Importance of Education

If the media is biased, the importance of education becomes even more pronounced so that those hearing the news of the day can determine whether what is being said makes sense or whether it does not. If they realize that they are only receiving one side of an issue, they can seek out the other side(s), weigh the arguments, and make an informed decision. They can also find a source of news that gives them both sides of an issue or the side that the liberal media does not.

Conservatives believe in the importance of education. Liberals, too, say they believe in the importance of education. But do they really. Liberals want a big government. What is the best way to achieve a big government? It is by having more and more people dependent on the government for their well-being, more people in the ranks of those not paying taxes and, therefore, with the self-interest of continuing to get government money and not pay taxes.

How do you achieve these goals? By convincing people that they need the government in order to survive, that the reason for their position in life is due to someone else's fault, and that there is no other solution to a problem other than by government intervention. It is also by convincing people that they are entitled to have what other people have regardless of whether they work for it or not. If you believe in a federal solution to all problems, why do you need an educated public? *You don't want them educated on the issues.* You just want to promise them the moon so they will vote for you.

The only hope to stop that is an educated public. The conservative philosophy requires an educated public in order to succeed. It requires an educated public to understand the importance of history and how we have arrived at our present circumstance, the mistakes that have happened in the past so as not to repeat them, and the actions of those who have engaged in attempted conquests of the past so as to remain ever vigilant of that possibility again.

Conservatives understand the importance of economics, the importance of mathematics, the importance of fiscal responsibility, the importance of science and of business, and the importance of fewer regulations.

Citizens must also be aware of the biased media when opinion polls are conducted. Poll participants cannot answer properly if they only get their news from a biased media that writes the poll questions. Therefore, poll results are skewed.

Benjamin Franklin stated: "This will be the best security for maintaining our liberties. A nation of well-informed men who have been taught to know and prize the rights which God had given them cannot be enslaved. It is in the religion of ignorance that tyranny begins." [20]

Freedom of Speech

In addition to the biased liberal media, the liberals are also doing everything they can to stifle freedom of speech. While the president and the Congress cannot do anything to abridge the freedom of speech, in theory anyway, the liberals are trying to do that themselves. One of the greatest examples of this occurs on college campuses. When conservatives are invited to speak on a campus, the liberal professors and students demand that the invitation be withdrawn and that the person not appear. They threaten to not permit the speaker to speak by disrupting the proceedings or by rioting. The sponsors of the speaker, or the college, often capitulate to these demands.

The common childhood chant, "sticks and stones may break my bones but words will never hurt me," apparently needs to be repeated on liberal college campuses. They must be afraid that words will hurt them. Are they afraid that when given another point of view, thinking about it will give them a headache? Are they afraid of being hurt? Or, are they afraid that if a conservative speaks, people will be convinced by the argument and go over to the conservative side?

If that is the case, isn't that the very reason that freedom of speech should permit the discussion? College is a place where ideas are supposed to be shared and debated. One should not be afraid to hear an argument they believe they will not agree with. But why else would they protest a speaker unless they believe that the speaker will be persuasive?

Other examples of liberal attempts to inhibit free speech occur when liberals accost people in restaurants who work for President Trump, or are Republican Members of Congress, and tell them they are not welcome and force them to leave or to simply refuse to serve them. Maxine Waters, a Democrat congresswoman representing Los Angeles, California, urged attendees at a Los Angeles rally to keep pushing back against members of the Trump administration with whom they disagree. She told the people that if they see a member of President Trump's Cabinet in a restaurant, in a department store, or at a gasoline station, they should create a crowd, push back on them and, tell them they are not welcome anymore, anywhere.

Democrats have also released the names of individuals who have donated money to the Trump Campaign and have urged their supporters to confront them and harass them.

In other words, if you are not a liberal, keep your mouth shut or we will get you!

In the "Freedom of Religion" section it was noted that liberals have also encouraged their supporters to boycott businesses that do not support their point of view. This is a "free speech" issue, also. They tried to boycott Chick Fil A and Home Depot. Liberals have also tried to get advertisers on conservative radio/TV programs to cease their advertising with them to get rid of the host and shut them down, just because they disagree with their viewpoints.

Conservatives have also been attacked and injured. Conservative writer Andy Ngo, who is from Asia, has described himself as a gay journalist of color. He was attending a demonstration in Portland, Oregon, in June 2019 when he was kicked, beat in the face and the back of his head with fists and weapons, and hit with milkshakes, eggs, rocks, and possibly pepper spray. "Milkshaking" is a new weapon in terror attacks by liberals and they added quick-drying cement here. In the attack he let go of his camera which was stolen from him. He was taken to the hospital where he was told he may have six months of memory loss from a hemorrhage in his brain. He also had a ripped earlobe. The attack was made by members of Antifa.

The Antifa … movement is a conglomeration of left-wing autonomous, militant anti-fascist . . . groups in the United States. . . The principal feature of antifa groups is their use of direct action, . . . with conflicts occurring both online and in real life. . . They engage in varied protest tactics, which include digital activism, property damage, physical violence, and harassment against those whom they identify as fascist, racist, or on the far-right. . .

Activists involved in the movement tend to be anti-capitalists . . . and subscribe to a range of ideologies, typically on the left. They include anarchists, socialists and communists along with some liberals and social democrats. . .[21]

It is telling that the leaders of the Democrats in the House and Senate, Representative Nancy Pelosi and Senator Chuck Schumer, along with other current Democrat members of the House and Senate, have done nothing to stop these attempts to stifle free speech. It is also telling that former Presidents Obama and Clinton, Vice President Joe Biden, and former Senator and Secretary Hillary Clinton, have done nothing to stop these attempts.

All of the candidates campaigning to be the Democrat nominee for President have, also, not spoken out against these actions.

One has even suggested that President Trump's twitter account be suspended.

If the Democrats succeed in winning the election of 2020 for President and if they get control of the House and the Senate, in conjunction with the liberal media, the conservative point of view will be limited even more.

With that much power, there will be nothing to stop the Democrats from taking whatever actions they want against con-servatives–except the Constitution. Democrats, and their media, will certainly attempt to limit the conservatives message and to stop them stop them from saying anything against the Democrats. Conservatives will be seriously impacted.

Centrist Democrats and Independents must vote with conser-vatives to see that this does not happen.

To which philosophy is education of the most importance? The liberal philosophy, which is afraid of a discussion of ideas, or the conservative philosophy, which welcomes a discussion of ideas?

Political Correctness and Hate Speech

Conflicting with the guarantee of free speech and freedom of the press is the "political correctness" mantra that the liberals have been using to suppress free speech—as always, with the help of their colluding media.

Political Correctness is being defined as: "Adj. Conforming to a belief that language and practices which could offend political sensibilities (as in matters of sex or race) should be eliminated." [22]

"Noun—Avoidance of expressions or actions that can be per-ceived to exclude or marginalize or insult people who are socially disadvantaged or discriminated against." [23]

To outward appearances, the goal of political correctness advo-cates is to not offend anyone. But political correctness is really an attack on free speech. If you have an opinion that differs from others, throughout our history you have been guaranteed the right to speak that opinion. Now however, if you speak your mind, and if that differs from someone else's opinion, they can either engage in a debate or profess to be offended. In the case of a conservative expressing an opinion to which a liberal disagrees, it is easier for the liberal to respond by saying the conservative is being politically incorrect as opposed to discussing the issue on its merits.

The purpose of free speech is to have a free flow of ideas—to find out who is correct and who is incorrect on an issue. You never hear a conservative argue that some argument made by a liberal is not politically correct. A conservative understands the value of free speech. A liberal only understands the value of free speech if he or she agrees with what is being said. By arguing that something is not politically correct, a liberal is trying to cut-off debate on an issue. A liberal is basically conceding that they don't have a legitimate response to counter the argument. It is a way of avoiding a discussion of the matter on its merits.

Again, this is an attempt to muzzle and eliminate discussion on important issues. Conservatives need to have the courage to stick up for, and speak up for, what they believe.

"PC is a doctrine fostered by a delusional, illogical liberal minority, and rabidly promoted by an unscrupulous mainstream media, which holds forth the proposition that it is entirely possible to pick up a turd by the clean end."[24] Another site says this was the winning entry in an annual contest at Texas A& M University in 2007, calling for the most appropriate definition of a contemporary term. [25]

In addition to political correctness, liberals have also come up with the label—"hate speech." The terms *political correctness* and *hate speech* are attempts by liberals to stifle opposition. A person may not believe that people of the same sex should be allowed to marry. A person may not believe that a transgender person should use a public restroom of the sex to which they now identify. A person who owns a bakery may not want to bake a cake for a same-sex couple's wedding. That does not mean that one side hates the other people. It just means that they have different beliefs.

A person may believe in having strong border enforcement and that immigrants should only come into the country by legal means. That does not mean that they hate the immigrants. It just means they disagree on policies.

However, a liberal does not want to debate what is right or wrong. They want to shut off the debate by switching the discussion to attack their opposition personally with the hate argument. Once the hate argument is made, liberals cease arguing a matter on its merits. Liberals believe that everyone should conform to all of their beliefs, that there is no room for disagreement, and that any disagreement with them should be silenced!

The problem is that the *hate tactic* is effective. Who wants to be accused of hating another person or group for whatever reason? Besides, it is easier for those using the hate tactic to outshout those with whom they disagree, especially with the help of the biased media. Liberals would have us believe that they don't hate anyone. But the fact of the matter is that they do. They hate rich people. They hate large financial institutions and the people that work in them. They hate the National Rifle Association (NRA) that works to preserve the right to bear arms. The NRA has millions of members of both political parties, which is thereby non-partisan, but they take on a lobbying group rather than the millions of NRA members.

And, liberals hate conservatives! Liberals have said that Rush Limbaugh, a conservative radio commentator, should go blind and that he should be dead. They said that former Vice President Dick Cheney should not have received a heart transplant which saved his life. As noted earlier, they have accosted members of the Trump administration and Republicans in Congress in restaurants and elsewhere, and they are urged to seek out other conservatives and to make it known that they are not welcome anywhere. They have urged that businesses be boycotted because of the owner's religious beliefs.

Hillary Clinton infamously called people that did not support her "the deplorables" during her campaign for the presidency. Deplorable is defined as "deserving censure or contempt: wretched."[26] That is "hate speech."

Joy Behar, panelist on the ABC show "The View," admitted on television that the reason that the media is so negative toward President Trump is because they hate him!

But does anybody ever call them out on it? Do the liberals get called out on that by the media? They do not! The support of the media is a major aid to those using "political correctness" and "hate" tactics.

Accusing conservatives of "racism" or "sexism" is another way that the liberals and their colluding media are trying to further their agenda. Whenever a conservative disagrees with a liberal of color they are accused of being racist—that the only reason the conservative disagrees with the person is because of their race. Conservatives that did not vote for Barack Obama were accused of doing so because they were racist. Nothing could be further from the truth. Just as when they had not voted for other liberals like Jimmy Carter and Bill Clinton, they voted against President Obama because they disagreed with his positions—not because they were racists. Conservatives who did not vote for Hillary Clinton did not vote because for her because they were sexists, but because they did not agree with her positions just like when they had not voted for other liberals.

The liberals and their media are arguing that any time a Republican white man, or white woman, disagrees with a black man or black woman, that is evidence of racism. If a Democrat white man or white woman, disagrees with a black liberal, that is not racism.

Democrats are claiming that all of President Trump's supporters are also racists. President Trump received about 63 million votes in the 2016 election. Those supporters included men and women of all ages, people of all races and sexual orientation, and Democrats.

The claim is ridiculous!

But the Democrats keep repeating this and their colluding media keeps supporting them

All of these are additional evidence of their attempts—the Democrats and their colluding media—to stifle free speech.

Any attempts to stifle freedom of speech must be stopped. It keeps people from saying what they think. It puts a muzzle on them and hinders or stops any discussion of important issues.

As Thomas Paine, one of the Founders of the United States said: "He who dares not offend cannot be honest."[27]

Here is the irony: the censurers, the radicals who are all too ready to deny freedom to those who disagree with them are perceived in our culture as "tolerant," and we, who want to express our views, are viewed as "intolerant." In other words, the philosophy of the left is preach tolerance, but practice inflexible intolerance to anyone who has the courage to express a different point of view.[28]

Journalism Ethics and Standards

Journalism ethics and standards comprise principles of ethics and good practice as applicable to journalists. This subset of "media ethics" is widely known to journalists as their professional "code of conduct" or the "canons of journalism." The basic codes and canons commonly appear in statements drafted by both professional journalism associations and individual print, broadcast, and online news organizations.

While various existing codes have some differences, most share common elements including the principles of truthfulness, accuracy, objectivity, fairness, and public accountability. . .

Journalism is guided by five values:

1. Honesty: journalists must be truthful. It is unacceptable to report information known to be false, or report facts in a misleading way to give a wrong impression;
2. Independence and objectivity: journalists should avoid topics in which they have a financial or personal interest . . .
3. Fairness: journalists must present facts with impartiality and neutrality, presenting other viewpoints and sides to a story where these exist. It is unacceptable to slant facts;
4. Diligence: a journalist should gather and present pertinent facts to provide a good understanding of the subject reported;
5. Accountability: a journalist must be accountable for their work, prepared to accept criticism and consequences. . .

One of the leading voices in the U.S. on the subject of journalistic standards and ethics is the Society of Professional Journalists. The Preamble to its Code of Ethics states:

. . . public enlightenment is the forerunner of justice and the foundation and democracy. The duty of the journalist is to further those ends by seeking truth and providing a fair and comprehensive account of events and issues. Conscientious journalists from all media and specialties strive to serve the public with

thoroughness and honesty. Professional integrity is
the cornerstone of a journalist's credibility.[29]

Daily, the "principles of truthfulness, accuracy, objectivity, fairness, and public accountability are violated by liberal print, broadcast and online reporters and organizations. They do not meet their
duty of providing fair and comprehensive accounts, of serving with
thoroughness and honesty, and serving with professional integrity that is the cornerstone of a journalist's credibility. They are so
wrapped up in their biases that they are violating the principles
that govern them.

They either have no appreciation for the freedom of the press
and the freedom of speech, and its importance in the working of
this republic, or they are so governed by their biases that they do not
care. They are feeding the citizens that listen to them with a biased
view of only one side of an issue. It is impossible for a republic to
work under these circumstances. The only hope for the republic is
for the citizens who listen to them to be smart enough to look for
the other side of the issues by listening to other sources. If they have
not listened to or watched conservative outlets, they should at least
give them a try. While some of them concentrate on the conservative principles, others, through panels made up of both liberals and
conservatives, air both sides of an issue.

Where are the deans and the professors in the journalism
schools? Where are the heads of the networks and other media
networks who should be preventing their anchors and reporters
from supporting the liberals across the board? The obvious answer
is that they have the same biases of their reporters and anchors.
Where are those that should be speaking out about all of the violations of journalism ethics?

The liberals are obviously taking this course of action because
they do not have the arguments that can counter what President
Trump and the Republicans are accomplishing. And they do not

care what parts of the Constitution, and our rights, that they trample on and eliminate in the process.

Conservative commentators and reporters are pointing out these wrongs, but will it be enough?

The Liberal Media is Colluding with the Democrats

But there is a further problem with the liberal bias. The liberal media is "colluding" with the liberals to reach the goals of the liberals. "Colluding" means to "cooperate in a secret or unlawful way in order to deceive or gain an advantage over others. . . Synonyms are: "conspire, connive, intrigue, be hand in glove, plot, participate in a conspiracy, collaborate, scheme. . . ." [30]

Robert Mueller was appointed special prosecutor to investigate Russian's involvement in the 2016 election. Daily, the liberals and their media argued that there was "collusion" between the Trump Campaign and the Russians to influence the 2016. Mr. Mueller concluded after a two-year investigation and after spending millions of dollars, that there was no collusion between the Trump Campaign and the Russians.

The only "collusion" going on was between the liberals and the biased media to bring down President Trump.

Media Bias Favors the Democrats

Investor's Business Daily published an editorial entitled "Media Bias: Pretty Much All Of Journalism Now Leans Left, Study Shows" on November 16, 2018.

> Media Bias: Ask journalists, and they'll tell you they play things right down the middle. They strive to be "fair." They're "centrists." Sorry, not true. The profound leftward ideological bias of the Big Media

is the main reason why America now seems saturated with "fake news." Journalists, besotted with their own ideology, are no longer able to recognize their own bias.

Despite journalist's denials, it's now pretty much a fact that journalism is one of the most left-wing of all professions...

Researchers from Arizona State University and Texas A & M University questioned 462 financial journalists around the country. They followed up with 18 additional interviews. The journalists worked for the Wall Street Journal, the New York Times, Washington Post, Associated Press and a number of other newspapers...

When you add it up, 58.47 % admit to being left of center. Along with that, another 37.12 % claim to be "moderate."

What about the mythic "conservative" financial journalist? In fact, a mere 0.46% of financial journalists called themselves "very conservative," while just 3.94 % said they were "somewhat conservative." That's a whopping 4.4 % of the total that lean right-of-center.

That's a ratio of 13 "liberals" for every one "conservative." Whatever happened to ideological diversity? Please remember this as you watch the business news or read a financial story in the paper. You might want to take its message with a grain of salt.

That's especially true if the piece seems unduly harsh on the free-market system and its many proven benefits. Or if it lauds socialism as the "answer" to society's ills.

This is an enormous problem for the media—perhaps bigger than they realize. A Rasmussen Reports survey in late October found that 45 % of all likely voters in the midterm elections believed "that when most reporters write about a congressional race, they are trying to help the Democratic candidate."

Just 11 % said the media would try to help the Republican. And only 35 % said they thought reporters simply try to report the news in an unbiased way.

Rasmussen notes that this "helps explain why Democratic voters are much bigger fans of election news coverage" than others. They see it is favorable to their own beliefs. . .

It wasn't always this way. A long-term study of reporters' leanings and attitudes, "The American Journalist in the Digital Age," shows that the drift toward liberalism has been going on for years within journalism. In 1971, Republicans made up 25.7 % of all journalists. Democrats were 35.5 %, and independents were 32.5 %. Some 6.3 % of responses were "other."

By 2014, the year of the last survey, the share of journalists identifying as Republican had shrunk to

7.1 %, an 18.6 % drop. From having near-parity with the journalist Republicans in the 1970s, Democrats outnumber Republicans today by four to one. . .

A Reader Turn Off?

Bad news for journalists, and bad news for journalism. Because as Americans continue down their path of growing mistrust of the mainstream media, they will start looking for alternatives.

Will they find new, more trustworthy sources of news? Or will they just turn it off entirely? Either one is not good for journalists, or good for America.

It's time the journalistic mainstream addresses this problem. Smug denial is no longer an option. It starts with owners, publishers and editors demanding fairness in their reporting and weeding out obvious bias. While they're at it, they should elevate the idea of unbiased news coverage to a goal, even if it's not attainable.[31]

Another article has concluded that:

As newspapers have dwindled, internet publishers have added employees at a bracing clip. . . In late 2015 . . . for the first time, the number of workers in internet publishing exceeded the number of their newspaper brethren. Internet publishers are now adding workers at nearly twice the rate newspaper publishers are losing them.

This isn't just a shift in medium. It's also a shift in sociopolitics, and a radical one. Where newspaper jobs are spread nationwide, internet jobs are not. Today, 73 percent of all internet publishing jobs are concentrated in either the Boston-New York-Washington-Richmond corridor or the West Coast crescent that runs from Seattle to San Diego and on to Phoenix. The Chicago area . . . captures 5 percent of the jobs, with a paltry 22 percent going to the rest of the country. And almost all the real growth of internet publishing is happening outside the heartland, in just a few urban counties, all places that voted for Clinton. . .

As the votes streamed in on election night, evidence that the country had further cleaved into two Americas became palpable. With few exceptions, Clinton ran the table in urban America, while Trump ran it in the ruralities. And as you might expect, Clinton dominated where internet publishing jobs abound. Nearly 90 percent of all internet publishing employees work in a county where Clinton won, and 75 percent of them work in a county that she won by more than 30 percentage points. When you add in the shrinking number of newspaper jobs, 72 percent of all internet publishing or newspaper employees work in a county that Clinton won. By this measure, of course, Clinton was the national media's candidate . . .

If current trends continue—and it's safe to predict they will—national media will continue to expand

and concentrate on the coasts, while local and regional media contract.[32]

Another report also studied the bias of journalists. The Center for Public Integrity:

> . . . which examined donations by journalists to Donald Trump and Hillary Clinton during the presidential primaries and the first month of the 2016 general election campaign reported that more than 96 percent of those donations were made to Clinton. . .

> In 2016 the trust in media by both Democrats and Republicans changed once again. According to Gallup news, "Democrats trust and confidence in the mass media to report the news "fully, accurately and fairly" has jumped from 51 % in 2016 to 72 % this year. . . while Republicans is unchanged at 14 %. . . In 2017, a Gallup poll found that the majority of Americans view the news media favoring a particular political party; 64 % believed it favored the Democratic Party, compared to 22 % who believed it favored the Republican Party.[33]

Educators' Bias Favors the Democrats

A 2018 study found that 10 professors are affiliated with the Democrat Party for every faculty member who is registered as a Republican. At 39 percent of the colleges there were no Republicans. Broken down by gender, there were 21 female Democrats for every female Republican and 7 male Democrats for every male Republican.[34]

There have also been studies of bias in K-12 schools:

> While it is unsurprising that among actors and actresses there are 90 Democrats for every 10 Republicans many would be amazed to discover that teachers are actually as liberal or even more so than those in acting...

> Dr. Greg Forster, Friedman Fellow at the school-choice organization Ed Choice and a top education researcher, last year wrote that university education schools indoctrinate future teachers in left-wing ideology.

> Peruse the course catalog of any major education school, or read the Twitter fees of the professors, observes Forster and you will "find yourself swimming in an ocean of hard-left ideology critical theory that says there is no truth only power; 'intersectionality' that says you're not allowed to be right about anything unless you're right (that is left) about everything; cheerleading for every fashionable left-leaning cause."

> Forster notes, "The central concept in the ideology that rules education schools, with an iron fist is that real pedagogy means the liberation of the oppressed."

> Forster emphasizes that in the prevailing worldview at education schools, "Liberation means left-wingery because left-wingery means liberation."...

A study by the then-chair of the education policy department at Boston university and the literacy director of the Bedford, MA public schools of top-ranked university schools of education, which was contemporaneous to my own research, found that The Pedagogy of the Oppressed was one of the most frequently assigned books in philosophy of education courses.

Is it any wonder then that the products of these schools and their courses are now manning strike lines and pushing leftist curricula on children? [35]

Bias from Cradle to Grave

From the first days of school children are confronted by liberal bias. That continues throughout their attendance in school from grade school through college. As they become interested in the world around them and start to listen to or read about the news of the day, they are then confronted by more bias by those providing network news or other mainstream media outlets.

It becomes imperative for them, as it is for all Americans, to seek out all of the news so that they can determine the facts—the truth.

The survival of the United States is at stake!

The Right To Keep And Bear Arms

The Second Amendment to the United States Constitution provides: "A well-regulated militia, being necessary to the security of a free State, the right of the people to keep and bear arms shall not be infringed."

The shooting at an elementary school in Newtown, Conn, stirred up a slew of gun-control sentiment in Hollywood. But Samuel Jackson, an actor who stars in perhaps the most gun-heavy movie of the season (when the shooting occurred), says that an abundance of firearms in this country isn't necessarily the problem, and that reducing them isn't automatically the answer.

> "I don't think it's about more gun control. . . I grew up in the South with guns everywhere and we never shot anyone. This (shooting) is about people who aren't taught the value of life. "Parents and role models who emphasize that value," he said, "will accomplish more than legislators reducing the number of firearms." [36]

Since then there have been more shootings at schools, theatres, offices and elsewhere. These are horrific events, causing parents and families to lose children, children to lose parents and siblings, spouses to lose spouses, friends to lose friends, and communities to lose teachers and others.

After these events there is hurt, sorrow, anger, other emotions, and a feeling of helplessness. Rightly, so. What to do?

When there is a shooting death, liberals cry for more gun control. They blame it on the gun. They blame it on an object that by itself is not harmful. The liberals make the weapon the issue, not the shooter. The liberal agenda always goes after the symptom, never the underlying issue

Chicago has one of the highest levels of gun violence and some of the strongest gun control laws in the country. A lot of their violence is due to gang activity involving blacks against other blacks. In 2019, there were 510 homicides and 358 of them were African Americans. Of those, 315 were African American males. But that receives very little national publicity. Rahm Emmanuel, who recently was the mayor of Chicago and who was once President Obama's chief of staff, is a black man. The current mayor is Lori Lightfoot, an African American woman. Shouldn't there be an outcry against this violence that happens every week, at least as loud as the outcries that occur when there is a shooting involving a police officer and a black person? The lack of an outcry leads one to conclude that they are either trying to cover it up, that they do not know what to do, or they just do not care.

On the weekend of August 3 and 4, 2019, there were mass shootings in El Paso, Texas, and Dayton, Ohio. In response, Ohio Governor Mike DeWine announced a number of new proposals to curb gun violence. A number of them involved mental health, to include: early intervention in schools where there are warning signals in school-aged children; using funds to tackle students' social and emotional issues and to increase access to behavioral and health professionals; a more active role for students and teachers in prevention; more teachers going through training to recognize threats of violence and tools to help them intervene; a larger role for mental health and addiction services in communities to help parents identify risk factors and connect them to resources to help their child's wellness; freeing up space in psychiatric hospitals for those who really need help; helping religious and nonprofit organizations to fortify their facilities; expanding the monitoring of social media to identify potential warning signs with a follow up on potential threats; and to increase penalties and minimum sentences to those who commit felonies with firearms, felons who illegally possess firearms, and those who sell firearms to minors or to those who cannot buy a gun themselves.

Kelly Guthrie Raley has been teaching for twenty years and currently educates kids at Eustis Middle School in Lake County, Florida. She was named the 2017–2018 Teacher of the Year. The day after the horrific shooting that took place at Marjorie Stoneman Douglas High School in Parkland, Florida, what she posted on

Facebook has gone viral. In the post, she talked about parental responsibility, compassion, and respect. Here is what Ms. Raley had to say:

> Okay, I'll be the bad guy and say what no one else is brave enough to say, but wants to say. I'll take all the criticism and attacks from everyone because you know what? I'm a TEACHER. I live this life daily. And I wouldn't do anything else! But I also know daily I could end up in an active shooter situation.
>
> Until we, as a country, are willing to get serious and talk about mental health issues, lack of available care for the mental health issues, lack of discipline in the home, horrendous lack of parental support when the schools are trying to control horrible behavior at school (Oh no! Not MY KID. What did YOU do to cause my kid to react that way?), lack of moral values, and, yes, I'll say it—violent video games that take away all sensitivity to ANY compassion for others' lives, as well as reality TV that makes it commonplace for people to constantly scream up in each other's faces and not value any other person but themselves, we will have a gun problem in school. Our kids don't understand the permanency of death anymore!!!
>
> I grew up with guns. Everyone knows that. But you know what? My parents NEVER supported any bad behavior from me. I was terrified of doing something bad at school, as I would have not had a life until I corrected the problem and straightened my ass out.

My parents invaded my life. They knew where I was ALL the time. They made me have a curfew. They made me wake them up when I got home. They made me respect their rules. They had full control of their house, and at any time could and would go through every inch of my bedroom, backpack, pockets, anything!

Parents: it's time to STEP UP! Be the parent that actually gives a crap! Be the annoying mom that pries and knows what your kid is doing. STOP being their friend. They have enough "friends" at school. Be their parent. Being the "cool mom" means not a damn thing when either your kid is dead or your kid kills other people because they were allowed to have their space and privacy in YOUR HOME.

I'll say it again. My home was filled with guns growing up. For God's sake, my daddy was an 82nd Airborne Ranger who lost half his face serving our country. But you know what? I never dreamed of shooting anyone with his guns. I never dreamed of taking one! I was taught respect for human life, compassion, rules, common decency, and most of all, I was taught that until I moved out, my life and bedroom wasn't mine; it was theirs. And they were going to know what was happening because they loved me and wanted the best for me.

There. Say that I'm a horrible person. I didn't bring up gun control, and I will refuse to debate it with anyone. This post wasn't about gun control. This was me, loving the crap out of people and wanting the best for them. This was about my school babies and knowing that God created each one for greatness, and just wanting them to reach their futures.

It's about 20 years ago this year I started my teaching career. Violence was not this bad 20 years ago. Lack of compassion wasn't this bad 20 years ago. And God knows 20 years ago that I wasn't afraid daily to call a parent because I KNEW that 9 out of 10 wouldn't cuss me out, tell me to go to Hell, call the news on me, call the school board on me, or post all over Facebook about me because I called to let them know what their child chose to do at school because they are a NORMAL kid!!!!!

Those 17 lives mattered. When are we going to take our own responsibility seriously? [37]

We are advised to not judge all Muslims by the actions of a few lunatics, but we are encouraged to judge all gun owners by the actions of a few lunatics!

2

UNITED STATES ECONOMY

Free Markets

Conservatives believe in free markets. There is no perfect free market. The freer the market the smaller the government involvement, the lower the taxes, and the fewer the regulations. That is what conservatives strive for. Liberals, on the other hand, believe in big government involvement, higher taxes, and higher regulations.

Two important parts of free markets are capitalism and entrepreneurship. "Capitalism generally means an economic system in which all or most of the means of production are privately owned and operated, and the investment of capital and production, distribution and prices of commodities (goods and services) are determined mainly in a free market, rather than by the state. In capitalism, the means of production are generally operated for profit."[38]

An entrepreneur is "a person who organizes and manages any enterprise, especially a business, usually with considerable initiative and risk.[39]

Entrepreneurs are, by nature, dreamers. They are willing to be leaders, to take risks, to try new things, to look for needs in the marketplace, and to determine how to fulfill those needs. And, importantly, they are willing to take action to pursue their dreams.

Entrepreneurship, broadly speaking, includes the processes used in discovering a need and then the processes after that to meet that need. It could be in products or services, it could be in social areas, or it could be in areas such as reaching for space or the moon.

Inventors have the same mindset. They are looking for products or machines that can make our lives better or safer. Their actions can precede or coincide with actions of entrepreneurs and/or capitalists.

The United States, and the world, are full of well-known examples of invention and entrepreneurship. Early examples can include developing the wheel, devising a buggy whip, electricity, internal combustion engines, flying machines, railroads, jet engines, rockets, and telephones. In more modern times, examples include computers, the internet, IBM, Microsoft, Apple, Google, Facebook, Intel, smart phones, and millions of other things we could name.

Just look around. Nearly everything that you see was developed by an entrepreneur, whether you are in your house, your office, your workplace, or driving down the street. Entrepreneurship is now being taught at a number of colleges and universities, to include the award-winning Center for Entrepreneurship and Innovation at the University of North Dakota. In addition, the Dakota Venture Group "is the first completely student run venture capital fund in the United States. It is unique because DVG is the first fund where students complete all due diligence, make the final investment decision, and negotiate the deal's term structure. By participating in Dakota Venture Group UND students receive an unheard of opportunity for experiential learning in the field of venture capital and angel investing." [40]

The entrepreneur could also be a capitalist, or he/she could team with a capitalist. The United States was built on capitalism and entrepreneurship. They are both based on freedom. The capitalists and entrepreneurs need to be free to think and to dream of how things can be done better. What better place to do that than in a new country that would throw off the yoke of oppression and taxation from a government that was just using them for its own goals and its own revenues? That freedom enabled the new economy to take root, to be nourished, and to grow into the economic engine that became the best in the world, something that had never been seen throughout history. It has become the biggest and most important economy in the world.

Capitalists and entrepreneurs can turn an investment into multiples of that investment. Within the United States, the economy enabled our citizens to reach a standard of living higher than any other place on earth. Our economy enabled us to send men to the moon and to ultimately see the end of the Cold War and the tearing down of the Berlin Wall. It enabled us to build roads and infrastructure and equip and maintain the best armed force in the world. It enabled us to develop the best health care system in the world and some of the best technology in the world. It has enabled us to provide billions of dollars in assistance to other countries around the world—not to expand our territory but to keep the hope of freedom alive throughout the world.

The United States economy is strong enough that it drives business cycles in other areas around the world. Everything we are able to do as a country requires a strong and vibrant economy. If we are going to improve our standard of living, improve our infrastructure, improve our education system, maintain our armed forces, and continue to provide our assistance to needy citizens and other nations, we are going to need a strong economy. Mess with the economy and mess with those who take chances to provide us products and services, take away the profit incentive, increase taxes and regulation, and watch the economy slow down to the level of the Union of Soviet Socialist Republics at the end of the Cold War.

With their big government philosophy, getting the government involved more and more in people's lives takes precedent to the liberals over a booming economy. People and businesses react to federal legislation and executive actions. If you raise the minimum wage, people will lose jobs and business will make do with fewer employees. If you pass a law requiring that businesses employing over a certain number of full-time employees must provide health insurance, businesses will reduce the number of full-time employees. Pass a law that permits a regulator to fine a bank for mistakes in trying to follow a regulation, and the banks may quit offering those services. Make the regulations on an industry so complicated that businesses live in fear of not complying with all of the regulations or make them so onerous that they are difficult to comply with, businesses will exit that industry or their owners will sell. But to liberals this is not important.

For entrepreneurs to exist and to do their work, the taxes and the regulations have to be bearable to them. They are in the business of taking risks. If taxes and regulations are too high, they will not take risks.

Throughout most of our country's history, the belief in individual freedom, limited government and limited regulations prevailed. This enabled the young and growing country to develop its towns, cities, and states and to have a citizenry that was concerned with taking care of themselves, their families, and their neighbors and retaining the money with which to do so. This enabled the capitalists and the inventors and the entrepreneurs to be born and to grow and to take their ideas and their money to establish businesses that were able to grow to hire tens if not hundreds or even thousands of people. It allowed those same entrepreneurs and capitalists to expand this country from the Atlantic to the Pacific, from Mexico to Canada, whether by horse and wagon, by train, by automobile and finally by airplane.

If the new country had not limited the size of the federal government, and if the citizens had been regulated by the government, none of the growth in the economy since our founding would have occurred. If our founders had been believers in a big federal government, their laws and regulations and willingness to tax-and-spend taxpayer dollars would have killed the economy before it even started.

In his first inaugural address, President Reagan stated, "In this present crisis, government is not the solution to our problem; government is the problem."

The United States Budget–Federal Debt and Deficit

President John F. Kennedy famously said: "Ask not what your country can do for you. Ask what you can do for your country."

The federal deficit is the amount of money that is spent each year that exceeds the amount of revenue. The federal debt is the cumulative amount of money that the federal government owes from the failure to have a balanced budget over the years.

During the 2008 election candidate Barack Obama blamed the $8 trillion in debt on President George W. Bush, the forty-third president of the United States, and said that that level of debt was unpatriotic. When the debt reached $16 trillion during his administration, President Obama said that level was not a problem, and his fellow Democrats said the same thing. When President Obama left office, the debt was over $20 trillion. The $8 trillion in debt was the total amount amassed under all of our presidents from George Washington to George W. Bush. It took over two hundred years to reach $8 trillion in debt, and it only took President Obama four years to increase it by a like amount, and only a few more years to reach $20 trillion.

Conservatives believe in a strong military. To fund the military we need a strong economy. One of the major benefits of a strong economy is to have low unemployment numbers so that the need for federal spending on welfare types of needs are reduced.

Democrats and liberals do not believe in a strong military. They would rather spend less money on defense and more money on welfare or entitlement types of programs. There is never an end to the projects that the liberals want to fund at the federal level, and they don't want to eliminate or cut existing programs. Now that they have made people dependent on the federal government in the different areas, they can't take existing programs away for fear of losing their constituents. Regardless, the rich do not have enough money to pick up the tab. The so-called rich are paying some 80 percent of the taxes now! Since about 50 percent of the people do not pay taxes, it is going to be difficult to start taxing them now. So, what is the alternative?

If you are not going to cut spending to reduce the deficits and the debt, the only alternative is growing the economy. By growing the economy, even at the same tax rates, tax revenues to the federal government will increase. However, without reducing spending or at least putting a cap on it, it is highly unlikely that increased revenues from a growing economy would be sufficient to eliminate the yearly deficit and the total federal debt. Even if the federal spending level was capped each year going forward, the deficit and the debt would continue to grow until the increased revenues from a growing economy were sufficient to make up the difference.

President Obama and the Power Democrats' solution to getting the economy moving in 2009 was using federal stimulus dollars—to spend more federal money than they were already spending. President Obama liked to point to the automobile industry as an indication of the success of the stimulus money. When the automobile industry received the stimulus money, some of the major benefits went to the automobile labor unions, one of the key Democrat constituencies. By choosing the unions, President Obama chose to force many business owners of dealerships to lose their franchises and their businesses, which is another instance of the Democrats choosing to help one of their constituency groups at the expense of businesspeople and entrepreneurs.

Additionally, some of the stimulus money was going to be spent on so-called "shovel-ready projects." President Obama learned after he spent so much time touting the money going to "shovel-ready projects" that there were no such things. Regulations prevented the "shovel-ready projects." Regulations cost time and money.

Federal regulations affect every area of our economy. Increasing regulations affect businesses and they increase costs, make it more difficult to make a profit, increase the risks of doing business, and may lead to businesses being sold. Regulations imposed on banks is one area where the federal government has gone overboard with regulations, to include the home mortgage area. Banks need to have compliance officers to cover all of the areas that are regulated. With regard to home mortgage regulations, fear of not complying with the regulations and the fines that may be imposed if they have not been in compliance have driven some banks, especially the smaller banks, out of the home mortgage business. Those laws and regulations do keep the Consumer Finance Protection Bureau in business and give them the time to think up more areas where consumers supposedly need to be protected from business. Those laws and regulations increase the size of the bureaucracy needed to handle them. In many cases, the weight of the regulations has led many small bank owners to merge or to sell, leading to the concentration of banking in larger institutions.

Spending and Morality

In July 2014, Walter E. Williams wrote the following essay on spending and morality. Mr. Williams is a black Professor of Economics at George Mason University.

> . . . let me offer you my definition of social justice: I keep what I earn, and you keep what you earn. Do

you disagree? Well then tell me how much of what I earn belongs to you—and why?

During last year's budget negotiation meetings, President Barack Obama told House Speaker John Boehner, "We don't have a spending problem." When Boehner responded with, "But, Mr. President, we have a very serious spending problem," Obama replied, "I'm getting tired of hearing you say that." In one sense, the president is right. What's being called a spending problem is really a symptom of an unappreciated, deep-seated national moral rot. Let's examine it with a few questions.

Is it moral for Congress to forcibly use one person to serve the purposes of another? I believe that most Americans would pretend that to do so is offensive. Think about it this way. Suppose I saw a homeless, hungry elderly woman huddled on a heating grate in the dead of winter. To help the woman, I ask somebody for a $200 donation to help her out. If the person refuses, I then use intimidation, threats, and coercion to take the person's money. I then pur- chase food and shelter for the needy woman. My question to you: Have I committed a crime? I hope that most people would answer yes. It's theft to take the property of one person to give to another.

Now comes the hard part. Would it be theft if I managed to get three people to agree that I should take the person's money to help the woman? What if I got 100, 1 million, or 300 million people to agree to take the person's $200? Would it be theft then? What if instead of personally taking the person's $200, I got together with other Americans and asked Congress to use Internal Revenue Service agents to take the person's $200? The bottom-line question is: Does an act that's clearly immoral when done privately become moral when it is done collectively and under the color of law? Put another way, does legality establish morality?

For most of our history, Congress did a far better job of limiting its activities to what was both moral and constitutional. As a result, federal spending was only 3 to 5 percent of the gross domestic product from our founding until the 1920s, in contrast with today's 25 percent. Close to three-quarters of today's federal spending can be described as Congress taking the earnings of one American to give to another through welfare, thousands of handout programs, such as farm subsidies, and business bailouts.

During earlier times, such spending was deemed unconstitutional and immoral. James Madison, the acknowledged father of our Constitution, said, "Charity is no part of the legislative duty of the government." In 1794, when Congress appropriated $15,000 to assist some French refugees, Madison stood on the floor of the House of Representatives to object, saying, "I cannot undertake to lay my finger on that article of the Constitution which granted a right to Congress of expending, on objects of benevolence, the money of their constituents." Today's Americans would crucify a politician expressing similar statements.

There may be nitwits out there who would assert, "That James Madison guy forgot about the Constitution's general welfare clause." Madison had that covered, explaining in a letter, "If Congress can do whatever in their discretion can be done by money, and will promote the general welfare, the Government is no longer a limited one possessing enumerated powers, but an indefinite one." Thomas Jefferson agreed, writing: "[Members of Congress] are not to do anything they please to provide for the general welfare... It would reduce the (Constitution) to a single phrase, that of instituting a Congress with power to do whatever would be for the good of the United States; and, as they would be the sole judges of the good or evil, it would be also a power to do whatever evil they please."

The bottom line is that spending is not our basic problem. We've become an immoral people demanding that Congress forcibly use one American to serve the purpose of another. Deficits and runaway national debt are merely symptoms of that larger problem.

...To find out more about Walter E. Williams and read features by other Creators Syndicate writers and cartoonists, visit the Creators Syndicate Webpage. [41]

President Obama—Increase in Government Entitlements

How much did government entitlements grow under Obama? by Rick Moran (January 15, 2017).

> As President Obama leaves office, one of his major legacies will be the huge increase in the number of Americans who receive benefits from entitlement programs...

> When Obama took office in 2009, there were 60,880,000 Medicaid beneficiaries, according to the Medicaid and CHIP Payment and Access Commission. As of March 2016, there were 74,059,221 enrollees, an increase of over 13 million.

> "Historically, Medicaid eligibility has generally been limited to low-income children, pregnant women, parents of dependent children, the elderly, and individuals with disabilities; however, the Patient Protection and Affordable Care Act included the ACA Medicaid expansion, which expands Medicaid eligibility to individuals under the age of 65 with income up to 133% of the federal poverty level at state option," explains the Congressional Research Service.

> Medicare, which offers coverage to individuals 65 years and older, will cost taxpayers about $701 billion in fiscal 2016. According to program trustees, the Medicare trust fund is projected to face insolvency.

> In 2009, average monthly enrollment for Medicare was 45,466,997. Enrollment rose to 56,873,505 beneficiaries in 2016, an increase of 25 percent...
>
> But by far the biggest increase in beneficiaries was in the SNAP program: The Supplemental Nutrition Assistance Program, otherwise known as the food stamp program, helps low-income individuals purchase food. The program cost taxpayers $70,866,830,000 in 2016.
>
> In 2009, when Obama entered office, 33,490,000 Americans were on food stamps. Eight years later that number had increased to 44,219,000, an increase of nearly 11 million. Recipients of the program received a monthly benefit of about $125. The Department of Agriculture has noted that changes to food stamp policies made it easier to receive benefits...
>
> And should someone living 133% above the poverty line be eligible for free medical care? It just doesn't make any sense.[42]

As a political motive, it was simply to increase the people on welfare, get more people receiving money from the federal government, and making them dependent on the federal government so they would continue to "need" federal money. That is a way to build up your political base and to increase your power. The Democrats are really buying votes. They are using tax dollars to buy votes for the liberals, but is that in the best interests of the United States?

Combine this with the fact that approximately 50 percent of the eligible United States taxpayers do not pay any federal taxes. The other 50 percent pay all of them, and the top 20 percent of earners pay most of the taxes. Isn't this another way of increasing your political base? When 50 percent of the taxpayers are not paying taxes, there is no incentive for them to vote for people who are trying to see that taxpayers' money is spent frugally and wisely, unless they are conservatives who know that the only way for the country to survive is by having a smaller federal government, fewer regulations, and a strong economy.

Power Democrats believe that a big federal government is more important than a strong economy. But, is a big federal government important to the future of the country, or to the future of the Power Democrats who have been using the poor and those they have made dependent upon the government to further their goal of a big federal government. Why else would the Power Democrats refuse to secure our borders in the belief that those who come here illegally will need federal help and thus would continue to vote for the Power Democrats? Power Democrats continue to sell their big federal government line to maintain their positions of power and their positions of wealth and entitlement themselves. As the federal government expands its influence, we become more a socialist system and even a communist system. These give more control over the ownership of the economy to the federal government and take it away from the free market—basically a takeover of the economy by the federal government and severe restrictions on the freedoms of its citizens. The Power Democrats cannot believe that they can do a better job of managing the economy than free markets. It is just a means to an end for them.

Alexis de Tocqueville (1805—1859) was a French historian, journalist, political scientist and government official. He wrote of the American political system in "Democracy in America." The following quote has been attributed to him: "The American Republic will endure until the day the Congress discovers that it can bribe the public with the public's money." [43]

Benjamin Franklin earlier said something similar: "When the people find that they can vote themselves money, that will herald the end of the republic." [44]

> It's not an endlessly expanding list of rights—the "right" to education, the "right" to health care, the "right" to food and housing. That's not freedom, that's dependency. Those aren't rights, those are the rations of slavery—hay and a barn for human cattle. [45]

To determine if this is true you need only to listen to Democrats campaigning for their party's nomination to run for President of the United States in the 2020 general election. They try to out-promise each other. They have promised, for example: I will give you all free college, I will forgive all of your college debts, I will give everyone more time off, I will have free Medicare and universal child care for all, and I will have a universal basic income for all. They makes these promises in exchange for votes.

Ben Franklin and Alexis de Tocqueville made these predictions that our republic will endure only until the citizens learn that they can vote themselves money from the public treasury over 150 years ago. Now, the people that are voting for a large federal government have already learned this and the politicians making promises of federal money have learned it as well.

These political promises in return for votes certainly look like bribes. Many elected officials have been fined and/or sentenced to jail for taking money or other items of value from a citizen in exchange for a vote on a particular issue or for getting them something else of governmental value.

Let's assume that the conversation at a political fund raiser goes like this. Voter says I will vote for you if you forgive my student debt. If he/she wins politician gets a nice salary and many perks.

Politician says I will see that it happens. Politician gets elected and voter receives forgiveness of his student debt worth $20,000.

Is there truly a difference between a politician promising something—money—from the government for a vote, and those instances where a politician has been convicted of taking a bribe.

It seems we constantly hear about how Social Security is going to run out of money. How come we never hear about welfare or food stamps—or aid to illegal aliens—running out of money? The first group "worked for" their money, but the next group did not.

The New Normal

President Obama gave us an example of an economy under a high tax and spend and high regulation environment. The fact is that in a high tax and spend, high-regulation environment under liberals, there is no hope that there will be a growing and robust economy. There may be some growth in Gross Domestic Product (GDP), but it will not be enough to change the standard of living of our citizens and maybe not even maintain the standard of living.

The President Carter years are also a perfect example of what happens under a Democrat administration. When Jimmy Carter was president, there were long lines at gas stations just to get gas. Speed limits on highways were reduced. President Carter went on television and told people to turn down their thermostats in the winter and to wear sweaters or sweatshirts around the house. President Carter was telling people that things were not going to get better, and they should get used to the way things were—the "new normal." There was general discouragement in the country about the future of the country. This led President Carter to give his famous "malaise speech" on July 15, 1979. He said in part:

> I want to talk to you right now about a fundamental
> threat to American democracy. I do not mean our

political and civil liberties. They will endure. And I do not refer to the outward strength of America, a nation that is at peace tonight everywhere in the world, with unmatched economic power and military might.

The threat is nearly invisible in ordinary ways. It is a crisis of confidence. It is a crisis that strikes at the very heart and soul and spirit of our national will. We can see this crisis in the growing doubt about the meaning of our own lives and in the loss of a unity of purpose for our nation.

The erosion of our confidence in the future is threatening to destroy the social and the political fabric of America.

The confidence that we have always had as a people is not simply some romantic dream or a proverb in a dusty book that we read just on the Fourth of July.

It is the idea which founded our nation and has guided our development as a people. Confidence in the future has supported everything else—public institutions and private enterprise, our own families, and the very Constitution of the United States. Confidence has defined our course and has served as a link between generations. We've always believed in something called progress. We've always had a faith that the days of our children would be better than our own.

Our people are losing that faith, not only in government itself but in the ability as citizens to serve as
the ultimate rulers and shapers of our democracy. . .

Looking for a way out of this crisis, our people
have turned to the Federal government and found
it isolated from the mainstream of our nation's life.
Washington, D.C., has become an island. The gap
between our citizens and our government has never
been so wide. The people are looking for honest
answers, not easy answers, clear leadership, not false
claims and evasiveness and politics as usual. . .

Often you see paralysis and stagnation and drift. You
don't like it, and neither do I. What can we do? [46]

At the heart of the internal debate over the administration's future was a memo by Patrick Caddell,
Carter's pollster and resident "deep thinker." "What
was really disturbing to me," he remembered, "was
for the first time, we actually got numbers where
people no longer believed that the future of America
was going to be as good as it was now. And that
really shook me, because it was so at odds with
the American character." Caddell argued that after
fifteen years filled with assassinations, Vietnam,
Watergate, and a declining economy, Americans
were suffering from a general "crisis of confidence."[47]

During the Obama administration, talk of the "new normal"
rose again. One of the proponents of this "new normal" was Robert
Reich, President Obama's Secretary of Labor. When things go
wrong during a Democrat administration, since their plans and

programs do not work, they need to convince people that the current economy is the "new normal" and they will just have to get used to a lower standard of living. The liberals will have to convince voters that they and future generations will have to get by with less because times are going to continue to be tough. They will have to convince voters to lower their expectations. They will have to convince voters that the only way to prosperity is by a bigger government and higher taxes that can give them more money and that "big brother" will always be there to help them and to look after them.

Under this scenario, the liberals believe that there is only so much money in the world and that if you want your share, the only way to get it is by taking it from someone else. They attempt to convince people that they are entitled to something for nothing and that it is okay—morally acceptable—to take from someone else in order to get the entitlement. The someone else is the rich.

Contrast this "new normal" under a Democrat administration with the economy that is happening all around us right now under a conservative Republican administration: historically low unemployment across all categories including women and minorities, rising wages, reduced regulations, increasing salaries and bonuses, increased investment by business, decreasing need for government programs, new trade deals, a stronger military, millions of jobs created, and the list goes on. (See the accomplishments under President Trump in later chapters.)

Redistribution of Wealth

Liberals won't talk about it but one of their primary tenets is the redistribution of wealth in the United States. You redistribute wealth by taking from those who have and by giving to those who do not. The taking is done by government, whether at the state or federal level. The taking is typically done by increasing taxes. High taxes and heavy regulations would lead to an economic slowdown.

The Democrats would bring out the "new normal" argument again and try to convince the citizens that this is the way things are going to be going forward. To paraphrase Pat Caddell, should United States citizens have to live in a country where our children and grandchildren will not have a future as bright as we have had in the past?

The only fix for this is a smaller government, less regulation and lower taxes—main tenets of the conservative philosophy.

Wisconsin

The fiscal problems that have built up over the years at the federal government level have also affected some of our states. Those states have done the same things that the federal government has done to get into a fiscal bind—too much spending, too much taxation, too much taking care of supportive groups, too many programs, too much red tape and regulation, and too much of any number of things.

In taking care of constituent groups and by buying votes, other responsibilities of government have suffered. They cannot be ignored any longer. Our infrastructure to a large extent has been ignored. Roads and bridges need to be repaired, flood protection in many areas needs to be completed, aging pipes under our streets need to be replaced, buildings need to be maintained, computer systems need to be updated, and our security needs to be strengthened, to name a few. There is hope and one need only look to one state for an example of hope, with principles and hard work correcting a situation that had been building for years.

In early 2011, Governor Scott Walker and the Wisconsin Legislature were working on solving the state's budget problems. On January 3, 2011, when he was being sworn in, Governor Walker declared that under his administration state government would do only what was necessary, no more, no less. The state had a deficit of $137 million that was projected to increase to $3 billion plus in the next two years. Of course, all that the Democrats wanted to do was ignore the budgetary problems, increase taxes, and continue their free-spending ways. Governor Walker, a Republican, and the Republicans in the legislature had the power to cut spending instead of raising taxes. In addition, they had the power to limit, if not strip, public unions in the state of the right to bargain collectively.

State unions were some of the persons opposing Governor Walker and the State Legislature in working to solve the problem.

The striking unions did not seem to care at all that the state was facing a budget crisis. They were assuming the state could just raise taxes to take care of their demands. But, that had been done too much in the past and that was the reason for the crisis. Governor Walker and the Wisconsin Legislature were elected to manage the state and its budget. In doing so, they were acting responsibly. They enacted big tax cuts, expanded private school vouchers and froze tuition at University of Wisconsin campuses. They passed laws on concealed carry for gun owners, voter identification at the polls, and work requirements for those receiving public benefits. During Governor Walkers' 8 years unemployment plummeted, they held the line on property taxes, they helped the state business climate to keep and attract businesses, and they started a "rainy day" fund to put the state in a good place financially.

One alternative, if they had not taken the action, was to drop 200,000 people from Medicaid. In taking the actions that he and the legislature took, Governor Walker did not want to cut people's salaries or to increase the amount they spend on health care.

Governor Walker withstood an attempt to recall him. In addition to working on the budget, Governor Walker and the state legislature, among other things, made Wisconsin a right-to-work state that guarantees that no person could be compelled to join a union or pay union dues as a condition of employment which helped the business climate. They also imposed requirements on those receiving public benefits.

Wisconsin ended every year with a budget surplus under Governor Walker. The state ended the 2018 fiscal year with a positive balance of $588.5 million. The state deposited $33.1 million into the state Budget Stabilization Fund. The balance is now $320.1 million, the largest balance in state history and190 times larger than the balance in fiscal year 2010. General fund tax collections and individual income taxes were higher than had been estimated. State expenditures were $174 million less than budgeted.

The policies that Governor Walker and the Legislature had put into place continued to work!

Socialism

A number of the persons campaigning to be the next Democrat to run for President of the United States are arguing that the United States should become a socialist or a democratic socialist country.

Socialism can be defined as:

1: any of various economic and political theories advocating collective or governmental ownership and administration of the means of production and distribution of goods

2a: a system of society or group living in which there is no private property

b: a system or condition of society in which the means of production are owned and controlled by the state

3: a stage of society in Marxist theory transitional between capitalism and communism and distinguished by unequal distribution of goods and pay according to work done. [48]

A few decades ago, Venezuela was one of the richest countries in the world. Daniel Di Martino, an expatriate now in the United States, wrote an article in March 2019 entitled: "How Socialism Destroyed Venezuela."

> Many in the media have blamed Venezuela's worsening humanitarian crisis on corruption, mismanagement, falling oil prices, or U.S sanctions—anything but the rise of socialism in what was once the wealthiest country in South America.
>
> Yet corruption and mismanagement were the direct result of increased government control of the economy—socialism—and in reality lower oil prices and U.S. sanctions have little to do with the crisis. Instead, the mass starvation and exodus faced by Venezuelans are the natural consequence of the socialist policies implemented by dictators Hugo Chavez and Nicolas Maduro.
>
> There are three main policies implemented by Chavez since 1999 that produced the current crisis: Widespread nationalization of private industry, currency and price controls, and the fiscally irresponsible expansion of welfare programs.
>
> One of Chavez's first actions was to start nationalizing the agriculture sector, supposedly reducing

poverty and inequality by taking from rich land-
owners to give to poor workers. From 1999 to 2016,
his regime robbed more than 6 million hectares of
land from its rightful owners.

Nationalization destroyed production in affected
industries because no government has the capacity
to run thousands of businesses or the profit motive
to run them efficiently. Instead, government officials
face incentives to please voters by selling products
at low prices and hiring more employees than necessary, even when that's the wrong industry decision.

Socialism run rampant—not cronyism, corruption,
falling oil prices, or U.S. sanctions—caused the
crisis in Venezuela.

As economic theory predicted, as state control of
the agricultural industry increased, Venezuela's food
production fell 75% in two decades while the country's population increased by 33%. This was a recipe
for shortages and economic disaster. After agriculture, the regime nationalized electricity, water, oil,
banks, supermarkets, construction, and other crucial
sectors. And in all these sectors, the government
increased payrolls and gave away products at low
cost, resulting in days-long countrywide blackouts,
frequent water service interruptions, falling oil production, and bankrupt government enterprises.

Yet taking over the most important sectors of the
economy was not enough for the socialist regime.
In 2003, Chavez implemented a foreign currency

control scheme where the government set an over-valued exchange rate between the Venezuelan currency and the U.S. dollar.

One goal of the scheme was to reduce inflation by overvaluing the currency, subsidizing imported products. But the currency control meant the regime had to ration available U.S. dollars to importers since, at an overvalued (cheap) exchange rate, there was more demand for U.S. dollars than supply. Naturally, a black market for foreign currency emerged and corrupt regime members and lucky individuals assigned cheap U.S. dollars obtained large profits. Even worse, the scheme actually increased inflation since overvaluing the currency reduced government oil revenues in Venezuelan currency, leading the regime to print money to cover the ensuing budget deficit.

The socialist regime also implemented price ceilings on hundreds of basic products such as beef, milk and toilet paper. At artificially low prices, more people were willing to buy these products but the few private factories left—not nationalized—could not profit at the government-capped price, so they reduced or halted their production. Instead of benefiting the poor, price ceilings predictably resulted in shortages that forced them to stand in lines for hours, while supermarket employees and the well-connected obtained the products they needed.

But perhaps the most harmful part of the Venezuelan socialist project is the part that the international

media and leftist figures used to praise most frequently: welfare programs. The socialist regime
created social "missions" aimed at tackling poverty,
illiteracy, healthcare, and more. But despite enjoying
higher government oil revenues due to a tenfold rise
in oil prices from $10 a barrel in 1999 to more than
$100 in 2008, the regime financed a growing deficit
by printing more currency. Expansive welfare programs and massive public-works projects provided
ever-growing opportunities for still greater corruption. Printing money to pay for endless state programs unsurprisingly led to high rates of inflation.

In this way, socialism run rampant—not cronyism,
corruption, falling oil prices, or U.S. sanctions—
caused the crisis in Venezuela. Welfare programs
that were supposed to help the poor actually
increased the cost of living. A foreign currency control that aimed to reduce inflation only increased it
and allowed for massive corruption. And national-
izations that should have given "power" to workers
only left them unemployed and hungry.

Corrupt regimes can certainly cause many problems,
but without socialism, hyperinflation and widespread
shortages are not usually among them. Moreover,
even at today's lower oil prices, Venezuelan oil sells
for two to three times as much as in 1999 adjusting
for inflation. And the only U.S. sanction with some
chance of affecting regular Venezuelans, the ban
on oil imports, has not been in effect for even two
months while inflation and shortages have plagued
the country for years.

So do not make excuses. As Venezuelans have learned over the past 20 years of socialism, "free things" come at a high price.[49]

Compare what has happened to Venezuela with what has happened since Donald J. Trump was sworn in as president in January 2017.

Since President Trump's election, more than 7 million jobs have been added to the economy.

For the first time on record there are more job openings than unemployed Americans.

There are more than 7 million job openings, outnumbering job seekers by more than 1 million.

Nearly two-thirds of Americans rate now as a good time to find a quality job, empowering more Americans with rewarding careers.

This year, the unemployment rate reached its lowest level in half a century.

The unemployment rate has remained at or below 4 percent for the past 21 months.

The unemployment rate for women reached its lowest rate in 65 years under President Trump.

Under President Trump, jobless claims hit their lowest level in half a century.

The number of people claiming unemployment insurance as a share of the population is the lowest on record.

American workers of all backgrounds are thriving under President Trump.

The unemployment rates for African Americans, Hispanic Americans, Asian Americans, veterans, individuals with disabilities, and those without a high school diploma have all reached record lows under President Trump.

The booming economy is putting more money in Americans' pockets.

Wages are growing at their fastest rate in a decade, with year-over-year wage gains exceeding 3 percent for the first time since 2009.

November 2019 marked the 16th consecutive month that wages rose at an annual rate of at or over 3 percent.

Median household income surpassed $63,000 in 2018—the highest level on record.

President Trump's policies are helping forgotten Americans across the country prosper, driving down income inequality.

Wages are rising fastest for low-income workers.

Middle-class and low-income workers are enjoying faster wage growth than high-earners.

When measured as the share of income earned by the top 20 percent, income inequality fell in 2018 by the largest amount in over a decade.

Americans are being lifted out of poverty as a result of today's booming economy.

Since President Trump took office, over 2.4 million Americans have been lifted out of poverty.

Poverty rates for African Americans and Hispanic Americans have reached record lows.

Since President Trump's election, nearly 7 million Americans have been lifted off of food stamps.

Americans are coming off of the sidelines and back into the workforce.

The prime age labor force has grown by 2.1 million under President Trump.

In the third quarter of 2019, 73.7 percent of workers entering employment came from out of the labor force rather than from unemployment, the highest share since the series began in 1990.

President Trump's pro-growth policies are helping businesses of all sizes thrive like never before.

Small business optimism broke a 35-year old record in 2018 and remains historically high.

The DOW, S&P 500, and NASDAQ have all repeatedly notched record highs under President Trump.

President Trump is following through on his promise to revitalize American manufacturing, with more than a half million manufacturing jobs added since the election. [50]

See more examples of President Trump's accomplishments in a later chapter.

The following has been circulating on the internet in various forms:

> An economics professor at a local college made a statement that he had never failed a single student before but had once failed an entire class. That class had insisted that . . . socialism worked and that no one would be poor and no one would be rich, a great equalizer.
>
> The professor then said, "OK, we will have an experiment in this class on the plan."
>
> All grades would be averaged and everyone would receive the same grade so no one would fail and no one would receive an A.
>
> After the first test, the grades were averaged and everyone got a B. The students who studied hard were upset and the students who studied little were happy. As the second test rolled around, the students who studied little had studied even less and the ones who studied hard decided they wanted a free ride too so they studied little.

The second test average was a D! No one was happy.

When the 3rd test rolled around, the average was an F.

As the tests proceeded, the scores never increased as bickering, blame and name-calling all resulted in hard feelings and no one would study for the benefit of anyone else. All failed, to their great surprise, and the professor told them that socialism would also ultimately fail because when the reward is great, the effort to succeed is great but when government takes all the reward away, no one will try or want to succeed.

Could not be any simpler than that.[51]

Daniel J. Mitchell has added the following to this lesson: There are five morals to this story:

1. You cannot legislate the poor into prosperity by legislating the wealthy out of prosperity.
2. What one person receives without working for, another person must work for without receiving.
3. The government cannot give to anybody anything that the government does not first take from somebody, else.
4. You cannot multiply wealth by dividing it.
5. When half of the people get the idea that they do not have to work because the other half is going to take care of them, and when the other half gets the idea that it does no good to work because somebody else is going to get what they work for, that is the beginning of the end of any nation.

I'll make one final point. There are five morals to the story, but there are dozens of nations giving us real-world examples every day.[52]

Will the America that has led in economic development, break-throughs in medicine, science, technology, transportation communication, industrialization and products to serve people, protecting individual rights, and fighting to protect freedom of persons all over the world, continue to provide opportunities for everyone in America and around the world? Will it continue to have a robust economy that will enable it to continue in a leadership capacity in the world?

Or, will all of this come to a screeching halt if those arguing for socialism have their way?

Big Government Run Amok – The Affordable Care Act

When he took office, President Obama promised to have the most transparent administration in history. Sadly, that did not occur. Instead, it became one of the least transparent administrations in history. The passage of Obamacare is a typical example of that lack of transparency. The negotiations on the bill took place behind closed doors by the Democrats. Republicans had no input into the bill since the Democrats controlled the House and the Senate at the time, with Obama as president. The Democrats rammed the bill through the Congress with no Republican votes in April 2010.

No one knew what was in the bill, including the Congress. This led Representative Nancy Pelosi, the Speaker of the House of Representatives and the leader of the Democrats in the House, to famously say: "We have to pass the bill, so we can find out what is in it!" Can you believe a legislator saying that, especially the Speaker of the House?

Republicans had their own ideas as to how to fix what was wrong with health care in the country. They wanted to change the laws without throwing out the entire health care system that had brought about the best health care in the world. It made no sense to throw out the best health care system in the world and start over with a whole new system.

It wasn't just that the Democrats were throwing out the best health care system in the world. They were also attempting to take over one-sixth of the United States economy.

Dr. Ben Carson warned about health care: "If the government can control *that* they can control everything." [53]

Republicans believed that the bill was going to be far more expensive than the Democrats were arguing and that there would be changes in health insurance coverage that would not be as the Democrats were promising.

President Obama promised over and over that if people liked their plan, they could keep their plan. If they liked their doctor, they could keep their doctor. In 2013 millions of Americans received cancelation letters from their insurers. President Obama was challenged on his promise so often that he finally stated "If you like your plan, you can keep it *Period.* If you like your doctor, you can keep your doctor *Period.*" This turned out to be untrue and President Obama and his administration knew that it was not true at the time they were making those promises.

In plain terms, they lied to the American people to accomplish one of their policy objectives—they lied solely for political reasons. Politifact named this claim the Lie of the Year in 2013.

President Obama took executive action to delay some portions of the law until after the 2014 election. He realized the extent of the unpopularity of the law and knew that, if some of these other provisions were implemented prior to the election, they would have a negative effect on voters and possibly cost the Democrats some seats in the Congress. Again, decisions were made based solely on politics. And, more important, decisions were made to deceive the voters into acting contrary to how they otherwise might have acted—the way they would otherwise act for the good of the country.

As the 2016 election was approaching, a number of insurance providers in different states were backing out of offering Obamacare because it was too expensive. Democrats want to have a single-payer system that would be run by the federal government. If they achieve that, your choice of insurance would be what the federal government says you have. You would not have the right to seek the insurance you want from private insurers. That means the government would make decisions about everyone's health care. No longer would the decision be made by a patient and his or her doctor. The decisions would be mandated from Washington.

Life-and-death decisions would be made by government bureaucracies—a faceless and soulless body hundreds or thousands of miles away from you and your doctor. In addition, the government could decide to ration health care. As an example, the government could decide that when you reach a certain age your health care would be limited. Pick an age when that would commence: 50 or 60 or 70 or 80. Or in individual cases, the government could have a "death panel" that could conclude that money should not be spent to help a certain person. The government could have a policy of taking money that would go to help an older person and give it to help younger people.

> This point deserves attention, for if a democratic republic similar to that of the United States were ever founded in a country where the power of a single individual had previously subsisted, and the effects of a centralized administration had sunk deep into the habits and the laws of the people, I do not hesitate to assert, that in that country a more insufferable despotism would prevail than

any which now exists in the monarchical States of Europe, or indeed than any which could be found on this side of the confines of Asia. . .[54]

At least there are still some private insurers in the system. The reduction in the number of carriers is going to adversely affect the cost of health insurance going forward. Conservatives want a health insurance market that has a number of private insurers that would have to compete for business. This would lead to competition in plan offerings, competition in pricing, and competition in customer service. Competition between insurers is the only way to control costs. In a "single payer" system there are no challenges to the cost and that "single payer" alone can set the coverages and the services and the prices to be paid.

Other promises have turned out to be untrue. President Obama promised that the average person would save $2,500 per year on health insurance. Not only did this not happen, but premiums and deductibles and co-pays all increased. In 2017 the Department of Health and Human Services reported that average health insurance premiums doubled since 2013. In 2018 they increased again, from 19 to 32 percent, depending whether they were high-cost plans or the cheapest plans. In addition, millions of people lost their plans, and many lost their doctors as well. Moreover, between 3 and 5 million people lost their company-sponsored health care plans because businesses believed it was more cost-effective to pay the penalty than to provide health insurance to their employees. Their workers could get a better plan through the exchanges.

With the cost of insurance going up, to get lower costs people choose higher deductibles which may lower the cost per month but the bills received later after insurance are higher.

In the years since Obamacare took effect Americans have experienced higher costs in the individual health insurance market. At the same time that premiums more than doubled deductibles also significantly increased. Choices for insurance coverage also fell. In 2019, half as many insurers offered plans through the Obamacare exchanges as offered plans before Obamacare That means that millions of Americans have fewer choices when it comes to doctors in their health care network and higher prices. It also led to a significant increase in the number of people dependent on government run health care. [55]

In a separate act after Obamacare passed, the Democrats passed a law requiring doctors' offices to computerize all medical records. As of October 1, 2013, doctors must choose from 140,000 codes when entering a diagnosis, up from 18,000 codes.

The vast majority of people who have received insurance under Obamacare have enrolled in Medicaid increasing enrollment from 55 million to 74 million from 2013 to 2018, an increase of 34.5 percent. The projected cost of Obamacare and subsidies and Medicaid expansions from 2018 to 2027 totals $4.8 trillion. Before Obamacare was passed health care amounted to 17.2 percent of the U.S. gross domestic product (GDP). It is forecast to reach almost 20 percent of GDP in 2025.

Many doctors, clinics, and hospitals do not accept Medicaid. The result is many millions of Americans will not be able to choose their doctor, their clinic, or their hospital and 30 million are still not insured.

The Democrats continue to push for more government control over health care. But more government involvement will not bring more affordable care to the insured. It would reduce access to care and increase wait times.

As an example, in Canada where the government runs health care in a single-payer system, some wait 10.6 weeks for an MRI, 4.3 weeks for a CT scan, and 3.9 weeks for an ultrasound.

Canada's single-payer healthcare system forced over 1 million to wait for necessary medical treatment last year. That's an all-time record.

Those long wait times were more than just a nuisance; they cost patients $1.9 billion in lost wages, according to a new report by the Fraser Institute, a Vancouver-based think-tank. . .

The leading proponent of transitioning the United States to a single-payer system is Senator Bernie Sanders . . . If Sanders and his allies succeed, Americans will face the same delays and low-quality care as their neighbors to the north.

By his own admission, Sen. Sanders' "Medicare for All" bill is modeled on Canada's healthcare system. On a fact-finding trip to Canada last fall, Sanders praised the country for "guaranteeing health care to all people," noting that "there is so much to be learned from the Canadian system.

The only thing Canadian patients are "guaranteed" is a spot on a waitlist. As the Fraser report notes, in 2017, more than 173,000 patients waited for an ophthalmology procedure. Another 91,000 lined up for some form of general surgery, while more than 40,000 waited for a urology procedure.

All told, nearly 3% of Canada's population was waiting for some kind of medical care at the end of last year.

Those delays were excruciating long. After receiving a referral from a general practitioner, the typical patient waited more than 21 weeks to receive treatment from a specialist. That was the longest average waiting period on record—and more than double the median wait in 1993.

Rural patients faced even longer delays. For instance, the average Canadian in need of orthopedic surgery waited almost 24 weeks for treatment—but the typical patient in rural Nova Scotia waited nearly 39 weeks for the same procedure.

One Ontario woman, Judy Congdon, learned that she needed a hip replacement in 2016, according to the Toronto Sun. Doctors initially scheduled the procedure for September 2017—almost a year later. The surgery never happened on schedule. The hospital ran over budget, forcing physicians to postpone the operation for another year.

In the United States, suffering for a year or more before receiving a joint replacement is unheard of. In Canada it's normal.

Canadians lose a lot of money waiting for their "free" socialized medicine. On average, patients forfeit over $1,800 in lost wages. And that's only counting the working hours they miss due to pain and immobility.

The Fraser Institute researchers also calculated the value of all the waking hours that patients lost because they couldn't fully function. The toll was staggering—almost $5,600 per patient, totaling $5.8 billion nationally. And those calculations ignore the value of uncompensated care provided by family members, who often take time off work or quit their jobs to help ill loved ones.

Canada isn't an anomaly. Every nation that offers government-funded, universal coverage features long wait times. When the government makes health care "free," consumers' demand for medical services surges. Patients have no incentive to limit their doctor visits or choose more cost-efficient providers.

To prevent expenses from ballooning, the government sets strict budget caps that only enable hospitals to hire a limited number of staff and purchase a meager amount of equipment. Demand inevitably outstrips supply. Shortages result.

Just look at the United Kingdom's government enterprise, the National Health Service, which turns 70 this July. Today, British hospitals are so overcrowded that doctors regularly treat patients in hallways. The agency recently canceled tens of thousands of surgeries, including urgent cancer procedures, because of severe resource shortages. And this winter, nearly 17,000 patients waited in the backs of their ambulances—many for an hour or more—before hospital staff could clear space for them in the emergency room.

Most Americans would look at these conditions in horror. Yet Sen. Sanders and his fellow travelers continue to treat the healthcare systems in Canada and the UK as paragons to which America should aspire.

Sen. Sanders's "Medicare for All" proposal would effectively ban private insurance and force all Americans into a single, government-funded healthcare plan. According to Sen. Sanders, this new insurance scheme would cover everything from regular check-ups to prescription drugs and specialty care, no referral needed—all at no charge to patients.

Americans shouldn't fall for these rosy promises. As Canadians know all too well, when the government foots the bill for healthcare, patients are the ones who pay the biggest price.

Sally C. Pipes is president, CEO, and Thomas W. Smith Fellow in Health Care Policy at the Pacific Research Institute. Her latest book is The False Promise of Single-Payer HealthCare. [56]

Maybe that's why almost 60,000 of them visit the United States and other countries for medical care each year.

Instead of changing the world's best health care by taking over 1/6 of the economy, Republicans wanted to keep existing health care with changes that would ensure that the patient and his/her doctor would be in charge instead of the government, that would rely on competition instead of regulation, and that would strengthen market forces rather than weaken them (with the goal of lowering prices). The following are examples of what would comply with these principles: 1) make health insurance completely portable so workers could take their plan with them when they switch jobs; 2) allow smaller companies to pool their risk to get the same discounts from insurance carriers that bigger companies do; 3) allow policies to be sold across state lines to increase competition, just as permitted for automobile insurance policies; 4) increase the amount of money families can save for medical expenses tax-free in a Health Savings Account; 5) medical liability reform to reduce the number of unjustified lawsuits; 6) increase transparency in pricing so patients can compare costs for procedures in an area and (7) turn the money over to the states and let them be free to find ways to reduce costs and provide better services.

> But politicians need to do more than simply oppose. Instead, they must offer a compelling alternative for all Americans, including those with pre-existing conditions. Exit polls show that Americans care deeply about how this country will protect people with pre-existing conditions and make sure they have the care they need.

> Fortunately, conservative policy experts, working together at the national, state, and grassroots levels, have developed just such an alternative.

> The Health Care Choice Proposal would make coverage far more affordable—lowering premiums by up to 32 percent, according to the Center for Health and Economy. Moreover, it would ensure that everyone could access a quality, private coverage arrangement of their choice.

> The proposal relies on a fresh framework. Patients would be able to choose the coverage arrangement

that works best for them from a wide array of options, including direct primary care, short-term limited duration plans, catastrophic coverage, or "gold-plated Cadillac" coverage. Everyone who gets a government subsidy for health care would get new control over those dollars and be able to apply them to a plan of their choice rather than the one a bureaucrat picks for them.

The proposal also would do away with Obamacare's flawed subsidy structure in which insurance companies receive taxpayer subsidies, dollar for dollar, as they raise prices. Instead, federal funds would be placed on a budget and sent to states to help people access a quality private coverage arrangement of their choice—including the vulnerable poor and sick.

Data show that this proposal builds on a promising emerging trend. A Heritage Foundation study found that, when states have been given even a little bit of freedom from Obamacare's mandates, they've been able to lower projected 2019 premiums—in one state by up to 43 percent—while still ensuring that the sick retain access to care. And they're able to do all this without new federal money or micromanagement of the market.

Ninety leading conservatives have already endorsed the Health Care Choice Proposal as the path forward on health reform. This is a sharp change from 2017, when Congress fell short and failed to unify behind an Obamacare replacement plan. Our families cannot afford continued failure.

That's why conservatives created a strong framework on which to build. Efforts to refine and improve this proposal can and will continue. But even in its current form, it offers a way to help Americans suffering under high health costs and fewer choices, a clear alternative to the progressive agenda, and a serious plan to alleviate the health care anxiety in the country. [57]

Finally, there is one more factor that must be considered. Just remember the Democrats' attempts during the Obama administration to use the IRS to limit the activities of non-profit conservative groups. The controversy began in 2013 when an IRS official admitted the agency had been aggressively scrutinizing groups with names such as "Tea Party" and "Patriots." Isn't it interesting that no liberal non-profit groups have "Patriot" in their name! In one case, the IRS agreed in a consent order that it wrongly used heightened scrutiny and inordinate delays and demanded unnecessary information as it reviewed applications for tax-exempt status. The IRS apologized for the treatment.

For the first time, the IRS admitted their discrimination against conservative groups was wrong and unlawful. A three-point declaratory judgment in the case declares "it is wrong" to apply federal tax laws based only on an entity's name, positions on issues or political viewpoint. The judgment says the IRS must act evenhandedly, and politically based discrimination in administering the tax code "violates fundamental First Amendment rights. [58]

The Power Democrats used the power of the United States government, through the Internal Revenue Service, to limit the effectiveness of conservatives. If they are in charge, what's to stop them from cutting or limiting medical treatment to conservatives/Republicans? Look out if you are associated with the Tea Party or some other conservative organization. If the power of the Internal Revenue Service could be used against their enemy, the health care system could as well.

Nobody lost their job over it, and nothing else happened to ensure that it never happens again. The higher-ups in the Democrat Party said it was not their intent to limit the activities of nonprofit conservative groups. If you drink the Democrat tea, I guess you would believe that. But any thinking American knows it is not true.

They tried to use a powerful government agency to stifle opposing political views—another attempt to stifle free speech. If they used health care as their weapon, it would affect the health and the life of their target(s).

3

DEMOCRAT LEADERSHIP OF OUR LARGEST CITIES

Big Democrat Cities—Big Democratic Poverty

I n 2013, Richard Ahlert penned an article entitled "Big Dem Cities—Big Dem Poverty." The Startling Truth about America's Biggest Poverty Centers and the Politics That Produces Them.

> On Sunday's ABC This Week telecast, former House Speaker Newt Gingrich squared off with former Clinton Labor secretary Robert Reich, who tried to blame the increase in poverty over the last five years on the GOP. "Here's the baloney," Gingrich fired back. "Every major city which is a center of poverty is run by Democrats. Every major city. Their policies have failed, they're not willing to admit it, and the fact is it's the poor who suffer from bad government." Unfortunately for the millions of Americans, Gingrich is right on the money.

Here is a breakdown of the ten cities with populations above 250,000 that have borne the brunt of Democratic ideology.

St. Louis's poverty rate is 26 percent overall, and four-in-ten children live in poverty. Like Detroit, the city has experienced a major population decline, from 850,000 in the mid-20th century to 318,000 in 2013. Last year's Annual Performance Report gave the city's public schools a rating of 24.6 percent on a scale of zero to 100 percent. The city, which is also reeling from $640 million in unfunded pension liabilities, is currently rated the third most dangerous large city in the nation. St. Louis's current mayor is Francis G. Slay, who has served since 2001. There hasn't been a Republican mayor in St. Louis since 1949.

Newark, New Jersey's poverty rate is 26.1 percent. Its former mayor, Cory Booker, who was recently elected to the United States Senate, was the latest in a long, unbroken line of Democratic mayors dating back 106 years to 1907. Former Newark Mayor Sharpe James was convicted of five counts of fraud in 2008. Yet he is hardly an anomaly: with the exception of Booker, every Mayor of Newark since 1962 has been indicted for crimes committed during their tenure in office. Between 2005 and 2012, the city's population declined from 281,063 to 278,906, while violent crime totals increased from 2,821 to 3,219.

The residents of Cincinnati, OH are afflicted by a poverty rate of 27.4 percent overall, with a staggering 53.1 percent child poverty rate as of 2012. Former Democratic Mayor Mark Mallory left recently-elected Democrat Mayor John Cranley a $60 million deficit throughout 2012, and an annual budget shortfall of 20 percent, leading many to believe that bankruptcy is imminent. Cincinnati's last non-Democrat mayor, Charter Party member Arnold L. Bortz, served until 1984.

In Philadelphia, Pennsylvania, 28 percent of city residents overall live in poverty, a number that balloons to 40 percent in terms of child poverty. Democratic voter registration outnumbers Republican registration by a six-to-one margin in a city where the last Republican mayor to hold office, Bernard Samuel, was voted out in 1952. Current mayor Michael Nutter is presiding over a city with the lowest credit rating of the country's five most populous cities ($8.75 billion in outstanding debt) and a pension system that is only funded at a level of 47.6 percent. Last March, city officials voted to close 9 percent of the city's public schools due to a five-year $1.35 billion spending gap.

Milwaukee, Wisconsin sports a poverty rate of 29.9 percent overall, including 42.6 percent of children under 18. Like Camden, Milwaukee boasts a track record of non-Republican mayors going back 105 years to 1908. But they weren't all Democrats. In 2011, the city marked the 101st anniversary of the election of Emil Seidel, the first of three Socialist

Party mayors of Milwaukee. Current Mayor Tom Barrett claims the poverty experienced in his city is a "regional problem," but 71 percent of those who live in poverty in a four-county area were concentrated in Milwaukee.

In Buffalo, New York, 29.9 percent of residents overall are living below the poverty level, with children enduring a poverty rate of 46.8 percent, third highest in the nation behind Detroit and Camden. Mayor Byron Brown presides over a city that has lost 11 percent of its population over the last dozen years, due in large part to a stagnating economy. Buffalo's last Republican mayor served until 1965.

In El Paso, Texas, one-in-four live in poverty, rising to 35 percent for children. Oscar Leeser is the 53rd mayor of that city, whose history dates back to 1873. In all that time, the city has never elected a Republican mayor. The proposed 2014 budget asked a 4 percent tax increase, due to what City Manager Joyce Wilson characterizes as "a budget gap too extensive to overcome without significant impact to existing service levels." El Paso's current debt level stands at $893 million.

In Cleveland, Ohio, 36 percent of its residents live in poverty. In 1978, when current U.S. House of Representatives Democrat Dennis Kucinich was mayor, the city became the first one since the Great Depression to default on its debt. It remained in default until 1987. In 2011, the city's credit rating was downgraded by Fitch, due to concerns about the city's struggling economy and shrinking population. Cleveland, whose current mayor is Frank G. Jackson, hasn't had a Republican mayor since 1989. During Jackson's tenure, the police, fire and sanitation departments have been cited for excessive use of force, payroll abuse, and chronic billing problems, respectively.

And then, there is Detroit, Michigan, in a class by itself, with 36.2 percent of residents living in poverty, along with an astounding 60 percent of the city's children in the same boat. The city itself is utterly dysfunctional with $20 billion of debt, 78,000 abandoned homes, collapsing or nonexistent municipal services, and 47 percent illiteracy rate. It is also the most dangerous city in the nation. Yesterday, U.S. Bankruptcy Judge Steven Rhodes allowed his rulings declaring the city eligible for bankruptcy and leaving public employee pensions systems vulnerable to cuts for retirees, to proceed to the U.S. 6th Circuit Court of Appeals. Detroit is on track to becoming the largest city in the nation to go bankrupt. Democrat Dave Bing is the current mayor, representing an unbroken string of Democrats going back to 1962.

Camden, New Jersey rounds out the top ten, with a poverty rate of 42.5 percent, and child poverty rate of 56.7 percent. In one poll, Camden was rated the second most dangerous city in the nation, with gang violence cited as a chief contributing factor. Democrat Dana Redd is the current mayor of the city. Frederick Von Nieda was Camden's last Republican Mayor—he served until 1936.

That's the lineup regarding poverty. Yet there are also eight large American cities facing bankruptcy, a reality that would undoubtedly exacerbate each city's poverty rate. Cincinnati and Camden hold the distinction of being on both lists. The other six cities are Baltimore, Washington, D.C., San Diego, San Jose, San Francisco, and Los Angeles. Note that the last four are in California, the nation's foremost Democratic stronghold. As for Baltimore, it has been run by Democratic mayors and city councils since 1967. Since Washington, D.C's home rule began in 1975, every mayor has been a Democrat...

It's a shame Gingrich didn't have more time to educate Robert Reich. It's even sadder that millions of poor Americans are forced to endure their own "education" regarding poverty on a daily basis, even as Reich and his fellow Democrats refuse to recognize, much less admit, that their odious policies are responsible for it.[59]

Twenty Cities That May Face Bankruptcy after Detroit

Stephen Moore wrote an article entitled "Twenty Cities That May Face Bankruptcy after Detroit."

What do most of these ailing cities all have in common? Well, consider that the vast majority are located in states with forced labor unions, non-right-to-work states.

"Right-to-work laws attract people and businesses," says labor economist Richard Vedder of Ohio University. "Non-right-to-work states repel them." His statistics show that cities in states with right-to-work laws have sturdier tax bases and higher employment levels.

Unions control state legislatures and city halls in non-right-to-work states, so it can become politically paralyzing to try to fix the problem of runaway labor costs.

Another common trait of financially troubled cities: years and years of liberal governance.

For at least the last 20 years major U.S. cities have been playgrounds for left-wing experiments—high taxes on the rich; sanctuaries for illegal immigrants; super-minimum wage rules; strict gun-control laws (that actually contribute to high crime rates); regulations and paperwork that make it onerous to open a business or develop on your own property; crony capitalism with contracts going to political donors and friends; and failing schools ruled by teacher unions, with little competition or productivity.

Starting in the 1970s, Detroit became inhospitable if you wanted to raise a family and send your kids to good schools. Criminal predators also made cities like Detroit unlivable for families with children.

Businesses that provide jobs often faced citywide income taxes that were layered on top of state income taxes.

"Declining cities are jurisdictions that levy local income taxes," a Cato Institute report concluded. Detroit levies a 2.5 percent income tax; New York's is 5 percent.

Another problem has been the decline in family structure that has become acute in so many big cities across the country, from Los Angeles to New York. In many cities, as many as two out of three children are born to a family without a father. As Charles Murray of the American Enterprise Institute has warned, "Single-mother families are a recipe for social chaos."

They are a major factor in high-poverty levels of many U.S. cities, again with Detroit being exhibit A. Welfare reforms have helped, but much work needs to be done to reinstall a culture of traditional two-parent families in urban areas. This would lead to less crime, fewer school dropouts, more businesses, and more social stabilization.

But for all these problems, cities could see a potential renaissance. More empty-nesters in their 50s and 60s are moving back into central cities like Chicago and Boston, New York and Washington, D.C., because of the cultural amenities—fine restaurants, the theater, sports, fashion, and river or lakeside condominium properties. As baby boomers retire, cities may see new populations moving in.

But this creates a Catch 22 for American cities trying to recapture their glory days and attract new residents.

Who wants to pay taxes for retired city workers when they don't provide any services?

These legacy costs are a fiscal millstone. They put cities in a service decline spiral, because current taxes go to retired teachers and other municipal retirees, while city managers and mayors are forced to lay off firefighters, police, and teachers. Detroit has three retired city workers collecting a pension for every two currently working.

The Vallejo, Calif., city manager once told me when that city couldn't pay its bills several years ago, "You have no idea how bad it is here. We are now paying for three police forces: one that is working and two that are retired."

Given that payment of the benefits are often legally guaranteed contracts, bankruptcy may be a salvation for some cities. It is a way to hit the reset button and erase those costs so cities can start over...

So can America's great and iconic cities make a financial and population comeback? The answer is certainly yes, if they can erase from their books the mistakes of 50 years of labor-union political control.

Bankruptcy, strangely enough, may not be the end for cities, but perhaps the dawning of a new urban revival."

Stephen Moore is senior economics writer and member of the editorial board for The Wall Street Journal. [60]

On March 09, 2016, Investor's Business Daily published an article entitle "How Decades of Democratic Rule Ruined Some of our Finest Cities." After describing Flint, Michigan; Detroit, Michigan; Chicago, Illinois; St. Louis, Missouri; Philadelphia, Pennsylvania; Baltimore, Maryland; Oakland, California; and Newark, New Jersey; the Editors reached the following conclusions: "When Democrats are in control, cities tend to go soft on crime, reward cronies with public funds, establish hostile business environments, heavily tax the most productive citizens and set up fat pensions for their union friends. Simply put, theirs is a Blue State blueprint for disaster." [61]

On August 5, 2019, Robert B. Charles, wrote an article entitled "America's 25 Worst Cities are Democrat-Led—The Answer, New Leaders"

What did I discover? America is experiencing the best economy in 50 years, lifting every major minority group with record low unemployment, growth, dollar valuation, and accelerating wages. This should turn the tide in America's cities—but the turn is slow. . .

So what does this tell us. On the numbers, ten incontrovertible things.

First, the top ten homeless cities are sanctuary cities, all led by Democrats

Second, the top ten "most dangerous" are led by Democrats.

Third, the top-25 "most dangerous" are mostly Democrat-led, and among the poorest and least employed, with weak infrastructure, tax base and incentives for private investment.

Fourth, among the 25 "most dangerous," most face stifling poverty of 18 and 39 percent, against a national average of 12.3 percent. These democrat-led cities are America's poorest.

Fifth, most of these cities suffer unemployment rates for 4.4 and 9.3 percent, versus 3.7 nationally.

Sixth, of the 20 "least healthy" cities, all but four are Democrat-led.

Seventh, while these mayors wrestle difficult issues, most oppose policies promoted by President Trump that are bringing prosperity to the rest of the country, such as lower taxes, less regulation, incentives for business investment, stronger law enforcement, cooperation with federal immigration officials, border security, comprehensive anti-drug policies, and local responsibility for declining tax base.

Eighth, most are in anti-gun coalitions, focused on restricting Second Amendment rights, favoring policies at cross-purposes with allowing citizens to protect themselves. While each is different, many favor gun-control, bans on concealed carry and higher minimum wages—all proven misfires.

Ninth, taken as a whole—the mayors are pursuing conflicted policies, on the numbers not breaking cycles of intergenerational crime, poverty, unemployment, dependence, employers fleeing tax burdens, untrained employees, accessible private health care, environmental stewardship and personal fitness.

Tenth, in closing: These cities can do better. That is what democracy is for. If the policies and leadership are not working, there is an option—especially as America's economy is thriving and cities are seeing a renaissance in investment, employment, income, health, and safety. Elect new leaders. The numbers are compelling, so are elections. [62]

4

EDUCATION AND THE FEDERAL
DEPARTMENT OF EDUCATION

This country offers a wonderful education. Throughout most of
our history, the states and local governments were responsible
for education. Nothing in the Constitution gives the federal government the power to regulate or fund education. In fact, the word
education does not even appear in the Constitution. Since there is
no provision in the Constitution authorizing the federal government to spend money on education, that power was reserved to the
states or to the people under Article 10.

From the Civil War era on, Congress occasionally took action
to establish a national department of education, which actions were
opposed by those against establishing a national department.

During the Carter administration in the 1970s, a call for a cabinet-level department was put into law.

> Once again, opponents objected on various grounds,
> including the ability of a national department to
> oversee education programs for tens of millions
> of school children. Rep. Lawrence H. Fountain

(D-NC) was particularly outspoken in his objection, arguing that:

I find it disappointing that the administration has not given attention to another management option—namely, a critical review of those 150 plus education programs to determine how many of them are really needed today.... It would be more useful, in my judgment, to concentrate on weeding out programs that have outlived their usefulness, that duplicate another, or that simply don't work, than to devote our energies to creating a new organizational structure which might well help to perpetuate many off these programs. Vicky E. Alger, Federal Department Finds U.S. Department of Education a Massive Failure, 2–20–19. [63]

The Department of Education has an annual budget of about $70 billion. At the state and federal level, another $620 billion is spent on K–12 education each year.

Federal Agencies Are Not Built for Performance

A leading reason for re-establishing a cabinet-level U.S. Department of Education in 1979 was better coordination and administration of hundreds of federal education programs. The latest GAO report, however, adds to a growing body of evidence that far-off bureaucracies in Washington, D.C., are ill-suited to this task.

The department is just one of numerous federal entities operating nearly 300 federal, social, education, and training programs. In a separate report published nearly a decade ago the GAO concluded that no uniform definition for "education program" even exists across 25 federal departments and agencies. Not much has changed since then...

The OMB's revised inventory published in 2013 revealed that more than half of all education department programs were either deemed ineffective or their results were unproven. Yet, in 2014, the results of that inventory were deemed unreliable, largely because of inconsistencies in how federal agencies define education programs. As of the fall of 2017, the GAO estimated that, at best just 1 percent of federal agencies had submitted consistent program and budget data. Then, in December 2018, the GAO noted ongoing problems with data integrity and public accessibility of the OMB's program inventory.

We Shouldn't Spend Billions to Get Bad Results

It shouldn't be this hard to figure out whether specific education department programs are working. What we do know from publicly available spending and achievement data is that, since 1970, education spending has roughly tripled in real, inflation-adjusted terms, but student achievement has remained flat...

(T)he fundamental problem with the Department of Education is that it removes the decision-making authority from the real education experts: parents and taxpayers in local communities.

Currently, the federal government provides just 8 percent of total K-12 education funding. Yet, states and school officials have to agree to myriad federal mandates to access that funding. Given the on-going problems with the department, in contrast to the growth of successful state-level parental choice programs, it is well worth considering abolishing the U.S. Department of Education once and for all. [64]

To have a successful system of education, parents and the local community must be very active in the schools and in their children's education. Is the nation being served by removing much of the power from the local officials and school personnel and transferring it to the federal government? Why should the Federal Department of Education have such a key role in our children's education? Those bureaucrats are hundreds, if not thousands, of miles away from the teaching of our children. What does a federal bureaucrat know about the needs of education in your town or in your school? Chances are they have never been there and don't know anything about your town or your school.

Education requires serious work. It is up to parents, teachers, school boards, and mentors to see that their kids put in the work necessary to learn. Children will use the educational foundation they receive for the rest of their lives. Their work habits, or lack of them, will also follow them. Classes, such as English, mathematics, history, economics, accounting, and others will be necessary for them to find a job, to manage their finances, to interact with others, to make decisions (to include decisions necessary to exercise their rights in a democracy), and to raise children of their own.

Young people must not be given excuses for not succeeding. They cannot be told that the world is against them, that because of the way they look or their background they do not have a chance in life. Because children are born into a poor family, they cannot be told that there is no hope of moving out and moving up and bettering themselves. Parents must exercise discipline in seeing that their children stay on a path that leads to progress and success, not to gang activity, criminal activity, or a life in poverty. Children must not be taught that they are owed a living by the rest of society. They cannot be told by their leaders that society has been cruel to them and that whatever their problem, it is society's fault or that society owes them a living.

Are the children being properly served because not everyone has the same abilities? Is the achievement level required being lowered for everyone so as not to offend anyone? Is the education of our children being promoted by having pass/fail courses instead of graded courses? Is the process being helped by not declaring winners because you don't want to hurt the feelings of the others? Is the process served by not rewarding success? Is excelling at something to be avoided and discouraged?

Are parents and teachers and educators on the same side when making demands on students? Are parents being supportive of the teachers when teachers are demanding of their students? Are parents asking their children what they are learning at school and asking about homework and requiring that they do it?

Do teachers and educators have the disciplinary tools they need, and the support they need, when they exercise those tools to ensure that the students get the message that they are expected to learn? Are parents teaching their children to obey the rules of the schools, and are they supporting the teachers when they discipline their students? Are parents teaching their children to respect their teachers, or are they complaining that their children are being picked on by the school?

Are we advancing students because it is just easier to do that than to put up with them? Are we eliminating those teachers and educators who do not require enough of our students so that we can give proper support to those teachers and educators who are requiring enough?

Are teachers teaching their students in a biased way because of the teachers' own political biases? Administrators and school boards must ensure that this is not happening. If it is happening and if a teacher's liberal views are affecting his/her teaching, conservatives must become more active and resist the teaching of bias. While it is normally not in the DNA of a conservative to be an activist, we must occasionally use some liberal tactics to accomplish our goals.

When our education system fails kids, liberals say we just need to spend more money on education. Beyond throwing more money at the problem, the best they can come up with is to move students along, institute pass/fail, lower the education goals, discourage excellence, and take some religions out of schools. They don't like alternatives such as charter schools and school vouchers.

In his speech at the National Prayer Breakfast on February 7, 2013, Dr. Ben Carson had this to say about education:

> If you really want to be impressed, take a look at the chapter on education in my latest book, America the Beautiful, which I wrote with my wife—it came out last year, and in that education chapter you will see questions extracted from a sixth grade exit exam from the 1800's—a test you had to pass to get your sixth grade certificate. I doubt most college graduates today could pass that test. We have dumbed things down to that level and the reason that is so dangerous is because the people who founded this Nation said that our system of government was designed for a well-informed and educated populace,

and when they become less informed, they become vulnerable. Think about that. That is why education is so vitally important. [65]

Before more money is spent on education, shouldn't we ensure that our educational system is requiring—forcing—our students to learn. Our students are falling further and further behind other areas of the world. This is happening despite the trillions of dollars that have been spent on education. But after a time, when more and more money does not seem to solve the problem, wouldn't it be prudent to examine the system and see if there is a way to fix the problem without spending endless amounts of money?

There have been attempts to eliminate the Department of Education over the years. President Ronald Reagan argued that welfare and education are two functions that should be primarily carried out at the state and local levels. The 1996 Republican platform stated: "The federal government has no constitutional authority to be involved in school curricula or to control jobs in the marketplace. This is why we will abolish the Department of Education." Former Education Secretary William J. Bennett, Former Speaker of the House of Representative Newt Gingrich, Senators Ted Cruz and Rand Paul and Marco Rubio, and President Donald J. Trump have all called for elimination of the department. [66]

Poverty Habits Parents Teach Their Children of Whatever Race

On October 21, 2017, Thomas Corley wrote an article entitled "15 Poverty Habits Parents Teach Their Children."

When I travel the country speaking to high school and college students about exactly what they need to do to become financially successful in life he always begins his presentation by asking three questions:

"How many want to be financially successful in life?"

"How many think they will be financially successful in life?"

Almost every time I ask the first two questions every hand rises in the air.

Then he asks the magic third question:

"How many have taken a course in school on how to be financially successful in life?"

Not one hand rises in the air, ever. Clearly every student wants to be successful and thinks they will be successful but none have been taught by their parents or their school system how to be financially successful in life. Not only are there no courses on basic financial success principles but there are no structured courses teaching basic financial literacy. We are raising our children to be financially illiterate and to fail in life.

Is it any wonder that most Americans live paycheck to paycheck? That most Americans accumulate more debt than assets? That many Americans lose their homes when they lose their job? Is it any wonder that most Americans cannot afford college for their children and that student loan debt is now the largest type of consumer debt?

What's worse is what our children are being taught by their parents, the school system, politicians and the national media. They are teaching our children that the wealthy are corrupt, greedy, have too much wealth and that this wealth needs to be redistributed.

What kind of a message do you think that sends to America's future generation? It is teaching them that seeking financial success is a bad and evil thing.

Here are some statistics from my five-year study on the daily habits that separate the wealthy from the poor:

1. 72% of the wealthy know their credit score vs. 5% of the poor.
2. 6% of the wealthy play the lottery vs. 77% of the poor.
3. 80% of the wealthy are focused on at least one goal vs. 12% of the poor.
4. 62% of the wealthy floss their teeth every day vs. 16% of the poor.
5. 21% of the wealthy are overweight by 30 pounds or more vs. 66% of the poor.
6. 63% of the wealthy spend less than 1 hour per day on recreational Internet use. 74% of the poor spend more than an hour a day in the Internet.
7. 83% of the wealthy attend back-to-school night for their kids vs. 13% of the poor.
8. 29% of the wealthy had one or more children who made the honor roll vs. 4% of the poor.
9. 63% of wealthy listen to audio books during their commute vs. 5% of the poor.
10. 67% of the wealthy watch less than 1 hour of TV per day vs. 23% of the poor.

11. 9% of the wealthy watch reality TV shows vs. 78% of the poor.
12. 73% of the wealthy were taught the 80/20 rule vs. 5% of the poor (live off 80%; save 20%).
13. 79% of the wealthy network 5 hours or more per month vs. 16% of the poor.
14. 8% of the wealthy believe wealth comes from random good luck vs. 79% of the poor.
15. 79% of the wealthy believe they are responsible for their financial circumstances. 82% of the poor believe they are victims and not responsible for their poverty.

The fact is, the poor are poor because they have too many poverty habits and too few rich habits. The best parents teach their children good habits that lead to success and the poor parents teach their kids bad habits that lead to poverty.

We don't have a wealth gap in this country, we have a parent gap.

We don't have income inequality, we have parent inequality.

Parents and our schools need to work together to instill good daily success habits. They need to be teaching children specific rich habits that lead to success.

Here are some examples:

- Limit TV, social media, video games, and cell phone use to no more than one hour a day.

- Require that children read one nonfiction book a week and write a one-page summary of what they learned for their parents to review.
- Require children to aerobically exercise 20–30 minutes a day.
- Limit junk food to no more than 300 calories a day.
- Teach children to dream and to pursue their dreams. Have them write a script of their ideal future life.
- Require that children set monthly, annual, and long-term goals.
- Require working-age children to work or volunteer at least ten hours a week.
- Require that children save at least 25% of their earnings or the monetary gifts they receive.
- Teach children the importance of calling family, friends, teachers, coaches, and so forth on their birthday.
- Teach children the importance of calling family, friends, teachers, coaches, and so on when anything good or bad happens in their lives. Examples include births, deaths, awards, illnesses, and so forth.
- Teach children to send thank-you cards to individuals who helped them in any way.
- Reassure children that mistakes are good and not bad. Children need to understand that the very foundation of success is built upon the lessons we learn from our mistakes.
- Discipline children when they lose their temper, so they understand the consequence of not controlling this very costly emotion. Anger is the most costly emotion. It gets people fired or divorced and destroys relationships.
- Teach children that the pursuit of financial success is a good thing and not a bad thing.
- Children need to learn how to manage money. Open up a checking account or savings account for children and force them to use their savings to buy the things they want. This

teaches children that they are not entitled to anything. It teaches them that they have to work for the things they want in life, like cell phones, computers, fashionable clothes, video games, and so on.

- Require children to participate in at least one nonsports-related extracurricular group at school or outside of school.
- Parents and children need to set aside at least an hour a day to talk to one another, not on Facebook, not on the cell phone, but face to face. The only quality time is quantity time.
- Teach children how to manage their time. Teach them how to create a daily to-do list. They can put their to-do list on their bedroom door so parents can check it each day.

Obviously, it is not possible to follow every rich-habit recommendation I listed above.

From my research, I learned that all it takes is one or two rich habits to completely transform a life.

The reading habit, on its own, can set you up for career success.

The savings habit, on its own, can set your children up to be financially independent. The exercise habit, on its own, can set your children up for a long, healthy life.

The happy birthday or life event calls, on their own, can set your children up to forge strong relationships. Pick just two habits to teach you kids and stay on top of them for six months. After six months the habits should stick. [67]

Another writer, Hank Didier, has added to Mr. Corley's advice:

> High schools should be teaching financial educa-
> tion to their students beginning in freshman year. It
> needs to be a multi-prong curriculum that includes
> the following courses:

- How to Pay Bills and Balance a Checkbook (freshman year)
- How to Save and Invest your Savings (sophomore year)
- How Insurance Works—Auto Insurance, Home Owners Insurance, Health Insurance (junior year)
- Understanding Student Loans (junior year)
- Personal Income Tax Fundamentals (senior year)

> Schools teach what they are required to teach. It's
> unfortunate, but financial education is not a require-
> ment in most schools and, thus, it is up to the par-
> ents to teach their kids to be money smart. [68]

Other writers have concluded the following about poor families:

> In poor families, however, children tend to spend
> their time at home or with extended family . . . They
> are more likely to grow up in neighborhoods that
> their parents say aren't great for raising children, and
> their parents worry about them getting shot, beaten
> up or in trouble with the law . . . Poorer parents
> have less time and fewer resources to invest in their
> children, which can leave children less prepared for
> school and work, which leads to lower earnings. . .
> People used to live near people of different income
> levels; neighborhoods are now segregated more by
> income. More than a quarter of children live in

single-parent households—a historic high . . . and these children are three times as likely to live in poverty as those who live with married parents. [69]

They're malnourished. Even if they're getting enough (or too many) calories, their nutrition is terrible . . . The types of food these kids are subsisting on are terrible for both their body and their mind.

They're under stimulated. They've got an iPad or a tablet or mom or dad's old phone now. But no one is spending time helping them to learn the skills they need to be successful in school. Yes, the parents are tired and often they don't even know how to help. Many of them only had a third or fourth grade education themselves. English is their second language. Their child is already more proficient than they are—how can they help?

They're neglected. At home, at school, at daycare. They're abused. Physically, sexually, emotionally.

This list is not applicable to every poor child, but poor children who also do poorly in school (or who are difficult to teach) often count multiple factors I've mentioned as part of their story. They're vulnerable and often don't have even a parent or guardian to advocate for them beyond the most basic of their needs. They fall through the cracks and are passed on to the next grade over and over again until catching up to the other kids becomes nothing short of a pipe dream. [70]

What can we do to change the cycle of poverty? A wide body of research shows teaching poor parents to stimulate their children can have significant long-term impact on the kids' earning power... The amount of time a father spends with young children has long-term impact on brain development. For example, a father's presence in a baby's live improves the child's vocabulary, in a way that a constant day-care provider or school teacher does not . . . We can't solve the rich-poor gap with school. We have to solve it with family.

All the data we have says we need to help poor parents invest more time and energy into their kids. That begs the questions: How do those parents get the money to stay home to do that? Or how do poor parents find the money to hire the high-quality child care that rich parents hire to make up for their absence? Or how do parents get more financial resources so they can keep their marriages together? (Single parents live in poverty and rich, educated couples do not get divorced)... Rich parents are figuring out how to have one parent home with the kids. Poor parents do not have the tools to make that happen in their family. We need to reduce that disparity more than we need to improve schools... We spend so much money on schools, and that money does nothing to bring kids out of poverty. So we should shift the spending to create jobs to bring the kid's parents out of poverty in a respectful, family-friendly way. [71]

5

How Big Government Enslaves African Americans And The Poor

There are an increasing number of black people who are speaking out against the continuing effort to keep black people down.

Star Parker, freedom fighter and social policy activist, has written a blistering indictment of today's culture of government dependency.

"Uncle Sam's Plantation: How Big Government Enslaves America's Poor and What You Can Do About It" traces the benign origins of the welfare state and its evolution into a $400 billion plus monstrosity of programs that effectively enslave America's poor.

Parker, a former welfare mother, has seen first hand the damage that a life of dependency renders. Years of massive government spending have left America's inner cities in shambles, black families destroyed, and youth uneducated and directionless.

It's time to cut our losses, get government and bureaucrats out of the way, and return our precious and limited resources to where Americans know how to use them best—to the control of private citizens. Perpetuation of the lie, says Parker, that government programs can solve the problems of individuals has left a generation of black Americans with a loss of a sense of self, hope, and responsibility. Parker reveals how:

- The welfare system enslaves the poor on a subsidized legal plantation.
- The left and right continue to look in error to government approaches to poverty.
- Government undermines the framework of morality and values without which poverty and adversity cannot be overcome.
- Politicization of welfare, education, our tax system, and our retirement system perpetuates the cycle of poverty.

Thirty-five years of Great Society engineering have forced the disadvantaged to live under the control of the federal government.

Politicians control their housing, their food supply, their schooling, their wages, and their transportation.

A centralized government makes decisions about their childcare, healthcare, and retirement. It controls their reproduction through abortion and wants to control their deaths through euthanasia.

Through the welfare system, "Uncle Sam has developed a sophisticated poverty plantation, operated by a federal government, overseen by bureaucrats, protected by media elite, and financed by the taxpayers. The only difference between this plantation and the slave plantations of the antebellum South is perception."

America has two economic systems: capitalism for the rich and socialism for the poor. This double-minded approach seems to keep the poor enslaved to poverty while the rich get richer. Let's face it, despite its $400 billion price tag, welfare isn't working. [72]

Professor Carol M. Swain has noted: "As a black person, it bothers me that the America I love is being destroyed by a black man. It bothers me that blacks are being deceived into supporting programs and policies that are destroying them." [73]

Ludmya "Mia" Love served as a member of the United States House of Representatives for Utah's Fourth Congressional District. As a Haitian American, she was the first black female Republican elected to Congress and the first Haitian American elected to Congress from the state of Utah. She has stated: "Government is not your salvation. Government is not your road to prosperity. Hard work and education will take you far beyond what any government program can ever promise." [74]

Afrocity Brown has implored: "Tell me one thing that the Democrats have done for Blacks that does not involve entitlements, lowering standards, or any other measure that proves we are nothing more than a weak race who cannot and will not ever be able to contribute to society in a positive manner that does not involve the Government." [75]

Louisiana State Senator Elbert Guillory is an African American, who had been a Democrat. After making the announcement that he was leaving the Democrat Party to become a Republican, he released a video. Here is a transcription of the video:

> I'm Elbert Lee Guillory, the senator for the 24th district right here in beautiful Louisiana. Recently I made what many are referring to as a bold decision to switch my party affiliation to the Republican Party. I wanted to take a moment to explain why I chose to become a Republican and also to explain why I don't think it was a bold decision at all. It is the right decision. Not only for me, but for all my brothers and sisters in the black community. You see, in recent history, the Democrat Party created the illusion that their agenda and their policies are what's best for black people.
>
> Somehow it's been forgotten the Republican Party was founded in 1854 as an abolitionist movement with one simple creed that slavery is a violation of the rights of man. Fredrick Douglas called Republicans the party of freedom and progress. And the first Republican president was Lincoln, the author of the Emancipation Proclamation. It was Republicans who offered the 13th, 14th, and 15th amendments giving former slaves citizenship, voting rights, and due process of law. The Democrats, on the other hand, with the party of Jim Crow, it was Democrats who defended the rights of slaves'

owners. It was the Republican President Dwight Eisenhower who championed the Civil Rights Act of 1957, but it was the Democrats in the Senate who filibustered the bill.

At the heart of liberalism is the idea that only a great and powerful big government can be the benefactor of social justice for all Americans. But the left is only concerned with one thing: control, and they disguise control as charity. Programs, such as welfare, these programs aren't designed to lift black Americans out of poverty. They were always intended as a mechanism for politicians to control the black community. The idea that blacks or anyone, for that matter, need the government to get ahead in life is despicable.

And even more important, this idea is a failure. Our communities are just as poor as they have always been. Our schools continue to fail children, our prisons are filled with young black men who should be at home, being fathers. Our self-initiative and our self-reliance have been sacrificed in exchange for allegiance to overseers who control us by making us dependent on them. Sometimes I wonder if the word freedom is tossed around so frequently in our society that it has become a cliché. The idea of freedom is complex and all-encompassing. It's the idea that the press must operate without government intrusion. It's the idea that e-mails and phone records of Americans should remain free from government search and seizure. It's the idea that parents must be the decision-makers in regards to their

children's education, not some government bureaucrat. But most importantly, it is the idea that the
individual must be free to pursue his or her own
happiness, free from government dependence and
free from government control, because to be truly
free is to be reliant on no one, other than the author
of our destiny.

These are the ideas at the core of the Republican Party,
and it is why I am a Republican. So my brothers and
sisters of the American community, please join with
me today in abandoning the government plantation
and the party of disappointment so that we may
all echo the words of one Republican leader who
famously said, "Free at last, free at last, thank God
almighty, free at last." [76]

Senator Guillory credited President Dwight D. Eisenhower
for the 1957 Civil Rights Bill, but President Eisenhower was also
responsible for the 1960 Civil Rights Bill.

Bill Cosby should need no introduction, at least to those of
us who have been around for a while. He was a comedian and
actor who, among other accomplishments, blazed the way for black
people in television. He starred opposite Robert Culp in a television series called *I Spy* and was the first African American to have
a starring role in a television series. As a comedian, he was a master
at just having a conversation with the audience. His routines were
always free from profanity and off-color jokes. Later he starred in
another television show where he played a lovable and kindly patri-
arch of his family as Dr. Huxtable. His TV family was a role model
for millions of families of whatever race. Once one of the nations
most admired and respected men, he was convicted of three counts
of sexually assaulting a woman and sentenced to three to ten years.

Words that he spoke at the height of his popularity still have meaning today. In May 2004, he gave a speech before the NAACP on the 50th anniversary of Brown v. Board of Education.

> Ladies and gentlemen, I really have to ask you to seriously consider what you've heard, and now this is the end of the evening so to speak. I heard a prize fight manager say to his fellow who was losing badly, "David, listen to me. It's not what's he's doing to you. It's what you're not doing."

> . . .ladies and gentlemen, in our cities and public schools we have 50% drop out. In our own neighborhood, we have men in prison. No longer is a person embarrassed because they're pregnant without a husband. No longer is a boy considered an embarrassment if he tries to run away from being the father of the unmarried child.

> Ladies and gentlemen, the lower economic and lower middle economic people are not holding their end in this deal. In the neighborhood that most of us grew up in, parenting is not going on. In the old days, you couldn't hooky school because every drawn shade was an eye. And before your mother got off the bus and to the house, she knew exactly where you had gone, who had gone into the house, and where you got on whatever you had one and where you got it from. Parents don't know that today.

> I'm talking about these people who cry when their son is standing there in an orange suit. Where were you when he was two? Where were you when he

was twelve? Where were you when he was eighteen, and how come you don't know he had a pistol? And where is his father, and why don't you know where he is? And why doesn't the father show up to talk to this boy?

The church is only open on Sunday. And you can't keep asking Jesus to ask doing things for you. You can't keep asking that God will find a way. God is tired of you...

Fifty percent drop out rate, I'm telling you, and people in jail, and women having children by five, six different men. Under what excuse? I want somebody to love me. And as soon as you have it, you forget to parent. Grandmother, mother, and great grandmother in the same room, raising children, and the child knows nothing about love or respect of any one of the three of them. All this child knows is "gimme, gimme, gimme." These people want to buy the friendship of a child, and the child couldn't care less. Those of us sitting out here who have gone on to some college or whatever we've done, we still fear our parents. And these people are not parenting. They're buying things for the kid — $500 sneakers — for what? They won't buy or spend $250 on Hooked on Phonics.

...Looking at the incarcerated, these are not political criminals. These are people going around stealing Coca Cola. People getting shot in the back of the head over a piece of pound cake! Then we all run out and are outraged: "The cops shouldn't have shot him." What the hell was he doing with the pound cake in his hand? I wanted a piece of pound cake just as bad as anybody else. And I looked at it and I had no money. And something called parenting said if you get caught with it you're going to embarrass your mother." Not, "You're going to get your butt kicked." No. "You're going to embarrass your mother." "You're going to embarrass your family." If you knock that girl up, you're going to have to run away because it's going to be too embarrassing for your family. In the old days, a girl getting pregnant had to go down South, and then her mother would go down to get her. But the mother had the baby. I said the mother had the baby. The girl didn't have a baby. The mother had the baby in two weeks. We are not parenting.

Ladies and gentlemen, listen to these people. They are showing you what's wrong. People putting their clothes on backwards. Isn't that a sign of something going on wrong? Are you not paying attention? People with their hat on backwards, pants down around the crack. Isn't that a sign of something or are you waiting for Jesus to pull his pants up? Isn't it a sign of something when she's got her dress all the way up to the crack — and got all kinds of needles and things going through her body. What part of Africa did this come from? We are not Africans. Those people are not Africans; they don't know a damned thing about Africa. With names like Shaniqua, Shaligua, Mohammed and all that crap and all of them are in jail. (When we give these kinds names to our children, we give them the strength and inspiration in the meaning of those names. What's the point of giving them strong names if there is not parenting and values backing it up).

Brown versus the Board of Education is no longer the white person's problem. We've got to take the neighborhood back. We've got to go in there. Just forget telling your child to go to the Peace Corps. It's right around the corner. It's standing on the corner. It can't speak English. It doesn't want to speak English. I can't even talk the way these people talk: "Why you ain't where you is . . .?" I don't know who these people are. And I blamed the kid until I heard the mother talk. Then I heard the father talk. This is all in the house. You used to talk a certain way on the corner and you got into the house and switched to English. Everybody knows it's important to speak English except these knuckleheads. You can't land a plane with, "Why you ain't..." You can't be a doctor with that kind of crap coming out of your mouth. There is no Bible that has that kind of language. Where did these people get the idea that they're moving ahead on this. Well, they know they're not; they're just hanging out in the same place, five or six generations sitting in the projects when you're just supposed to stay there long enough to get a job and move out.

Now, look, I'm telling you. It's not what they're doing to us. It's what we're not doing. 50 percent drop out. Look, we're raising our own ingrown immigrants. These people are fighting hard to be ignorant. There's no English being spoken, and they're walking and they're angry. Oh God, they're angry and they have pistols and they shoot and they do stupid things. And after they kill somebody, they don't have a plan. Just murder somebody. Boom. Over what? A pizza? And then run to the poor cousin's house. . .

Five or six different children — same woman, eight, ten different husbands or whatever. Pretty soon you're going to have to have DNA cards so you can tell who you're making love to. You don't know who this is. It might be your grandmother. I'm telling you, they're young enough. Hey, you have a baby when you're twelve. Your baby turns thirteen and has a baby, how old are you? . . .

I'm telling you Christians, what's wrong with you? Why can't you hit the streets? Why can't you clean it out yourselves? It's our time now, ladies and gentlemen. It is our time. And I've got good news for you. It's not about money. It's about you doing something ordinarily that we do — get in somebody else's business. It's time for you to not accept the language that these people are speaking, which will take them nowhere. What the hell good is Brown v. Board of Education if nobody wants it?

What is it with young girls getting after some girl who wants to still remain a virgin. Who are these sick black people and where did they come from and why haven't they been parented to shut up? . . .

So, ladies and gentlemen, I want to thank you for the award — and giving me an opportunity to speak because, I mean, this is the future, and all of these people who lined up and done — they've got to be wondering what the hell happened. Brown V. Board of Education — these people who marched and were hit in the face with rocks and punched in the face to get an education and we got these knuckleheads walking around who don't want to learn English. I know that you all know it. I just want to get you as angry that you ought to be. When you walk around the neighborhood and you see this stuff, that stuff's not funny. These people are not funny anymore. And that's not my brother. And that's not my sister. They're faking and they're dragging me way down because the state, the city, and all these people have to pick up the tab on them because they don't want to accept that they have to study to get an education.

We have to begin to build in the neighborhood, have restaurants, have cleaners, have pharmacies, have real estate, have medical buildings instead of trying to rob them all. . .

Basketball players — multimillionaires can't write a paragraph. Football players, multimillionaires, can't read. Yes. Multimillionaires. Well, Brown v. Board of Education, where are we today? It's there. They paved the way. What did we do with it? . . .

You got to tell me that if there was parenting — help me — if there was parenting, he wouldn't have picked up the Coca Cola bottle and walked out with it to get shot in the back of the head. He wouldn't have. Not if he loved his parents. And not if they were parenting! Not if the father would come home...

Well, you're probably going to let Jesus figure it out for you. Well, I've got something to tell you about Jesus. When you go to the church, look at the stained glass things of Jesus. Look at them. Is Jesus smiling? Not in one picture. So, tell your friends. Let's try to do something. Let's try to make Jesus smile. Let's start parenting. Thank you, thank you. [77]

Bill Cosby has not repudiated his controversial pronouncements or attempted to distance himself from them. Instead, he chose to expand upon his theme on subsequent occasions and to make himself a spokesperson for black self-empowerment through education and better parenting. He said:

This is a problem of epic proportion. Then, in a statement released shortly after the NAACP gala, he made clear his purpose. "I think that it is time for concerned African-Americans to march, galvanize and raise the awareness about this epidemic, to transform our helplessness, frustration and righteous indignation into a sense of shared responsibility and action." In another interview, he said: "I feel that I can no longer remain silent. If I have to make a choice between keeping quiet so that conservative media does not speak negatively or ringing the bell to galvanize those who want change in the lower economic community, then I choose to be a bell ringer."

In July 2004, he again took to the public soapbox to expound upon his theses. In a speech given at Reverend Jesse Jackson's Rainbow Coalition/PUSH conference in Chicago, he said: "You've got to stop beating up your women because you can't find a job, because you didn't want to get an education and now you're (earning) minimum wage. You should have thought more of yourself when you were in high school, when you had an opportunity."

In December 2004, he addressed a panel at Medgar Evers College in Brooklyn, telling them: "Stop waiting for a leader. Get up! Tell your friends. And if they can't get up, we must see about them because they are true victims . . . It's time to study four hours a day with your children. Teach them how much they'll be worth when they have A's instead of F's. We cannot blame the white people any longer." [78]

Larry Elder is a talk show radio host, syndicated columnist, author, and attorney. He wrote the following:

> Years ago, I interviewed Kweisi Mfume, then the president of the NAACP. "As between the presence of white racism and the absence of black fathers," I asked, "Which poses the bigger threat to the black community?" Without missing a beat, he said, "The absence of black fathers."

> It was President Barack Obama who said, "We all know the statistics. That children who grow up without a father are five times more likely to live in poverty and commit crime; nine times more likely to drop out of school and twenty times more likely to end up in prison." The Journal of Research on

Adolescence confirms that even after controlling for varying levels of household income, kids in father-absent homes are more likely to end up in jail. And kids who never had a father in the house are the most likely to wind up behind bars.

In 1960, 5 percent of America's children entered the world without a mother and father married to each other. By 1980 it was 18 percent, by 2000 it had risen to 33 percent, and fifteen years later, the number reached 41 percent. For blacks, even during slavery when marriage for slaves was illegal, black children were more likely than today to be raised by both their mother and father. Economist Walter Williams has written that, according to census data, from 1890 to 1940, a black child was more likely to grow up with married parents than a white child.

For blacks, out-of-wedlock births have gone from 25 percent in 1965 to 73 percent in 2015. For whites, from less than 5 percent to over 25 percent. And for Hispanics, out-of-wedlock births have risen to 53 percent. What happened to fathers? The answer is found in a basic law of economics: If you subsidize undesirable behavior, you will get more undesirable behavior. In 1949, the nation's poverty rate was 34 percent. By 1965, it was cut in half, to 17 percent—all before President Lyndon Johnson's so-called War on Poverty. But after that war began in 1965, poverty began to flatline. From 1965 until now, the government has spent over $20 trillion to fight poverty.

The poverty rate has remained unchanged, but the relationship between poor men and women has changed—dramatically. That's because our generous welfare system allows women, in effect, to marry the government. And this makes it all too easy for men to abandon their traditional moral and financial responsibilities. Psychologists call such dependency "learned helplessness" (Free Courses for Free Minds.com).

How do we know that the welfare state creates disincentives that hurt the very people we are trying to help? They tell us. In 1985, the *Los Angeles Times* asked both the poor and the non-poor whether poor women "often" have children to get additional benefits. Most of the non-poor respondents said no. However, 64 percent of poor respondents said yes. Now, who do you think is in a better position to know?

Tupac Shakur, the late rapper, once said: "I know for a fact that had I had a father, I'd have some discipline. I'd have more confidence." He admitted he began running with gangs because he wanted the things a father gives to a child, especially to a boy: structure and protection. "Your mother cannot calm you down the way a man can," Shakur said. "You need a man to teach you how to be a man."

In my book *Dear Father, Dear Son,* I write about my rough, tough World War II Marine staff sergeant dad. Born in the Jim Crow South of Athens, Ga., he was 14 at the start of the Great Depression.

Growing up, I watched my father work two full-time jobs as a janitor. He also cooked for a rich family on the weekends—and somehow managed to go to night school to get his GED. When I was 10, my father opened a small restaurant that he ran until he retired in his mid-80s.

He was never angry or bitter—and insisted that today's America was very different from the world of racial segregation and limited opportunity in which he grew up. "Hard work wins," he told me and my brothers. "You get out of life what you put into it. You can't control the outcome, but you are 100% in control of the effort. And before blaming other people, go to the nearest mirror and ask yourself, 'what could I have done to change the outcome?'" This advice shaped my life.

Fathers matter. Until we have a government policy that makes that its first priority, nothing will. [79]

Martin Luther King, Jr., gave his famous "I have a dream" speech in 1963. This was one of the greatest speeches ever given by any person, man or woman, black or white, or any other source of difference. The country was moved by him and by this speech. One of the major tragedies in our country's history was his assassination. It is too bad that we will never know what else he could have accomplished had he lived.

Those people who believe that there is a better future for black people and others who have not partaken fully in the American economy need to add their voices to the people quoted here. They need to convince African Americans and poor people and those in positions of power that there is hope for the future–that there is hope for them to participate in the American dream. That hope does not lie in continuing to try to get more and more from the federal government. Slavery ended 160 years ago. The Civil Rights Act was passed sixty years ago. It is time that black and poor people step up and do what they individually can do to reach the dream that Martin Luther King had fifty years ago.

There are spokespersons in the black community that speak for the status quo. Jesse Jackson and Al Sharpton are two of the most prominent ones. Their continued prominence is dependent on race. The same can be said about some politicians who play the race card and try to keep African Americans dependent upon the federal government. The same can be said about the Democrat party, which is dependent in large measure on race for its continued level of prominence. When listening to those who play the race issue, you would think that the only hope for black people is continuing dependence upon the federal government.

If they can continue to convince African Americans that they cannot do anything about their situation, that their situation is not their fault, and that the only way to better themselves and their situation is to support the Democrats, they will continue to have their stage and their power, regardless of whether their continuing positions are in the best interests of the country and of black people. This may be good for the persons playing the race card, and it may be good for the Democrat Party, but it is certainly not good for black people or for the nation. The blame for that falls squarely on the race baiters, on liberals and on the Democrat Party.

Black Lives Matter

Should Black People Tolerate This?
By Walter E. Williams
May 23, 2012

Each year, roughly 7,000 blacks are murdered. Ninety-four percent of the time, the murderer is another black person. According to the Bureau of Justice Statistics, between 1976 and 2011, there were 279,384 black murder victims. Using the 94 percent figure means that 262,621 were murdered by other blacks. Though blacks are 13 percent of the nation's population, they account for more than 50 percent of homicide victims. Nationally, black homicide victimization rate is six times that of whites, and in some cities, it's 22 times that of whites. Coupled with being most of the nation's homicide victims, blacks are most of the victims of violent personal crimes, such as assault and robbery.

The magnitude of this tragic mayhem can be viewed in another light. According to a Tuskegee Institute study, between the years 1882 and 1968, 3,446 blacks were lynched at the hands of whites. Black fatalities during the Korean War (3,075), Vietnam War (7,243) and all wars since 1980 (8,197) come to 18,515, a number that pales in comparison with black loss of life at home. It's a tragic commentary to be able to say that young black males have a greater chance of reaching maturity on the battlefields of Iraq and Afghanistan than on the streets of Philadelphia, Chicago, Detroit, Oakland, Newark and other cities.

A much larger issue is how might we interpret the deafening silence about the day-to-day murder in black communities compared with the national uproar over the killing of Trayvon Martin. Such a response by politicians, civil rights organizations and the mainstream news media could easily be interpreted as "blacks killing other blacks is of little concern, but it's unacceptable for a white to kill a black person."

There are a few civil rights leaders with a different vision. When President Barack Obama commented about the Trayvon Martin case, T. Willard Fair, president of the Urban League of Greater Miami, told The Daily Caller that "the outrage should be about us killing each other, about black-on-black crime." He asked rhetorically, "Wouldn't you think to have 41 people shot (in Chicago) between Friday morning and Monday morning would be much more newsworthy and deserve much more outrage?" Former NAACP leader Pastor C.L. Bryant said the rallies organized by Al Sharpton and Jesse Jackson suggest there is an epidemic of "white men killing black young men," adding: "The epidemic is truly black-on-black crime. The greatest danger to the lives of young black men are young black men."

Not only is there silence about black-on-black crime; there's silence and concealment about black racist attacks on whites—for example, the recent attacks on two Virginian-Pilot newspaper reporters set upon and beaten by a mob of young blacks. The story wasn't even covered by their own newspaper. In March, a black mob assaulted, knocked unconscious, disrobed and robbed a white tourist in downtown Baltimore. Black mobs have roamed the streets of Denver, Chicago, Philadelphia, New

York, Cleveland, Washington, Los Angeles and other cities, making unprovoked attacks on whites and running off with their belongings.

Racist attacks have been against not only whites but also Asians. Such attacks include the San Francisco beating death of an 83-year-old Chinese man, the pushing of a 57-year-old woman off a train platform and the knocking of a 59-year-old Chinese man to the ground, which killed him. For years, Asian school students in New York and Philadelphia have been beaten up by their black classmates and called racist epithets—for example, "Hey, Chinese!" and "Yo, dragon ball!" But that kind of bullying, unlike the bullying of homosexuals, goes unreported and unpunished.

Racial demagoguery from the president on down is not in our nation's best interests, plus it's dangerous. As my colleague Thomas Sowell recently put it, "if there is anything worse than a one-sided race war, it is a two-sided race war, especially when one of the races outnumbers the other several times over."

Walter E. Williams is a professor of economics at George Mason University. To find out more about Walter E. Williams and read features by other Creators Syndicate writers and cartoonists, visit the Creators Syndicate Web page at www.creators.com. [80]

Professor Williams wrote a book entitled *Up from the Projects*. In an interview regarding the book, Jason L. Riley, notes:

Even in the antebellum era, when slaves weren't permitted to wed, most black children lived with a biological mother and father. During Reconstruction and up until the 1940s, 75 % to 85 % of black children lived in two-parent families. Today more than 70 % of black children are born to single women. "The welfare state has done to black Americans what slavery couldn't do, what Jim Crow couldn't do, what the harshest racism couldn't do," Mr. Williams says. And that was to destroy the black family." . . .

(I)n 1982 he published his first book, "The State Against Blacks," arguing that laws regulating economic activity are far larger impediments to black progress than racial bigotry and discrimination. Nearly 30 years later he stands by that premise.

"Racial discrimination is not the problem of black people that it used to be" in his youth, says Mr. Williams. "Today I doubt you could find any significant problem that blacks face that is caused by racial discrimination. The 70 % illegitimacy rate is a devastating problem, but it doesn't have a damn thing to do with racism. The fact that in some areas black people are huddled in their homes at night, sometimes serving meals on the floor so they don't get hit by a stray bullet—that's not because the Klan is riding through the neighborhood." . . .

Mr. Williams says that "if there is anything good to be said about the Democratic White house and the previous Congress and their brazen attempt to take over the economy and control our lives, it's that the tea party movement has come out of it. But we have gone so far from the basic constitutional principles that made us a great country that it's a question of whether we can get back.". . .

"You find more and more black people—not enough in my opinion but more and more—questioning the status quo," he says. "When I fill in for Rush, I get emails from blacks who say they agree with what I'm saying. And there are a lot of white people questioning ideas on race, too. There's less white guilt out there. It's progress." [81]

There have been some shootings by police officers. Some of the officers have been white, and some have been black. Some of the shootings have been of white men, and others have been of black men. Black officers have shot white and black men, and white officers have shot white and black men. Sometimes the suspect has had a weapon, and other times the officer thought he had a weapon. When a white officer has shot a black man, there has been an immediate outcry by African Americans to have the white officer prosecuted. Their outrage is understandable. They wanted the officer(s) prosecuted no matter what the circumstances. The claim is made that the white officer shot the black man just because he was black. After investigations have been held, in most instances, the officers were found to have acted within the law. Even one finding that the officer did not act within the law is too many. Regardless, the protests have continued and they have kept the issue alive. Hopefully, this will ensure that the training and awareness of officers will continue. This led to the Black Lives Matter movement.

Of course, black lives matter. Before the civil rights movement in the middle of the twentieth century, it is clear that black people were discriminated against and oftentimes wrongly killed by white people, sometimes by white police officers. Were black people wronged? Absolutely. Do they have the right to be upset and angry for those things? Absolutely. It has taken a long time for civil rights to reach African Americans. There is no question that progress has been made. There is also no question that we have not reached the point of eliminating all discrimination.

As a part of the anger and the frustration, black people were encouraged to stand up for their rights. Who can disagree with that? However, that included encounters with police officers, white or black. When you try to claim your rights with an armed police officer, however, there is a different circumstance. Police officers are armed and have the legal right to use their weapons. Police officers are taught to control the encounter with a suspected law breaker. They give orders, which they expect to be obeyed. If those orders are not obeyed, the officer will attempt to enforce the order(s). This could lead to a physical altercation. If that happens, emotions escalate and turn to anxiety and probably fear on both sides. Two people fearing one another with a pistol in the mix will likely not have a good outcome.

There have been a number of incidents where white officers have killed black persons in instances where the officers were clearly in the wrong. These have been incidents of at least gross callousness for human life and, to some writers. the dehumanization of black people. These incidents have been caught on officers' body cameras or on cell phones of private citizens. We are fortunate that these have been recorded. Hopefully the perpetrators will be brought to justice. Police departments must get rid of racists and officers who exhibit callous behavior and/or dangerous tactics. They must be reminded of the value of human lives in all of their training.

As a result of officers killing black men, black men have begun to target officers. In many instances, the officers were lured to an area where they were basically assassinated. They did not have anything to do with the earlier killing. Will men and women continue to join police forces in this atmosphere? While they are trying to do their jobs, they could be targeted and shot. Or, they could be fired, charged, and prosecuted and perhaps spend time in jail if they are determined to have acted illegally. They need to really want to be police officers to take the risks that they face every day.

Those promoting the black lives matter movement were incensed when countered with the idea that white lives matter or all lives matter. But, the fact of the matter is *black lives matter, white lives matter,* and *all lives matter. To believe otherwise is to be a racist.*

Jussie Smollet

Jussie Smollet is an American actor.

On January 22, 2019, a letter arrived at the Chicago studio of Smollett's employer that was addressed to Smollett and depicted a stick figure hanging from a tree with a gun pointing toward it. It read "Smollett, Jussie you will die" and "MAGA" and contained a white powder determined to be Tylenol. On January 29, 2019, Smollett said that he was attacked in the early morning in the 300 block of East Lower North Water Street in Chicago's Streeterville neighborhood, in what was initially investigated as a hate crime. . . Smollett told police that he was attacked by two people he described as white men who were "yelling out racial and homophobic slurs" and who "poured an unknown chemical substance on him and began to beat him "about the face with their hands" and used their hands, feet, and teeth as weapons in the assault. According to a statement released by the Chicago Police Department, the two suspects then "poured an unknown liquid" on Smollett and put a noose around his neck. . . Smollet said that the attack may have been motivated by his criticism of the Trump administration and that he believed that the alleged assault was linked to the threatening letter that was sent to him earlier. . .

On January 30, 2019, public figures expressed support for Smollett on social media. Entertainment industry figures, including Shonda Rhimes and Viola Davis, tweeted their outrage over the attack and support for Smollett. Democratic senators and presidential candidates Kamala Harris and Cory Booker both described the attack as an attempted modern-day lynching. Booker urged Congress to pass a federal anti-lynching bill co-sponsored by him and Harris. In an interview with April Ryan of AURN, President Trump was asked about Smollett being attacked and said, "I think that's horrible. It doesn't get worse." Smollett faced skepticism regarding his claim of being attacked; he responded by saying that he believed that, if he had said his attackers were Mexicans, Muslims, or black people, "the doubters would have supported me much more ... And that says a lot about the place that we are in our country right now."

On February 13, Chicago police raided the home of two "persons of interest" in the case. The men are brothers, of Nigerian descent, who have acted as extras on *Empire*. Police recovered bleach and other items from the home. The brothers were held in police custody on suspicion of battery but were not charged. . .

The Chicago Police Department later told ABC News: "Police are investigating whether the two individuals committed the attack—or whether the attack happened at all"...

On February 20, 2019, Smollett was charged by a grand jury with a class 4 felony for filing a false police report. Smollett's felony count charge in Illinois carries a maximum sentence of three years in prison...

Chicago PD believe that Smollett staged the attack as a publicity stunt meant to further his career, ... by tying the incident to racism and President Trump, ...

On March 8, Smollett was indicted on 16 counts of "false report of offense" related to the incident... On March 26, 2019, all charges filed against Smollett were dropped . . . and the public file sealed. First Assistant States Attorney Joseph Magats said the office reached a deal with Smollett in which prosecutors dropped the charges upon Smollett performing sixteen hours of community service and forfeiting his $10,000 bond.

Chicago Police Superintendent Eddie T. Johnson held a press conference in which he spoke about Smollett, asking, "Why would anyone, especially an African American man, use the symbolism of a noose to make false accusations? ...Chicago police spokesman Anthony Guglielmi said "Allegations against Mr. Smollett are shameful and if proven, they are an afront to the people of Chicago...

The Mayor of Chicago, Rahm Emmanuel, strongly criticized the decision saying it was a "whitewash of justice" and that "From top to bottom, this is not on the level"...

... the city of Chicago filed a lawsuit ... against Smollett for the cost of overtime authorities expended investigating the alleged attack, specified in the complaint as $130,105.15. The suit further asked that Smollett be found liable for $1,000 "for each false statement he made to the city, in addition to three times the amount of the damages that the city sustained"...

On April 23, 2019, the Osundairo brothers filed a federal defamation lawsuit against Smollett's legal team. [82]

This was not the first racial hoax that occurred.

Claimed Racist Assaults That Turned Out to Be Hoaxes

Tawana Brawley, a black teenager in 1987, claimed that she had been raped and kidnapped by a group of white men in Dutchess County, New York. She alleged she had been attacked, smeared with feces, written on with racial slurs, and left along a road in a plastic bag. Reverend Al Sharpton supported her, and her allegations were placed on front pages across the nation. A special state grand jury later determined that her claims were fabricated, perhaps to avoid punishment for staying out late.

The county prosecutor at the time, Steven Pagones, who had been accused of being among Brawley's attackers, won a defamation suit against Sharpton, Brawley, and her attorneys. Sharpton paid his debt ($65,000), but Brawley, who was ordered to pay $190,000, had her wages garnished to pay the debt. Mr. Pagones has said that he is more interested in Ms. Brawley telling the truth than in receiving the cash from her.

Other hoaxes have also been investigated.

> Wilfred Reilly is an Assistant Professor of Political Science at Kentucky State University, a historically Black college in Frankfort, Kentucky. He holds a PhD in Political Science from Southern Illinois University and a law degree from the University of Illinois. Reilly's research focuses on empirical testing of political claims which are often very influential but, he claims, rarely well-supported by scientific data.
>
> Reilly's book *Hate Crime Hoax: How the Left Is Selling a Fake Race War,* was published by Regnery Publishing in February 2019. For the book, Reilly assembled a data set of 409 allegedly false or dubious hate crime allegations (concentrated during the past five years), which he describes as hoaxes on the basis of reports in mainstream national or regional news sources. [83]

In an article, he has identified other reported race crimes that also turned out to be hoaxes. He has concluded that there are three possible motivations for hate crime hoaxes. One is that some hoaxers have the same motivations as others who file false police reports, which make them criminals. Collecting insurance money is often a factor in false reports. Second, hoaxers may think they are doing something noble, for example, by reporting it to call attention to a real problem. Third:

. . .there is a very large and established grievance industry in the West. I don't want to blame individual institutions, as they do some good, but you cannot ignore something like the Southern Poverty Law Center, which has an endowment of $470million. They made $139million in profit last year. It's the size of a Fortune 500 business. And they don't stand alone. These groups have a vested interest in promoting the idea that the race war never ended. In fact, affirmative action, minority set-asides and funding for NGOs are all dependent on the existence of an ongoing ethnic conflict.

The problem with this argument is that there is not a great deal of ethnic conflict in the USA. Eighty-five per cent of white murder victims are murdered by whites, while 94 per cent of black people are killed by other black people. We desegregated in 1964, we had the Civil Rights Act in 1965, and affirmative action in favor of minorities began in 1967. The problem is often that the demand for bigots exceeds the supply. [84]

Black America Wrong to Blame White Racism for Woes

L. Todd Wood, a graduate of the US Air Force Academy, flew special operations helicopters supporting SEAL Team 6, Delta Force, and others. After leaving the military, he pursued his other passion, finance, spending eighteen years on Wall Street, trading emerging market debt, and later writing. The first of his many thrillers is *Currency*. Mr. Wood is a contributor to Fox Business, Newsmax TV, *Moscow Times,* the *New York Post,* the *National*

Review, Zero Hedge, and others. For more information about L. Todd Wood, visit LToddWood.com.

I'm mad as hell and I'm not taking it anymore. Black America wrong to blame white racism for woes.

I know of no white person alive today in the United States who has ever legally owned a black slave, or any slave for that matter. Almost 700,000 mostly white men died 160 years ago to end slavery. Jim Crow ended generations ago. Yet black America, for the most part, is still locked in inner-city gang violence and economic hardship. Why?

Is it because America is racist? Is it because of some overhanging white supremacy? Is it because of the Illuminati?

No, unfortunately, it is because of black culture and the adoption of Democratic Party government dependency. We have just had eight years of the first black president. Black athletes, and entertainers, routinely earn multi-million-dollar incomes. I can easily name several black billionaires without even trying too hard. A large percentage of black America is very successful. But, it is not enough. Too many black youth are being left behind.

And it is no one but black America's fault. No one can solve this problem but black America. No one can throw enough money at it. We've tried that.

Black America needs to look in the mirror and stop blaming others, especially white people.

I am obviously white and conservative, and I served in the military, which, during my time, was as color blind as you could be. I can also honestly say I don't give a damn what color your skin is, neither do any of my friends. I do care about your actions.

Blacks are around 15 percent of the population. Depending on what study you look at, they commit around 40 percent to 50 percent of violent crime in America. Of course, there is going to be a problem with police. And, of course, there are some bad policemen. However, those bad apples do not kill black people statistically any more than they kill white people. Even Harvard said that recently. If you were a cop, and you had to work in a neighborhood infested with crime and murder, wouldn't you act differently than in a neighborhood where there was little crime? The most effective thing black America could do to improve its relationship with police is to significantly reduce violent crime where they live. Yes, that means change the culture of where you live and your community.

I for one am tired of being blamed. I am tired of dealing with people who only want something from others. I don't oppress anyone. I don't hold anyone down. I'm tired of getting on the D.C. metro and seeing white people being harassed by roaming gangs of black youth with their pants around their knees. Yes, you want a white person uncomfortable? That makes me uncomfortable.

It's our nation's capital and it's embarrassing. Blacks have nothing but opportunity in America. Try finding the same opportunity anywhere else in the world. If you are born in America you've won life's economic lottery. Take advantage of it.

The problem is this generation has been taught an agenda of cultural Marxism by our education system. They've been taught to be a victim, and it's still going on. All you have to do is watch the young black, female student at Yale screaming at the college president to understand that. Blacks in America don't even know how good they got it.

Don't kneel when my anthem is played. Too many people died for that flag. You are free to protest but not then. I am free to not watch or pay to watch you play if you do that. The NFL should make it a rule that you stand for the national anthem. There is no free speech to disobey a private employer on private property. This would solve the problem immediately. The NFL has deeply offended most of America. They will pay an economic and reputational price, as they should.

We have a real cultural problem in this country, the result of the Leftist multicultural agenda. Multi-ethnicity is perfect and should be encouraged. Having more than one American culture is destroying the country. But then again, that is what the Left wants. [85]

Presidents Abraham Lincoln and Dwight D. Eisenhower

While black voters generally vote in favor of Democrat candidates, Republicans and Republican presidents have had significant roles in helping to end segregation.

"Racial segregation, as a general term, includes the segregation along racial lines of access to facilities, services and opportunities such as housing, medical care, education, employment, and transportation. The expression most often refers to the legally or socially enforced separation of African Americans from other races." [86]

President Abraham Lincoln

President Abraham Lincoln served from 1861 to 1865 as the first Republican president of the new Republican Party. On January 1, 1863, he issued the Emancipation Proclamation as an executive order issued by the president. It had been signed on September 15, 1862. There were a number of issues that led to the Civil War, including slavery in the economy and society, states and federal rights, slave and non-slave states, the abolitionist movement, and the election of Abraham Lincoln. It changed the federal legal status of more than 3.5 million enslaved blacks in the designated areas of the South from slave to free. President Lincoln was assassinated on April 4, 1865, near the end of the Civil War because of his role in freeing the slaves.

Here is the Emancipation Proclamation. It is one of the most important actions ever taken by a president of the United States!

January 1, 1863
A Transcription
By the President of the United States of America:

A Proclamation.

Whereas, on the twenty-second day of September, in the year of our Lord one thousand eight hundred and sixty-two, a proclamation was issued by the President of the United States, containing, among other things, the following, to wit:

That on the first day of January, in the year of our Lord one thousand eight hundred and sixty-three, all persons held as slaves within any State or designated part of a State, the people whereof shall then be in rebellion against the United States, shall be then, thenceforward, and forever free; and the Executive Government of the United States, including the military and naval authority thereof, will recognize and maintain the freedom of such persons, and will do no act or acts to repress such persons, or any of them, in any efforts they may make for their actual freedom.

That the Executive will, on the first day of January aforesaid, by proclamation, designate the States and parts of States, if any, in which the people thereof, respectively, shall then be in rebellion against the United States; and the fact that any State, or the people thereof, shall on that day be, in good faith, represented in the Congress of the United States by members chosen thereto at elections wherein a majority of the qualified voters of such State shall have participated, shall, in the absence of strong countervailing testimony, be deemed conclusive evidence that such State, and the people thereof, are not then in rebellion against the United States.

Now, therefore I, Abraham Lincoln, President of the United States, by virtue of the power in me vested as Commander-in-Chief, of the Army and Navy of the United States in time of actual armed rebellion against the authority and government of the United States, and as a fit and necessary war measure for suppressing said rebellion, do, on this first day of January, in the year of our Lord one thousand eight hundred and sixty-three, and in accordance with my purpose so to do publicly proclaimed for the full period of one hundred days, from the day first above mentioned, order and designate as the States and parts of States wherein the people thereof respectively, are this day in rebellion against the United States, the following, to wit:

Arkansas, Texas, Louisiana, (except the Parishes of St. Bernard, Plaquemines, Jefferson, St. John, St. Charles, St. James Ascension, Assumption, Terrebonne, Lafourche, St. Mary, St. Martin, and Orleans, including the City of New Orleans) Mississippi, Alabama, Florida, Georgia, South Carolina, North Carolina, and Virginia, (except the forty-eight counties designated as West Virginia, and also the counties of Berkley, Accomac, Northampton, Elizabeth City, York, Princess Ann, and Norfolk, including the cities of Norfolk and

Portsmouth[)], and which excepted parts, are for the present, left precisely as if this proclamation were not issued.

And by virtue of the power, and for the purpose aforesaid, I do order and declare that all persons held as slaves within said designated States, and parts of States, are, and henceforward shall be free; and that the Executive government of the United States, including the military and naval authorities thereof, will recognize and maintain the freedom of said persons.

And I hereby enjoin upon the people so declared to be free to abstain from all violence, unless in necessary self-defence; and I recommend to them that, in all cases when allowed, they labor faithfully for reasonable wages.

And I further declare and make known, that such persons of suitable condition, will be received into the armed service of the United States to garrison forts, positions, stations, and other places, and to man vessels of all sorts in said service.

And upon this act, sincerely believed to be an act of justice, warranted by the Constitution, upon military necessity, I invoke the considerate judgment of mankind, and the gracious favor of Almighty God.

In witness whereof, I have hereunto set my hand and caused the seal of the United States to be affixed.

Done at the City of Washington, this first day of January, in the year of our Lord one thousand eight hundred and sixty three, and of the Independence of the United States of America the eighty-seventh.

(By the President: ABRAHAM LINCOLN)
WILLIAM H. SEWARD, Secretary of State. [87]

President Dwight D. Eisenhower

President Dwight D. Eisenhower served from 1953 to 1961. He played a significant role in freeing blacks from racial segregation and in ending segregation that had been ongoing in the United States since its founding and even before.

Eisenhower favored a patient, constitutionalist approach that would avoid a violent disruption of Southern society. However, by the mid-1950s he realized that he would have no control over the pace of integration, and he responded with actions and proposed legislative initiatives to provide racial equality. He was not successful in getting sweeping reforms passed by Congress, but he did build a sturdy foundation upon which more comprehensive changes were made in the years following his presidency. Consider the following:

Eisenhower appointed California Governor Earl Warren as Chief Justice of the Supreme Court. Warren molded a unanimous decision in Brown v. Board of Education, striking down public school segregation. Eisenhower also appointed outstanding jurists such as Potter Stewart, William

Brennan, John Marshall Harlan II, and Charles
Evans Whittaker to the Warren Court.

Eisenhower was consistently careful to appoint to
the southern districts federal judges who were sol-
idly committed to equal rights, fighting southern
senators to get them confirmed. When enforcement
of future civil rights laws came before the district
courts in the 1960s, they were upheld by progressive
judges—Frank Johnson, Jr., and Elbert Parr Tuttle,
for instance, appointed by Eisenhower years earlier.
Eisenhower's judicial appointments constitute a significant contribution to civil rights.

Eisenhower achieved Congressional passage of the
first civil rights legislation in the 82 years following
Reconstruction. The Senate at first refused to pass
the bill, which included both voting rights and a
provision authorizing the Attorney General to protect all civil rights. Eventually, Congress approved
the Civil Rights Act of 1957 without overall civil
rights protection. This was a much weaker law
than what Eisenhower had advocated. In 1960,
Eisenhower was successful in getting Congress to
pass additional voting rights legislation. These laws
were the precedents for the civil rights legislation
of the 1960s.

Eisenhower implemented the integration of the
U.S. military forces. Although President Truman
issued Executive Order 9981 (1948) to desegregate the military services, his administration had
limited success in realizing it. As a life-long soldier,

Dwight Eisenhower knew intimately the reality of racial intolerance in the military. As president, he commanded compliance from subordinates and was able to overcome the deeply rooted racial institutions in the military establishment. By October 30, 1954, the last racially segregated unit in the armed forces had been abolished, and all federally controlled schools for military dependent children had been desegregated.

Eisenhower sent elements of the 101st Airborne Division to carry out the mandate of the U.S. Supreme Court, when Orval Faubus of Arkansas openly defied a federal court order to integrate Little Rock Central High, an all-white high school. This act, the first time since Reconstruction that federal troops were deployed to a former Confederate state, was condemned by many at the time, but it established that southern states could not use force to defeat the Constitution.

Eisenhower was the first president to elevate an African American to an executive level position in the White House. In July 1955, President Eisenhower appointed E. Frederic Morrow, a graduate of Bowdoin College and the Rutgers University Law School, as Administrative Officer for Special Projects.

Eisenhower worked to achieve full integration in the nation's capital from his first day in office until the end of his administration. The President approached this task from several different angles.

He appointed pro-desegregation district government officials and directed the Justice Department to argue in favor of desegregation in the Supreme Court. One of the results of judicial actions he instigated was the Supreme Court's Thompson decision which desegregated Washington restaurants. He personally cajoled, persuaded, and pressured local government administrators, motion picture moguls, and businessmen in meetings at the White House. By the time Eisenhower left Washington, the Capital of the United States was transformed from an entirely segregated to an almost fully integrated city.

Eisenhower established the first comprehensive regulations prohibiting racial discrimination in the federal workforce. He established presidential committees that set standards and pressured government agencies and businesses with government contracts to end racial discrimination in employment.

Eisenhower was the first president since Reconstruction to meet personally in the White House with black civil rights leaders. He discussed national policy on civil rights with Martin Luther King, Jr., A. Philip Randolph, Roy Wilkins, and Lester B. Granger. [88]

The Racist History of the Democrat Party

Wayne Perryman, an inner city minister in Seattle and the author of Unfounded Loyalty, in an editorial circulating on the Internet (Feb. 2004), wrote:

Most people are either a Democrat by design, or a Democrat by deception. That is either they were well aware of the racist history of the Democrat Party and still chose to be Democrat, or they were deceived into thinking that the Democratic Party is a party that sincerely cared about Black people.

History reveals that every piece of racist legislation that was ever passed and every racist terrorist attack that was ever inflicted on African Americans, was initiated by the members of the Democratic Party. From the formation of the Democratic Party in 1792 to the Civil Rights movement of 1960's, Congressional records show the Democrat Party passed no specific laws to help Blacks, every law that they introduced into Congress was designed to hurt blacks in 1894 Repeal Act (sic). The chronicles of history shows that during the past 160 years the Democratic Party legislated Jim Crow laws, Black Codes and a multitude of other laws at the state and federal level to deny African Americans their rights as citizens.

History reveals that the Republican Party was formed in 1854 to abolish slavery and challenge other racist legislative acts initiated by the Democratic Party.

Some called it the Civil War, others called it the War Between the States, but to the African Americans at that time, it was the War Between the Democrats and the Republicans over slavery. The Democrats gave their lives to expand it, Republicans gave their lives to ban it.

During the Senate debates on the Ku Klux Klan Act of 1871, it was revealed that members of the Democratic Party formed many terrorist organizations like the Ku Klux Klan to murder and intimidate African Americans voters. The Ku Klux Klan Act was a bill introduced by a Republican Congress to stop Klan Activities. Senate debates revealed that the Klan was the terrorist arm of the Democratic Party.

History reveals that Democrats lynched, burned, mutilated and murdered thousands of blacks and completely destroyed entire towns and communities occupied by middle class Blacks, including Rosewood, Florida, the Greenwood District in Tulsa Oklahoma, and Wilmington, North Carolina to name a few.

After the Civil War, Democrats murdered several hundred black elected officials (in the South) to regain control of the southern government. All of the elected officials up to 1935 were Republicans....

History reveals that it was Thaddeus Stevens, a Radical Republican that introduced legislation to give African Americans the so-called 40 acres and a mule and Democrats overwhelmingly voted against the bill. Today many white Democrats are opposed to paying African Americans trillions of dollars in

Reparation Pay, money that should be paid by the Democratic Party.

History reveals that it was Abolitionists and Radical Republicans such as Henry L. Morehouse and General Oliver Howard that started many of the traditional Black colleges, while Democrats fought to keep them closed. Many of our traditional Black colleges are named after white Republicans.

Congressional records show it was Democrats that strongly opposed the passage of the 13th, 14th and 15th Amendments. These three Amendments were introduced by Republicans to abolish slavery, give citizenship to all African Americans born in the United States and, give Blacks the right to vote.

Congressional records show that Democrats were opposed to passing the following laws that were introduced by Republicans to achieve civil rights for African Americans:

Civil Rights Act 1866
Reconstruction Act of 1867
Freedman Bureau Extension Act of 1866
Enforcement Act of 1870
Force Act of 1871
Ku Klux Klan Act of 1871
Civil Rights Act of 1875
Civil Rights Act of 1957
Civil Rights Act of 1960

And during the 60's many Democrats fought hard to defeat the

1964 Civil Rights Act
1965 Voting Rights Acts
1972 Equal Employment Opportunity Act

Court records shows that it was the Democrats that supported the Dred Scott Decision. The decision classified Blacks as property rather than people. It was also the racist Jim Crow practices initiated by Democrats that brought about the two landmark cases of Plessy v. Ferguson and Brown v. The Board of Education.

At the turn of the century (1900), Southern Democrats continued to oppress African Americans by placing thousands in hard-core prison labor camps. According to most historians, the prison camps were far worst (sic) than slavery. The prisoners were required to work from 10–14 hours a day, six to seven days a week in temperatures that exceeded 100 degrees and in temperatures that fell well below zero. The camps provided free labor for building railroads, mining coal mines and for draining snake and alligator infested swamps and rivers. . .

History reveals that it was three white persons that opposed the Democrat's racist practices who started the NAACP. . .

Over the strong objections of racist Republican Senator Jessie Helms, Republican President Ronald Reagan, signed into law, a bill to make Dr. Martin Luther King's birthday a national holiday. Several Republican Senators convinced President Reagan this was the right thing to do.

Congressional records show after signing the 1972 Equal Employment Opportunity Act and issuing Executive Order 11478, Richard Nixon, a Republican, started what we know as Affirmative Action. . .

After exclusively giving the Democrats their votes for the past 25 years, the average African American cannot point to one piece of civil rights legislation sponsored solely by the Democratic Party that was specifically designed to eradicate the unique problems that African Americans face today. . .

Today both parties must remember their past. The Democrats must remember the terrible things they did to Blacks and apologize and the Republicans must remember the terrific things they did for Blacks and re-commit to complete the work that their predecessors started and died for. [89]

A retired professor has also written a paper on:

The Party of Lincoln's Record on Racial Justice
Spielberg's Critically Acclaimed Film Avails Historical Reality Check
BY PAUL TROUT, Ph D

With the release and critical acclaim of Steven Spielberg's stunning film Lincoln, one wonders if Blacks, Whites, Democrats and Republicans are not confused.

> As this movie makes clear, it was the Republican Party (frequently labeled as racist) that passed the constitutional amendment ending slavery (in 1865) against the strident opposition of northern Democrats. But isn't it the Democrat Party that is the protector of civil rights?

> Well, the historical record tells a different story, and raises the question about how the party of segregation got the right to tattoo the party of Lincoln with the scarlet "R".

> The Republican Party (1854) was created to protect Blacks from Democrats (sorry, but that's the only way to put it). The Democrat Party passed the Fugitive Slave Law (1854), the Kansas/Nebraska Act (1854), which allowed territories to vote to allow slavery, and it supported the Dred Scott decision (1857), that proclaimed Blacks to be non-citizens.

> Republicans wanted none of this. Besides passing the Thirteenth Amendment, Congressional Republicans also passed the Fourteenth Amendment (1868), making Blacks full citizens of the United States, and the Fifteenth Amendment (1870), guaranteeing Blacks the right to vote. It also passed the first civil rights bill (1866) and several measures protecting Blacks in the post-war South. In gratitude, Blacks overwhelmingly voted for Republicans.

Democrats wanted none of this. So, the Party came up with the best vote-suppressing device it ever devised—the Ku Klux Klan (1866). Historian Eric Foner describes the Klan as "a military force serving the interests of the Democratic Party." Thanks to Klan lynchings, the Republican vote in six heavily Black counties in Mississippi in the election of 1876 plunged from over 14,000 to a mere 723. By 1904, the number of Black Republican voters in Louisiana had shrunk from 130,000 to a mere 1,342. By 1877, the Democrat party had seized control in every southern state, and for nearly a hundred years the "solid South" was reliably Democrat and opposed to civil rights for Blacks ("Jim Crow" segregation laws, etc.).

Naturally, I'm simplifying a complex historical record, but this summary does not distort the essential truth about the two parties in the nineteenth century. Coming to the twentieth century, we find that the past was prologue.

Let's start with the Dems. Since 1840, the Democrat Party has had 43 national political platforms, 25 of which defended slavery, warned of "negro supremacy," encouraged loyalty to segregation, expressed hostility to Black voting rights, opposed anti-lynching laws, and supported poll taxes. There were so many Klansmen at the 1924 National Democrat Convention in New York that it was dubbed the "Klan Bake."

All three post-Civil War Democrats elected president before Harry Truman—Grover Cleveland, Woodrow Wilson, and Franklin Roosevelt—were supported by southern segregationists. Roosevelt admitted that Klansmen were among his "best friends and supporters."

In 1894 President Cleveland eviscerated what was left of the civil rights bills passed by Republicans after the Civil War. "Progressive" Woodrow Wilson barred Blacks from serving in the Federal government. Roosevelt excluded a significant portion of Black workers from Social Security coverage, refused to support Republican-sponsored anti-lynching legislation, banned Blacks from White House press conferences, and segregated his Warm Springs retreat. All three Democrats appointed notorious racists and Klan members to everything from the Supreme Court to Cabinet positions.

Not to say that the Democrat Party didn't have moments of racial sanity. Democrat President Harry Truman did officially desegregate the military, but he was making official what General Eisenhower had started during WWII.

It's also true that Congress passed the Civil Rights Act under Democrat President Lyndon Johnson, but the bill never would have made it into law without the overwhelming support of Republicans. Only 6 Republicans voted against the bill, but 21 Democrats did (including Albert Gore Sr.). One of these 21 was Robert Byrd—a former "Keagle" in the

Klan and a long-serving Senator—who filibustered the bill for 54 days, and as late as March 2001, used the N-word publicly as a sitting U.S. Senator.

How did the Republicans begin the twentieth century? By founding Black colleges and universities throughout the South (Morehouse, Spelman, Fisk, Sam Houston, Howard, etc.), despite often brutal efforts by Democrats to stop them (see hiphoprepublicans.com). White and Black Republicans also founded the NAACP in 1908. Later, it was Republican President Dwight Eisenhower who signed the 1957 Civil Rights Act that not only further protected the right of Blacks to vote but established the U.S. Commission on Civil Rights, and formed the foundation of the Civil Rights Division of the Department of Justice.

Eisenhower's Department of Justice argued successfully for school desegregation before the Supreme Court while the Democrat Party supported school segregation ("separate but equal"). The 1956 platform of the Republican Party endorsed the "Brown" decision, but the platform of the Democrat Party did not. Not blowing smoke, Eisenhower had the moral courage to send troops to Little Rock, Arkansas in 1957 to enforce the Court's desegregation decision.

Behind the scenes, Republican Senator Everett Dirksen from Illinois performed yeoman service for the cause of Black civil rights by making sure Congressional Republicans remained true to their historic mission by voting for civil rights legislation in 1957, 1960, 1964, and 1965. Dirksen also wrote both the 1965 Voting Rights Act and the Civil Rights Act of 1968, which prohibited discrimination in housing. Democrats assert that the racist southern members of their party all jumped to the Republican Party in the 1960s. Why they would is not explained. In fact, the prevailing sentiment of these Dixiecrats was that it was better to vote for a "yellow dog" than for a Republican. Some of these Dixiecrats had long illustrious political careers as Democrats (e.g., Robert Byrd).

What about glower-puss Republican Richard Nixon? Well, Tricky Dick managed to accommodate southern sensibilities rhetorically while delivering desegregation substantively. To overcome 15 years of foot-dragging on school desegregation, Nixon formed a cabinet committee that negotiated within months the successful desegregation of local school systems in the South within a couple of years. He also laid the basis for affirmative action by imposing race-preference guidelines on government contractors. He also pioneered minority set-asides in federal procurement and contracting to boost Black ownership of businesses, trying to undo some of the damage done by Woodrow Wilson. The long-term merit of these programs aside, they continued the civil rights program of the party of Lincoln.

So, what happened in the twentieth century to explain how the party of Lincoln became stigmatized as racist, while the party with so many avowed racists did the stigmatizing?

It was the Fall of 1960, and Nixon (R) and Kennedy (D) were in a heated race for the presidency. In the South, Martin Luther King Jr. had just been arrested in Atlanta, Georgia. The situation was menacing. Democrat County officials allowed the Klan to march through the courthouse where King was being arraigned. Then King was sentenced to four months hard labor on a Georgia chain gang, a punishment tantamount to a death sentence. Alarm spread throughout the Black South and most of the country.

A staff member suggested to Kennedy that he call Coretta King as a courtesy. Kennedy replied, "What the hell. Why not?" The conversation lasted two minutes, with Kennedy saying, "If there is anything I can do to help, please feel free to call on me." That was it. But when news of the call leaked out (Kennedy was afraid of losing White voters) there was a sea-change in Black political allegiance. That telephone call flipped—and flipped off, as it were— racial history.

When King was released the next day, his father held a press conference. He announced that he was changing his vote from Nixon to Kennedy and was going to put all the Black votes he controlled in his church into a suitcase and dump it in Kennedy's lap. Ralph Abernathy told Blacks to "take off your Nixon buttons." And they did. In 1956, 60 percent of Blacks voted Republican. In 1960, 70 percent voted Democrat. Now 96 percent vote Democrat.

What does Kennedy's call have to do with the Republican Party being labeled racist?

Well, Democrats had to somehow secure the sudden and astonishing support of Blacks. What better way than by commandeering the term racist and slapping it on their political opponents? It was easy to do because the term can mean almost anything you want it to mean. For example, MSNBC's Chris Matthews, a Democrat, readily suggests Republicans who oppose Obama are racist. This negative branding is not only "good" politics but serves deeper needs.

Use of the term miraculously nullifies the Democrat Party's hideous history. The term also allows the Party to shame its shamers by besmirching them with the same racial mud that once coated Democrats.

Commandeering the term racist also magically immunizes Democrats from the charge. Democrats are free to call Black Republicans anything they want with impunity (Oreos, Uncle Tom's, etc.).

More importantly, by exploiting the epithet, the Democrat Party is able to shield its secular quest for racial atonement. Let me explain.

In an effort to atone for its racist past, the Democrat Party champions all kinds of programs intended to help Blacks. It doesn't matter that many of these programs are redundant and pernicious in the long term. What does matter is that these programs serve to exculpate Democrats from the racial sins of the past. As Black scholar Shelby Steele sees it, the real purpose of "redemptive liberalism" is not actually to improve the lives of Blacks but to assuage White guilt.

To question, interfere with, or obstruct any of these programs, one might say, is tantamount to impeding a quest for racial salvation, and cannot be tolerated. When the statesman-like Senator Daniel Patrick Moynihan—a scholar as well as politician—published a work in 1965 that correctly argued that federal welfare policies dear to Democrats were helping break-up Black families, he was roundly denounced as a bigot and racist, and he was a Democrat. By branding Republicans as racist, impugning their motives, and undermining their right to help organize a decent society, Democrats prevent cogent criticism of their "good works," not all of which have turned out good—$7 trillion dollars, for example, having been poured into inner cities since the 1960s with little decline in poverty or demoralization, and an increase in dependency. It is not unfair therefore to assert that by delegitimizing the right of the Republican Party to honestly vet social policy and legislation, the Democrat Party (however good its intentions) has again wound up doing damage to Blacks.

Moreover, even if we should parse the political record right up to yesterday, we won't find any law, policy, or secret sin so egregious as to warrant the defamation of the Republican Party as "racist." Quite the opposite.

Since its creation, the GOP has struggled honorably to protect and extend civil rights and social well being, often against the rank hostility of Democrats.

Like it or not, the Republican Party has done nothing more than the Democrat Party to deserve the label "racist," and a good deal less.

Paul Trout is a retired professor of English at Montana State University, Bozeman. [90]

Wikipedia reports the following regarding Jim Crow Laws:

Jim Crow laws were state and local laws that enforced racial segregation in the Southern United States. All were enacted in the late 19th and early 20th centuries by white far-right Democratic-dominated state legislatures after the Reconstruction period. The laws were enforced until 1965. In practice, Jim Crow laws mandated racial segregation in all public facilities in the states of the former Confederate States of America and other states, starting in the 1870s and 1880s, and were upheld in 1896 by the U.S. Supreme Court's "separate but equal" legal doctrine for facilities for African Americans, established with the court's decision in the case of Plessy vs. Ferguson. Moreover, public education had essentially been segregated since its establishment in most of the South, after the *Civil War* (1861–65). [91]

Many African Americans Fought in the Civil War

Many African Americans fought in the Civil War on the Union side. None felt the purpose of the mission more than the African

American soldier for his efforts gave him a chance to strike a blow against slavery and prove himself equal to his white comrades.

Sergeant William Harvey Carney was the first African American to receive the Medal of Honor in the Civil War. Sergeant Carney was born a slave, but his father escaped slavery and worked hard to buy freedom for the rest of his family. He joined the Union Army and ended up in Company C of the 54th Massachusetts Infantry Regiment. The unit was commanded by Colonel Robert Gould Shaw and was an all African American unit except for senior officers and a few non-commissioned sergeants. The 54th went to battle on July 18, 1863, against Fort Wagner outside of Charleston, South Carolina. The 54th was ordered to advance against a heavy barrage of shelling and musketry from the fort. The flag bearer of the 54th was wounded, so Sergeant Carney dropped his gun and grabbed the flag and moved to the front of the attack. He was wounded by musket fire four times but, despite being seriously wounded, he refused to drop the flag until he was brought to the rear for medical treatment. The Union forces were repulsed at that battle, but the 54th was widely praised for its bravery, and that bravery spurred other black men to join the Union Army. Sergeant Carney was discharged from the Army because of his injuries. President Abraham Lincoln noted that the 54th's bravery during that battle was a key development that helped final victory for the North. When asked about his heroic actions during the Medal of Honor ceremony, he said, "I only did my duty." (This battle was the subject of the movie *Glory*, starring Matthew Broderick, Denzel Washington, and Morgan Freeman). [92]

African Americans also made some progress in national politics during the period of reconstruction after the Civil War. At least twenty-one (some accounts say twenty-three) African Americans served in the House of Representatives. They were all Republicans.

6

FOREIGN AFFAIRS

I t's dangerous out there! There are many nations and groups that would like to see the United States of America fail—to see it removed from the international stage.

Conservatives believe in having a strong military—the strongest in the world. They want a military that must be respected by the rest of the world. We have used our full military power in only a few instances—namely World War I and World War II—with great success. We won because of a combination of the strength of our military, the strength of our economy, and the strength of our collective will to win. The strength of our economy, in gearing-up for war and in producing military equipment, enabled us to have the military might we needed. The strength of our will to win led to men and women joining the military to fight, joining industry to produce supplies and equipment to bring our industrial capacity to full strength, and in enduring sacrifices in their family lives and in goods and services.

However, whenever we have gotten involved in war and won victory, we have never taken over as an occupying nation and stayed to govern the conquered. Instead, we have helped the countries recover and seen them become our allies. The strength of our will is as important as the strength of our military and the strength of our economy. A perfect example is Vietnam. Protestors undercut the ability to prosecute the war to a winning conclusion. The most despicable of their protests was to label our soldiers as "baby killers" and as murderers of innocent people because of a few well-publicized incidents. The result of the protests was that our soldiers were not honored when they returned home and instead were booed and spit upon. Many soldiers would not admit to having served in Vietnam for fear of the treatment they might receive.

It took years for their service to be recognized and for them to be honored for their service. The opening of the Vietnam Veterans Memorial in Constitution Gardens in Washington, DC in 1982, with the names of some 58,195 servicemen and servicewomen who lost their lives in Vietnam, was finally recognition of their honored service on behalf of our country.

If our strength were to falter—as it did during the President Obama years—there will be problems all over the world and in the United States.

Peace through Strength

Dwight D. Eisenhower ran for president of the United States as a Republican and won, becoming the 34th president of the United States. Prior to that he was an Army Five-Star General who served as Supreme Commander of the Allied Expeditionary Forces in Europe during World War II. His vice president was Richard M. Nixon.

President Eisenhower set forth a series of fixed principles in his first Inaugural Address in 1953. Among them, he stated the following:

> In our quest for an honorable peace, we shall neither compromise, nor tire, nor ever cease. . . We must be

ready to dare all for our country. For history does not long entrust the care of freedom to the weak or the timid. We must acquire proficiency in defense and display stamina in purpose.

Ronald Reagan, a former actor who had served as governor of California for eight years, was elected president of the United States in 1980 as a conservative Republican, becoming the nation's 40th president. Before his entry into politics, he was a Democrat. George H. W. Bush was his vice president.

The Inaugural Speech of President Reagan on January 20, 1981, included the following:

> To those neighbors and allies who share our freedom, we will strengthen our historic ties and assure them of our support and firm commitment. We will match loyalty with loyalty. We will strive for mutually beneficial relations. We will not use our friendship to impose on their sovereignty, for our own sovereignty is not for sale.

> As for the enemies of freedom, those who are potential adversaries, they will be reminded that peace is the highest aspiration of the American people. We will negotiate for it, sacrifice for it; we will not surrender for it, now or ever.

> Our forbearance should never be misunderstood. Our reluctance for conflict should not be misjudged as a failure of will. When action is required to preserve our national security, we will act. We will maintain sufficient strength to prevail if need be,

knowing that if we do so we have the best chance
of never having to use that strength.

"Peace through strength" became the guiding principle on foreign affairs of President Reagan.

Before him, Jimmy Carter, a Democrat, had served as the 39th
president of the United States with Walter Mondale as his vice
president. In late 1979, American citizens had been taken hostage
in Iran. With the exception of one failed attempt to rescue them,
President Carter had taken no action other than failed diplomatic
efforts to secure their release. During the entire time the hostages
were in Iranian custody, the most powerful nation in the world
was shown to not have the will to take action to get them back.
The most powerful nation in the world was itself held hostage by
a small country in the Middle East. The United States was shown
to be powerless.

On the day President Reagan was sworn in as president, the
hostages had been in custody for 444 days, nearly fifteen months.
One of the issues he campaigned on was the apparent inability of
the United States to take action to end the hostage crisis and to
bring the Americans home. He talked tough, and the terrorists listened. And, more important, because of Reagan's words and actions,
they knew that he would take action to get the hostages back when
he became president.

On the day of his inauguration, the Iranians released the
prisoners.

President Reagan started his administration by being feared by
the Iranians. Other nations took note of the same things President
Reagan had said during the period leading to his presidency and
of Iran's release of the hostages. If the commander-in-chief is
respected, the United States is respected. If the United States is
respected, the commander-in-chief is respected—at least until he
earns disrespect. President Carter had let that happen.

During President Reagan's time as president, the United States and the Union of Soviet Socialist Republics (USSR) were engaged in a cold war. "The Cold War is the name given to the relationship that developed between the USA and the USSR after World War Two." [93] It was a state of political hostility characterized by threats and propaganda short of open warfare. It began in earnest during the Cuban Missile Crisis of 1962 when John F. Kennedy was president.

President Kennedy had authorized the Bay of Pigs invasion after Fidel Castro had led a revolution and became president of Cuba. The Bay of Pigs Invasion was supposed to oust Castro from power, but it failed. The USSR was a sponsor/supporter of Castro and had started to deliver nuclear missiles to Cuba, which is about 105 miles from southern Florida in the United States. The missiles had been discovered by spy planes that had been flying over Cuba. In flight time, the missiles were only a couple of minutes from Florida, and they could reach some of our large population centers as well. At the time, both the United States and the USSR had nuclear weapons and the capability to deliver them by airplane and by missiles.

John F. Kennedy, in his inaugural address in January, 1961, when he was becoming president of the United States said: "Let every nation know, whether it wishes us well or ill, that we shall pay any price, bear any burden, meet any hardship, support any friend, oppose any foe, in order to assure the survival and the success of liberty."

President Kennedy ordered a blockade of Cuba to stop and prevent any further deliveries of missiles to Cuba with the demand that all missiles be removed from Cuba as well. This was a period of high tension, probably as tense as any period before or after. During this crisis, Premier Nikita Khrushchev was the leader of the USSR. At the time he famously, or infamously, said of the United States: "We will bury you!"

In deliberations leading to the blockade, President Kennedy and his advisors were deeply concerned that any military action could lead to retaliation from the USSR. Retaliation that could lead to the firing of nuclear missiles by the USSR, which would lead to retaliation by the United States. Since both countries had enough nuclear weapons to destroy each other many times over, the possible outcome of such action would lead to "mutually assured destruction." "Mutually assured destruction" was probably regarded as "MAD," its acronym, and maybe that was in the mind of whomever thought of the label.

Much has been written about the days in May when these events occurred, and a movie was made of it, entitled *Thirteen Days*. Suffice it to say that the world was on the brink of nuclear war. Premier Khrushchev was being stared down by President Kennedy, and Premier Khrushchev blinked. His ships did not try to run the blockade, and the missiles were withdrawn from Cuba. If they had remained there, just think of the leverage they would have given Castro and Khrushchev in all future dealings with the United States. The thought of missiles being so close to the United States was unpalatable to President Kennedy and his advisors. President Kennedy decided at that moment that it was of the utmost importance that the United States be strong during this confrontation.

He believed in "peace through strength."

The cold war continued until Ronald Reagan became president. Ultimately, the USSR collapsed while he was president. It was President Reagan's strength in not making bad deals with the USSR and the United States' economy that led to that collapse. The USSR simply could not keep up with our economic strength. President Reagan also believed that any deal with a foreign country should be constantly evaluated. He believed in verifying that they were following their agreements. "Trust but verify" was his mantra.

History, both world history and United States history, is one of the most important areas that must be taught in our schools.

Besides learning about our heritage and how the various societies and countries have evolved, one of the most important parts of history is learning about things that have happened in the past, good and bad. The idea is to learn from mistakes and to take steps to ensure that they are not repeated. Those who ignore the lessons of history will watch it being repeated and pay the price—a high price.

A philosophy of "peace through strength," if put into practice, discourages nations and others from testing our foreign policy and our commitment to our foreign friends. But to practice that philosophy requires not only strong words but strong action to support those words. That, on occasion, may require military action. Talking strong and taking strong action early has as its goal removing the need for stronger action later that could lead to even stronger reactions.

In his First Annual Message on January 8, 1790, President George Washington said: "To be prepared for war, is one of the most effectual means of preserving peace." [94]

If you do not believe in "peace through strength," in what do you believe? What are some alternatives?

Peace through weakness? Obviously not! Whether in your personal life or in the life of a country, if this is your philosophy, you will be taken advantage of. If you do not stop whatever is happening initially, it could get worse and worse until finally you have no options other than ones that are drastic.

How about peace through appeasement? "Appeasement in a political context is a diplomatic policy of making political or material concessions to an enemy power in order to avoid conflict." [95]

This is where you believe that by being nice to your enemies, they will treat you nicely as well.

In the late 1930s, Neville Chamberlain, who was the prime minister of Great Britain, thought that peace could be achieved by appeasing Adolph Hitler of Germany as he started his conquest of Europe. He took no action until Hitler had acquired enough strength to continue his conquests. At that point, Britain and Europe began to take serious notice of what he was doing and what he may do in the future. Prime Minister Chamberlain was replaced by Winston Churchill.

In 1940, Britain was engaged in a great debate in Parliament over what should be done about the Germans' aggression. There was a strong group that supported Chamberlain and that did not want to take on Germany. There was another group that supported Churchill who believed that Germany should be stopped then. The 2017 movie, *The Darkest Hour,* dealt with this event. Churchill was having trouble arranging the support he needed. In perhaps the most important scene in the movie, King George met with Churchill. He told Churchill that Germany needed to be stopped and that he supported Churchill's efforts. King George did not want England to become a puppet of Germany.

If Hitler had been seriously opposed early on in his conquests, he could have been stopped. If he had been opposed, it may have led to shooting and to war. When you believe in "peace through strength," that could happen. But one cannot be afraid of that, and one must be aware that your goal is to make sure that far worse events do not occur by your failure to act.

England entered the battle, and the United States entered the war after Japan attacked Pearl Harbor, Hawaii, on December 7, 1941. But, Hitler's ambition led to World War II that lasted until 1945, years after the time he could have been stopped. Hundreds of thousands of United States service men and women died or were wounded, and it led to the murder of over 6,000,000 Jews at the hands of Hitler's forces.

"Appeasement only makes the aggressor more aggressive!" (Dean Rusk, United States Secretary of State during the Cuban missile crisis, 1962). [96]

"They that can give up essential liberty to purchase a little temporary safety, deserve neither liberty nor safety" (Benjamin Franklin, Historical Review of Pennsylvania, 1759). [97]

Lack of courage, fear and a failure to be committed to action mandated by the events, cannot be allowed when the challenges merit action. As President Franklin D. Roosevelt said during his first inaugural address in 1933 when the depression was at its depth:

> So, first of all, let me assert my firm belief that the only thing we have to fear is...fear itself–nameless, unreasoning, unjustified terror which paralyzes needed efforts to convert retreat into advance. In every dark hour of our national life a leadership of frankness and of vigor has met with that understanding and support of the people themselves which is essential to victory. And I am convinced that you will again give that support to leadership in these critical days. [98]

Another option is peace through negotiation. This would certainly be desirable and would be a way to resolve crises, perhaps the best way. However, it must be coupled with a "peace through strength" policy—and reputation—and the ability and will to back up that reputation. If a country does not have that as a policy, it cannot hope to achieve any kind of result under negotiations that will lead to a long-lasting result in its favor. As President Reagan said in his first inaugural address: "We will maintain sufficient strength to prevail if need be, knowing that if we do so, we have the best chance of never having to use that strength."

Even if you have "peace through strength" as a policy and reputation, a country cannot allow deals to be made through negotiation if the reason for them is not the good of the country but, rather, a political agenda.

President Obama and Foreign Affairs

President Obama did not believe in the goodness of the United States in foreign affairs or that a strong United States was good for peace in the world. This is apparent from a September 23, 2009, speech he made to the United Nations General Assembly in which he said, "No world order that elevates one nation or group of people over another will succeed." [99]

President Obama did not like or respect the role that the United States played in world affairs. He did not believe in American exceptionalism, that the United States should be involved in ensuring peace in the world, or that the United States should be the leader of the free world.

Presidents before President Obama, with few exceptions, believed that protecting the United States against dangers from without was a highest priority. Along with that, they believed that it was in the United States' interest to influence events around the world to uphold the peace, prevent aggression, or to act when they believed that the United States could be at risk They all saw the world as a potentially dangerous place for the United States and its interests.

President Obama apparently never viewed the world in that light. Those who are not our friends and allies seized on this immediately.

President Obama and Appeasement

The Middle East

As discussed earlier, there are numerous problems with appeasement as a political philosophy, or reality, as evidenced by President Carter and President Obama. Starting when President Obama took office, he was on a path of appeasement toward our enemies. One of his first trips overseas to the Middle East was dubbed the "apology tour." He claimed that some policies of the United States toward the Middle East were wrong and that the United States bore some of the blame for relationships in that area.

During the 2008 election campaign and in his inaugural address, President Obama announced that he was going to remove all troops from Iraq. Then, during his 2012 reelection campaign, he announced that he was going to remove all troops from Afghanistan. Stating our withdrawal plans in advance tells our enemies that they should hang on, wait until we leave, and when we do leave, they can continue their efforts to take over the country and impose their will on the resident people. Once we told them our withdrawal plans—that our leaving was more important than staying until we finished the job—we told them that we no longer had the will to complete the task.

Were these promises made because it was the smart thing to do? Were they in the best interests of the United States? Or were they deemed necessary by President Obama to keep his base happy and win an election? If we do not have the will to complete the task here, why would any of our enemies believe that we will have the will to complete the task in the future? The liberals do not understand that terrorists *hate us!* They hate our way of life, they hate our freedoms, they hate our standard of living, they hate the status of our women, and they hate our movies and everything else that sets us apart from them. They are not some misguided souls who will like us if we are nice to them.

Other than changes to our way of life to be more like the radical Muslims, they are not—all of a sudden—going to like us! We are the infidels, and in their minds, their religion mandates that they kill us and that they not rest until they do. Appeasement will not make us safe or even safer from these radicals. It shows them weakness, which only encourages them more. Our strength is the only thing that protects us from them. They must know that if they take us on, we will retaliate with greater force than that which they visited upon us—that there is no place that they can go that will protect them from our wrath.

Syria

In August 2011, Obama said that Syrian President Bashar Assad had to go but he did not indicate how that should happen. When it did happen, he refused to give assistance to the Syrian opposition. Russia's President Putin intervened militarily in Syria, which secured President Assad's position.

In August 2012, President Obama drew a "red line in the sand" that Assad would cross if he used chemical weapons. Later, President Assad used chemical weapons, and President Obama admitted that in a letter to the Congress. Assad crossed the "red line in the sand," but President Obama did nothing. Assad is still there, supported by Russia and Iran, stronger than ever. When questioned about why he did not act when Assad crossed the "red line in the sand," Obama said that he did not draw the "red line in the sand"— the world did. But, the world did not!

By drawing a "red line in the sand" and then not doing anything about it when that line was violated, President Obama showed the world that he lacked the courage to act. A president who will not act as he promised will be taken advantage of on the world stage— and worse—the United States will be taken advantage of on the world stage.

Since Donald Trump became president, Assad has used chemical weapons on two occasions. President Trump warned that the United States would retaliate if chemical weapons were used. On both occasions, President Trump responded with bombing.

Libya

In Libya, President Obama supported a campaign to overthrow Muammar Gaddafi, and when that occurred, Obama again was absent. He had not planned for the aftermath. Libya went into turmoil. Obama later admitted that his worst mistake was "probably failing to plan for the day after, what I think was the right thing to do, in intervening in Libya" [100]

This ultimately led to an attack on our embassy in Benghazi on September 11, 2012. Ambassador Chris Stevens, the top United States representative in Libya, was assassinated along with three other Americans—Information Officer Sean Smith, and former Navy SEALs Tyrone Woods and Glen Doherty. Administration spokespersons, including Hillary Clinton, Secretary of State at the time, all stated, in an orchestrated way, that the attack was the result of an internet video that Muslims did not like that led them to attack our embassy. That story was proven to be false, and the administration and Secretary Clinton knew it to be false at the time. It was a terrorist attack.

Congress held hearings to investigate the circumstances surrounding the attack and the death of Ambassador Stevens and the others. At one point, when she was called to testify, Secretary Clinton said, "At this point, what difference does it make?" As Secretary of State, she believed that the murder in a foreign country of the senior representative of the United States and three others is not an important event.

It is a very important event.

Could the attack have been prevented in the first place? Once the attack began, what was done to ensure the safety of those in harm's way? Why were additional military troops and/or air power not sent to Benghazi to help prevent the deaths? Were President Obama and Secretary Clinton and others negligent in performing their responsibilities and in their duty to protect representatives of the United States? Moreover, in a gross failure to take action, President Obama and Secretary Clinton did nothing to capture those who had been identified as the killers of the Americans in Benghazi for more than a year. They knew who they were and where they were, and at least one of them had been conducting interviews with United States news outlets regarding the attack and his role therein.

Why was a raid, or a secret mission, not ordered to get those killers? Why was the world allowed to believe that the United States Ambassador, the representative of the United States to Libya, and three others could be murdered with no action being taken to avenge their deaths? Why was the United States made to look weak and indecisive? If you were an enemy of the United States, wouldn't you be encouraged to take similar actions because you knew that there would be no repercussions? In effect, President Obama and Secretary Clinton declared an open season on Americans? How sad!

Finally, about twenty months after the attack, President Obama finally allowed one of the attackers to be captured in Libya where he had been living in plain sight. President Obama directed that he be taken to Washington, DC, to be tried in federal court instead of sending him to Guantanamo Bay to be interrogated. As soon as he hit United States soil, they gave him his Miranda rights, he lawyered up, and the chance for more actionable intelligence was lost.

The Release of Guantanamo Bay Prisoners

Terrorists who were characterized as being at high risk of returning to terrorism against us were held at Guantanamo Bay. In a stunning deal in the early part of 2014, President Obama decided to release five of the most high-risk prisoners in exchange for one captured American serviceman in Afghanistan. This country has long had a policy of not negotiating with terrorists. All of a sudden, he released five of the worst terrorists for one serviceman. The five were sent to Yemen with the assurances of the government of Yemen that they would not be released for at least a year. Liberals defended the trade with an argument that these five were now older and that they therefore would not be rejoining the battle. They may not be picking up a weapon to go into battle, but they certainly could. They could also participate in the interrogation of any American prisoners who fell into the terrorist's hands, and they could certainly contribute to planning terrorist actions against the United States.

When the identity of the serviceman exchanged for these five was released, many of the members of his unit came forward to relate that he was a deserter and had left the Army of his own free will to seek out the terrorists. President Obama released five high-risk prisoners in exchange for a deserter!

Russia

President Obama canceled planned missile defense facilities in Poland and the Czech Republic. That alienated our allies in Europe and NATO. In doing so, President Obama got nothing in exchange from Russia's President Vladimir Putin. President Putin then invaded the Ukraine. The Ukraine was part of the old Union of Soviet Socialist Republics (USSR), and it is widely believed that President Putin wants to put the old USSR back together again—the old USSR that collapsed when Ronald Reagan was president.

He was emboldened to do that by his lack of respect for President Obama. Based on President Obama's words and actions, he knew that President Obama would not lead the free world in uprising against his actions, and President Obama did not.

At the time of this invasion, President Obama referred to Russia as a regional power. They have nuclear weapons and the means to deliver them, significant influence in the Middle East, and one of five nations that has veto power in the Security Council of the United Nations. Just a regional power? If he believed that, he was beyond naïve. President Obama refused Ukraine's request for weapons. He did offer some assistance for the military—MREs (meals-ready-to-eat).

President Obama later imposed some economic sanctions upon Putin and some of his top people, which were in the news for a day or two and then were largely forgotten. In any event, President Putin did nothing to change his course.

There was also a widely reported incident during a personal meeting between President Obama and President Medvedev of Russia, Putin's hand-picked interim president when Putin had to step aside for a term. An open microphone caught Obama asking for Medvedev to give him some "space" until after the 2012 election when he could be more flexible on national missile defense. That was heard not just by Medvedev (and Putin) but by all of America, and all our friends and allies and those who aren't, around the world. They interpreted President Obama's comment as applying to much more than just missile defense. Why would a United States president show such weakness to a long-time international foe like Russia? Why would a US president show such weakness to our friends, our allies, and others that do not share our interests?

Israel

Alan Dershowitz is an American lawyer, author, and academician in US Constitution and Criminal Law. He is also known as a civil libertarian. He wrote:

> Obama engineered the notorious December 2016 Security Council Resolution that declared the Western Wall, the Jewish Quarter, and the access roads to be illegally occupied by Israel, thus changing the status quo. This unwanted change—long

opposed by United States Administrations—made a negotiated peace more difficult, because it handed the Jewish holy places over to the Palestinians without getting anything in return, thus requiring Israel "buy" them back in any negotiation.

Why did Obama change the status quo to the disadvantage of Israel. Congress did not want the change. The American people did not support the change. Many in the Obama administration did not want the change. Obama did it as lame duck revenge against Israeli Prime Minister Benjamin Netanyahu, whom he hated. His motive was personal, not patriotic. His decision was bad for America, for peace, and for America's ally, Israel. He never would have done it except as a lame duck with no political accountability and no checks and balances.

This entire brouhaha about Jerusalem—including the staged tactical violence by Palestinians—is entirely the fault of a single vengeful individual who put personal pique over American policy: Barack Obama. [101]

President Clinton and his Nuclear Deal with North Korea

In 1994, Bill Clinton was the 42nd president of the United States. A Democrat, he was elected president in 1992 after running against President George H.W. Bush, the 41st president of the United States, who had succeeded President Reagan after the 1988 election. Al Gore was President Clinton's vice president

In that year, President Clinton negotiated a deal with North Korea. North Korea was and is a communist nation whose rulers ruled with an iron fist, tolerated no dissent, and managed every aspect of North Korea. It became known that its rulers were developing a nuclear weapon. President Clinton negotiated a deal to supposedly stop this from happening. America's commitments to North Korea under the formal agreement were estimated at $4 billion. President Clinton heralded this deal as a major accomplishment and a great deal for the United States and the world. He called it a very positive development and assured the people that North Korea consented to stopping key aspects of its nuclear program and to allowing the International Atomic Energy Agency to monitor a nuclear facility to verify North Korea's agreement and compliance.

> Former Democratic Congressman Stephen Solarz said at the time of the agreement that North Korea's commitments "have about the same value as Tsarist war bonds." The agreement most likely will not protect the important interests of the United States and that Washington should prepare to revisit this crisis. [102]

In 2006, it became known that North Korea had not stopped developing nuclear weapons and, in fact, had continued and was near to having nuclear weapons. Besides it being a bad deal, President Clinton did not continue to verify that the North Koreans were not developing a nuclear weapon. North Korea's first test of a nuclear weapon occurred in October 2006. At the time, Senator John McCain said:

I would remind Senator (Hillary) Clinton and other Democrats critical of the Bush Administration's policies that the framework agreement her husband's administration negotiated was a failure.

. . The Koreans received millions and millions in energy assistance. They've diverted millions of dollars of food assistance to their military. [103]

President Clinton may have been surprised by this. Others were not! Conservatives had argued against the negotiations and the deal because they did not believe that North Korea would stop its development activities—that it could not be trusted. They had used the time and the money given them by President Clinton to acquire nuclear weapons. Now the United States is faced with an adversary with nuclear weapons that is now developing a missile system to deliver those weapons, ultimately to the United States.

President Obama and His Nuclear Deal with Iran

More recently, in 2016, President Barrack Obama negotiated a deal with Iran to supposedly limit their ability to develop nuclear weapons. It was a deal that President Obama made but did not submit to the Senate for approval because he knew it would not be approved. Therefore, it was a deal of President Obama's making, not a deal that reached the status of a United States treaty. Once again, the president of the United States released money to a country to make the deal only, in this case, it was $150 billion. In addition, he agreed to lift the sanctions against Iran that had been in place for many years. Sadly, that money is not going to help the people of Iran. Iran will continue to build up its military and its nuclear capability and continue to be a major, if not the major, sponsor of terrorism around the world.

President Obama did this over bi-partisan objections and objections of conservatives who, once again, argued that Iran, like North Korea, would not follow the agreement. It was also strongly opposed by our Arab League partners and one of America's strongest allies—Israel. There is no reason to believe that Iran will limit its nuclear efforts just as North Korea had not limited its efforts.

President Obama's Secretary of State at the time was John Kerry, the negotiator of the deal and a former United States Senator. At the time that President Clinton negotiated his deal with North Korea, Secretary Kerry was in the Senate. He certainly knew of President Clinton's deal with North Korea when it was signed and when North Korea announced that they had disregarded it. Hilary Clinton had been Obama's Secretary of State, and she certainly knew of her husband's deal with North Korea, and she was in the Senate when North Korea conducted its first test of a nuclear weapon in 2006. I assume President Obama knew of the deal President Clinton made with North Korea and that North Korea disregarded it. If he did, his decision was a failure to acknowledge the past and to learn from the past.

When this North Korea disaster happened just ten years before, it made no sense to negotiate a similar deal with Iran. President Obama apparently wanted what he viewed as a foreign policy victory for political reasons and as part of his legacy. Republican Congressman Mike Rogers, Chairman of the House of Representatives Intelligence Committee, said Iran's continued enrichment of uranium was the one thing the whole world was trying to stop them from doing. "We made this mistake in Pakistan. We made this mistake in North Korea. . . History is a great judge here and a great teacher. Why would you make the same mistake to a nation that will proliferate a nuclear arms race in the Middle East if they are successful at getting a nuclear weapon?" [104]

Appeasement may feel good for a while. President Clinton must have felt that when he signed the deal with North Korea in 1994. The same thing was happening with Iran and its development of a nuclear bomb.

The problem with appeasement is that it only apparently works for as long as the appeased want it to apparently work. They can labor for years in violation of a deal and, when they are ready to come out from the appeasement curtain, they can do so at will.

Whatever concessions the United States made to put the deal in place are all of a sudden misguided and a huge mistake. The only thing the United States can do is to say oops, but by then it is too late.

If we want to go back to a world of nuclear brinkmanship, allow some of these countries to have nuclear weapons that they can deliver. Appeasement is a good way for liberals to skate through their terms in office without handling problems in foreign affairs. Let the next president handle it. If he or she happens to be liberal, they will continue the appeasement and live with the problem. The only problem with that is, at some point, somebody has to fix it.

Those who forget—or ignore—the mistakes of the past are bound to repeat them. Why should we believe in the sincerity of Iran when it did not work with North Korea? We are paying the price now as North Korea has nuclear weapons and is seeking the means of delivery. And, the leader of North Korea is Kim Jung Un who is widely regarded as being unstable, at least.

There is no question that Iran will end up with a nuclear weapon in the same way as North Korea. The only question is, how soon? President Obama survived his presidency while his agreement with Iran had not blown up on him, just as President Clinton had survived his presidency without the North Korea deal blowing up on him.

President Trump and the Deals with North Korea and Iran

Donald J. Trump, elected as the 45th president of the United States in 2016, with Mike Pence as his vice president, now has to deal with North Korea as a nuclear power. Wouldn't it have been better to deal with North Korea before it had a nuclear weapon?

We are fortunate that Donald Trump is president of the United States at this time, when it is the right time to deal with the threats from North Korea and Iran. The fact that he dramatically increased the defense budget in his first budget was a strong message that backs up his strong positions. In his State of the Union message on February 3, 2018, President Trump said: "Weakness is the surest path to conflict, and unmatched strength is the surest means to our true and great defense." President Trump put peace through strength into effect.

President Trump has warned Kim Jung Un and North Korea, in the strongest possible terms, that the United States will not allow North Korea to have nuclear weapons and the missile capability to deliver them. In addition to strong warnings, he imposed sanctions on North Korea, and he is working with China, North Korea's major sponsor and trading partner, to reduce their business with North Korea to help force North Korea to change its course. President Trump has also gone to the United Nations Security Council and received its condemnation of North Korea on a number of occasions, along with further sanctions. Other countries have applied sanctions as well.

Liberals decried President Trump's language and his strong warnings. They even raised questions as to whether he should have his finger on the button controlling our nuclear weapons and the means to deliver them. In doing so now, as they did during Vietnam, the liberals were telling our enemy not to listen to the president. That gives encouragement to Kim to ignore the president and continue down his current path. Despite these efforts to undercut the president, President Trump and Kim Jung Un agreed to hold a summit on June 12, 2018, in Singapore. After five hours of meetings, the two leaders signed an agreement in which Kim agreed in principle to the denuclearization of the Korean Peninsula.

The two also held a summit in Hanoi, Vietnam, on February 27–28, 2019. No agreement has yet been reached.

With regard to the Iran deal made by President Obama, President Trump announced that the United States was no longer bound by that agreement. President Trump and other countries increased sanctions on Iran and gave some time to fix the Iran Agreement before the United States bowed out. The liberals again complained about this action. The liberals are preaching that we should learn to live with North Korea and with Iran as nuclear powers and that we should "try to contain them." That is what we were trying to do after President Clinton signed the deal with North Korea. It did not work. It will not work with Iran either, as it did not work for Prime Minister Chamberlain in dealing with Germany.

Iran also increased its rhetoric against the United States because the sanctions that had been imposed were hurting its economy. Britain, France, and Germany were getting anxious because of threats that Iran had made toward them with regard to trade. Britain, France, and Germany were trying to set up a complex barter system that would allow some trade with Iran in order to try to keep Iran from exceeding the limit on low-enriched uranium that the country was allowed under the nuclear deal.

General Colin Powell, Secretary of State under President George W. Bush, was speaking to the World Economic Forum in Switzerland in January 2003. He was asked by George Carey, a former Archbishop of Canterbury in England, if the:

> United States was relying too much on "hard power" such as military action as opposed to "soft power" such as appealing to common values of the major religions and building trust based on those values. Powell responded by affirming the "soft power" of values but that it was the "hard power" of the military that, for example, helped free Europe so the "soft power" of peace and reconstruction could take place. Powell then said, "We have gone forth from our shores repeatedly over the last hundred years

and we've done this as recently as the last year in Afghanistan and put wonderful young men and women at risk, many of whom have lost their lives, and we have asked for nothing except enough ground to bury them in, and otherwise we have returned home to seek our own, you know, to seek our own lives in peace, to live our own lives in peace. But there comes a time when soft power or talking with evil will not work where, unfortunately, hard power is the only thing that works. [105]

Britain, France and Germany should keep this in mind when they contemplate breaking with us. In addition to only asking for "enough ground to bury" our dead, we have been paying more than our share to keep the North Atlantic Treaty Organization (NATO) alive and leading in the defeat of the terrorists. President Trump has persuaded some NATO members to increase their contributions to NATO. Let's hope they will not adopt a peace through appeasement strategy and that they will stick with us.

A world with these "rogue nations" having nuclear weapons and intercontinental ballistic missiles would be a far more dangerous place than it is right now. They could sell those capabilities to other nations that support their hatred for the United States, thus multiplying the number of countries that could threaten us. President Trump has drawn a line in a rice paddy and in the sand that these nations must not cross.

There is nothing to stop North Korea from sharing its technology with Iran. When they both become nuclear powers, they can share the weapons and the delivery systems with other governments or terrorist units. The questions are: Should we deal with North Korea and Iran now while they are still developing their nuclear weapons and the means to deliver them, or should we wait until they have ten nuclear weapons—or one hundred nuclear weapons?

Maintaining the peace is not going to be on their respective agendas. They will not be thinking about peace. They will be thinking about what they can do to hurt us and our allies. Keep in mind that North Korea is developing a missile that could reach the United States. Also, keep in mind, in the case of Iran, that they continue to call for death to America. They hate us! They will not have a policy of trying to contain us—they will have a policy of eliminating us, and, Israel would be at great risk.

If they took action against us or our allies and, if the United States responded, what would Russia and China do?

President Obama—Decrease in Defense Spending

(CNSNews.com)—Barack Obama was the first president of the United States to spend more on "means-tested entitlements"—AKA welfare—than on national defense, according to data published by his own Office of Management and Budget...

In every year from fiscal 1962 through fiscal 2014, total national defense spending exceeded means-tested entitlement spending. In fiscal year 1962, for example, the federal government spent more than twelve times as much money on national defense ($52,345,000,000) as it did on means-test entitlements ($4,300,000,000).

However, national defense spending peaked in 2011, when it hit $705,554,000,000. By contrast, means-tested entitlement spending has increased each year since 2012.

Finally, in fiscal 2015, it exceeded national defense spending for the first time. In fiscal 2014, according to OMB Historical Table 3.2, "total national defense" spending was $603,457,000,000. That same year, according to OMB Historical Table 8.1, "means-tested entitlement" spending was $601,700,000,000.

But in fiscal 2015, total national defense spending declined to $589,965,000,000 while means-tested entitlement spending climbed to $666,900,000,000. Thus, fiscal 2015 became the first year that means-tested entitlement spending—welfare spending— exceeded national defense spending. [106]

So, President Obama took the money away from defense. This was further evidence of the reduced role in world affairs that he wanted for the United States. Instead he gave it to Medicaid and Food Stamps, making all of those recipients dependent on the government, increasing the size of government, and adding millions to those likely to vote for the liberals and more federal spending.

And the question is, "What should be the priority for the federal government, national defense or welfare?" There is no alternative for defense than the federal government. There are alternatives for welfare. The states would be preferable to the federal government because they are closer to the needy and have better knowledge of the problems and who needs help. Private charities are also available. The citizens, foundations, and corporations of the United States are extremely generous. In 2018 they gave $428 billion to charities.

The most important alternative, however, is having a strong economy that employs all of the people who can work and therefore will not need welfare.

President Obama's Nobel Peace Prize

Shortly after taking office, President Obama was awarded a Nobel Peace Prize. The only thing he had done at that time was talk about drawing down our troops in the Middle East and scheduling the withdrawal of American troops. So, he got the Nobel Peace Prize after he had done nothing.

President Reagan ended the Cold War and decades of tension between the United States and the Soviet Union—decades of tension with both sides having nuclear weapons and the capability to deliver them—without firing a shot, and he got nothing.

I guess in the minds of the Nobel Peace Prize Committee, talk trumps action. It is not our strength that is provocative. It is our weakness that is provocative because it encourages our enemies to challenge us.

Jimmy Carter

President Obama was following the example of Jimmy Carter who was president from January 1977 to January1981. Many of the problems in the Middle East began during his presidency.

During his first years in office, President Carter was earning a reputation as a weak leader. It was during his term that the Shah of Iran, a staunch ally of the United States, was overthrown, and Iran became an Islamic fundamentalist terror state led by the Mullahs and Ayotallah Khomeni. This led to the hostage crisis that has been discussed earlier and to many other terrorist acts supported by Iran. At about the same time, Saddam Hussein took power in Iraq and launched the Iraq-Iran War. He recognized that the fall of the Shah led to political instability and that there was a void in power in the Middle East, and he wanted to be that power.

In 1979, the Soviets invaded Afghanistan and began a war with the Mujahideen, which led to the formation of Al Qaeda. These actions led to the current state of the Middle East, and all United States presidents since then have had to deal with the fallout.

Former Senator Eugene McCarthy, a Democrat who ran to be the Democrat candidate for president in 1968, later said that it had been right for him to vote for Ronald Reagan in 1980 because Carter simply abdicated the whole responsibility of the presidency while in office because he left the nation at the mercy of its enemies at home and abroad and was the worst president we ever had. [107]

7

THE GROWTH OF ISIL/ISIS

The Islamic State of Iraq and the Levant, also known as the Islamic State of Iraq and Syria, (ISIL or ISIS), a Muslim terrorist group, emerged from the remnants of al Queda in Iraq in 2004. The battle that the United States and other nations of the world are fighting against the terrorists is called "asymmetric warfare. "Asymmetric warfare (or asymmetric engagement) is war between belligerents whose relative military power differs significantly, or whose strategy or tactics differ significantly. This is typically a war between a standing, professional army and an insurgency or resistance movement militias who often have status of unlawful combatants. [108]

ISIS faded into obscurity for many years but began to reemerge in 2011 and carried out attacks in Iraq and Syria because of instability there. It took over much of northwestern Iraq and, in the process, captured the city of Mosul and the Mosul Dam. They planned to retake Iraq and Afghanistan as well. They are such a radical and cruel group that they were separated from Al Qaeda The leader of ISIS stated his goal was to establish a caliphate in the region. A "caliphate is government under a caliph. A caliph is a spiritual leader of Islam who claims succession from Muhammed." [109]

President Obama was warned of the dangers of leaving Iraq without leaving US forces behind. The Iraqis and our allies wanted an American military presence to remain in Iraq to protect them. President Obama said he did, too, but he did not make a deal with Iraq that would have permitted United States forces to remain. As a result, all United States forces were pulled out of Iraq in December 2011. When ISIS moved into Iraq, they were simply filling the void when the United States and its coalition left Iraq. Where there is a void, something always goes in to fill the void. Iran and Russia also went into Syria where there was also a void.

In January 2014 Obama referred to ISIS as the junior varsity and as only a regional threat. Once again, he was wrong. They captured at least seven oil fields and two refineries. They conquered territory and took over banks and took the money out of the banks. They had billions of dollars in assets and at least $2 million a day in oil revenues. They had an estimated 30,000 to over 200,000 fighters, some with British or American passports. They could show up in the United States or anyplace in Europe and fit in among the local populace with no one suspecting their potential for harm. If they succeeded in Iraq and its neighbors, they would have all the money needed to carry out terrorist activities.

The terrorists of ISIS took joy in beatings, beheadings, and burying people alive if they did not agree with their radical Muslim beliefs. Christians in particular suffered their wrath. The terrorists gave Christians the choice of paying a fine, leaving the area, converting to Islam, or being killed. Thousands of Christians fled the area in order to save their lives and keep their religion, leaving all of their property behind. Homes that had been in families for hundreds of years were left behind. The terrorists marked their homes with a Muslim symbol similar to the way Hitler and the Nazis marked the homes of Jews in Germany about seventy-five years before. The terrorists destroyed Christian landmarks and symbols that had stood for centuries. By chasing out the Christians and by destroying the vestiges of their religious beliefs, they were in effect removing all evidence that the religion had even existed in the region.

Iraq had been asking for increased United States military presence and action in Iraq for some time. In addition, the Kurds had also been asking for military assistance. They were located next to the area where the ISIS terrorists were operating and were in the best position to resist those incursions. The Kurds live in an autonomous region, Iraqi Kurdistan, and they have been long-time allies of the United States. They have a fierce, feared, and well-trained fighting force. Their military forces are called the Peshmerga which means "those who face death." [110] They had been the only resistance to the terrorists. Their problem was that they were using older and smaller weapons than the ISIS terrorists were using. ISIS had purchased Russian tanks and armaments on the black market. In addition, they had captured weapons left behind by the United States when President Obama withdrew the troops from Iraq. At least forty M1A1 main battle tanks, 2,300 Humvee armored vehicles, 74,000 machine guns, and as many as fifty-two M198 howitzer mobile gun systems, plus small arms and ammunition fell into enemy hands. That possibility was certainly foreseeable when the United States left. One commentator said: "U.S. shoots itself in the foot by accidentally arming ISIS." [111]

The Kurds were not asking for our military presence on the ground in northern Iraq. They were simply asking for newer, better, and bigger military equipment that they could use to resist and attack the terrorists. They were not afraid to take on the terrorists without United States military help and were confident in their ability to defeat the terrorists. They had been promised arms from the United States for months, but those arms had not been delivered.

A large number of the Christians escaped to Mount Sinjar in northern Iraq. There they were joined by another religious minority, the Yazidis, a part of the Muslim religion. It was not until it became apparent that the Yazidis were there with the Christians that the Obama administration even recognized the problem. The Christians and the Yazidis on top of Mt. Sinjar faced a humanitarian crisis. They were in danger of dying from lack of water and food and from attacks by the terrorists.

President Obama was already being accused of being weak in his foreign policy actions or, more correctly, his foreign policy inactions. Could he ignore the fact that thousands of Christians and Yazidis were in danger of dying or being killed on a mountaintop in north Iraq? In August 2014, he finally gave the order to provide humanitarian assistance to the surrounded refugees. That assistance took the form of water and food being airlifted to the refugees, a few hundred military advisors to train the Iraqis and others, and air strikes by a coalition led by United States forces on the assembled ISIS terrorists. With the airstrikes, the Kurds stepped up their efforts to drive the terrorists back with the help of the Iraqi forces.

President Obama and his spokespersons continuously refused to use the words terrorism or radical Islamic terrorists in describing acts of terrorists. In addition, the administration routinely redacted or scrubbed documents of any language that might be deemed offensive to Muslims such as references to "ISIS," "Muslim," "Islam," or "jihad." Documents where this occurred included such things as FBI law enforcement training manuals and law enforcement reports on terrorist attacks and activities. In some cases they didn't just modify the records, they eliminated them out of the system which bypassed security protocol in Homeland Security. Senator Ted Cruz made the point that "political correctness is jeopardizing our national security."[112]

Secretary of Defense Chuck Hagel, in August 2014, issued a warning regarding ISIS. He said they were extremely well-funded, extremely well-trained with good leadership, with a radical cause that they believed in, and that they were a threat to the U.S. and would be for a considerable period of time. This was the first time that anybody in the administration had actually admitted these conclusions, even though others had been arguing these same things. He ended up resigning as Secretary of Defense.

The success of ISIS has emboldened other groups around the world, so instead of confining the ISIS problem to the Middle East, we now have the problem all over the world. [113] When President Obama left office, it certainly appeared that they would be continuing their terrorist activities all over the world. They became experts at using the internet and social media in recruiting terrorists in the United States and elsewhere. They can radicalize them, train them, and have "lone wolf" attacks wherever and whenever they want. We have to be prepared to counter that, wherever we can, or be prepared to live with the knowledge that we can and will be attacked. Our president must be prepared to act accordingly.

The attacks of September 11, 2001, showed us and the world that the Unted States was not safe from dangers from foes sent from far away. The sacrifices that the United States and its allies made in Iraq and Afghanistan lessened the potential dangers from those countries and the entire Middle East. Maintaining the peace in those countries was imperative to continued and increased stability in the Middle East. We spent billions of dollars fighting the terrorists in Iraq and Afghanistan and lost some 3,000 lives. In addition, many of our fighting men and women were maimed or injured or suffered trauma, physical and mental, that continue to this day. The families of all of these military personnel continue to suffer as well. Despite all of this, we achieved significant positive results in the Middle East.

We were in the process of losing those positive results. President Obama said he would change the world. He certainly did! He said that he wanted to lessen the United States' role in the world and he did. He cut the defense-related budget items during his first term, and they continued to decrease thereafter. The dangers to the United States increased under President Obama.

ISIS Beheadings

ISIS beheaded American Daniel Pearl, a journalist, in 2002. In August 2014 James Foley, an American journalist, was beheaded by an ISIS terrorist. Steven Sotloff, an American – Israeli journalist, was beheaded by ISIS in September 2014. All of these sick actions were recorded and replayed around the world. In addition to these, ISIS has beheaded many other people from different countries all over the world.

When he learned of Mr. Foley's fate, President Obama was returning from the White House to his vacation on Martha's Vineyard. The next day he made a five-minute appearance before the press to deplore this horrible act. He was then immediately recorded outside of the hall where he made his appearance, in golf attire and heading to his golf game.

British Prime Minister David Cameron, who was on vacation when he heard the news regarding Mr. Foley, left his vacation and returned to No. 10 Downing Street in London because of the crisis. President Obama, upon hearing the news, continued on his vacation, took five minutes to deliver a statement, and then left for the golf course. He obviously thought his golf game was more important than Mr. Foley's beheading. The world got two contrasting pictures of how a crisis should be handled by the two leaders. The contrasting actions are striking!

> These fanatical religious and political views are clearly the logical foundations for hatred of all free and open societies which do not adhere to their central tenets . . . It is never in America's interest to constrain domestic freedoms to appease foreign

enemies . . . Obama's "success" in Libya, over-throwing Gadhafi without US casualties, now lies in tragic ruins in Benghazi. His narrative that the global war on terror is essentially over is revealed as a sham. And his claim that he could reverse decades of anti-American feelings through "outreach," concessions and apologies, is shattered irretrievably.

America's Middle East policy, and its foreign policy globally, needs a far stronger and more determined defense of its interests and values than Obama has provided or is capable of providing. In particular, we must be absolutely clear that the recent violence is caused not by the freedoms Americans cherish, but by the repression and hatred brought forth by extremist religious ideologies. American liberty is their problem, not ours." John Bolton, 9/25/12, Human Events, "No Surprise: America under Attack Again in the Mideast. [114]

President Trump and ISIL/ISIS

President Trump was sworn in as president on January 20, 2017. Shortly thereafter he issued the "America First Foreign Policy" paper. Defeating ISIS and other radical Islamic terror groups was the highest priority. The policy had a number of actions by which the United States was going to defeat ISIS:

- To be strong on vetting people that were trying to enter the country.
- To conduct raids against Al Queda/ISIS headquarters to kill leadership and to capture important intelligence.

- To pursue aggressive coalition military operations, to include major military operations, when necessary with a combined 68 nations and organizations.
- To work with international partners to cut off funding for terrorist groups, to expand intelligence sharing, and to engage in cyberwarfare to disrupt propaganda and recruiting.
- To raise over $2 billion in humanitarian, stabilization, and de-mining needs for liberated areas of Iraq and Syria.
- To liberate ground in Iraq and Syria from ISIS including at least 500,000 square kilometers and nearly 2.5 million people. It also included re-taking Mosul where Iraqi Security Forces and the Kurdish Peshmerga cooperated to ensure this happened.
- To utilize the UN-managed Funding Facility for Immediate Stabilization to help displace Iraqis return home.
- To have coalition members produce content in five languages to counteract ISIS's propaganda and to attack its online presence. [115]

By December 2017, ISIS had lost 95 percent of its territory, including Mosul, Iraq, and Raqqa, Syria, and most of the deputies of the ISIS leader, Abu Bakr al-Baghdadi, were dead.

A New York Times columnist wrote a piece on President Trump's successful approach at taking on the ISIS caliphate:

Ross Douthat, who previously endorsed Hillary Clinton, wrote that the Trump administration surprised him in foreign policy, namely in the war on ISIS that Trump has won.

"If you had told me in late 2016 that almost a year into the Trump era the caliphate would be all-but-beaten without something far worse happening in the Middle East, I would have been surprised and gratified," Douthat wrote in a column titled "A War Trump Won."

Douthat wrote that Islamic State militants in Syria and Iraq—which he calls "the defining foreign policy calamity of Barack Obama's second term"—were effectively routed by Trump without the need of a massive ground troop invasion and without getting into a war with Russia or Syrian dictator Bashar al-Assad."

Douthat wrote that it is a "press failure" for succumbing to "the narrative of Trumpian disaster" and ignoring the story.

"But this is also a press failure, a case where the media is not adequately reporting an important success because it does not fit into the narrative of Trumpian disaster in which our journalistic entities are all invested," he wrote.

Earlier this month, Iraq declared its war against the Islamic State was over after more than three years of combat operations drove extremist fighters from all of the territories they once held.

Prime Minister Haider al-Abadi announced Iraqi forces were in full control of the country's border with Syria during remarks at a conference in Baghdad, and his spokesman said the development marked the end of the military fight against ISIS.

"Trump has avoided the temptation often afflicting Republican upper-hawks, in which we're supposed to fight all bad actors on 16 fronts at once. Instead he's slow-walked his hawkish instincts on Iran, tolerated Assad and avoided dialing up tensions with Russia," Douthat wrote.

Lastly, Douthat gives credit for Trump's decision to recognize Jerusalem as the capital of Israel – a move condemned by multiple countries around the globe – as recognizing that the Middle East has changed its priorities since the 1990's.

He wrote "And the Trump strategy on Israel and the Palestinians, the butt of many Jared Kushner jokes, seems ... not crazy?"

"The relatively mild reaction to recognizing Jerusalem as Israel's capital may be a case study in expert consensus falling behind the facts; the Arab world has different concerns than it did in 1995, and Trump's move has helped clarify that change."

Douthat ended the article: "So very provisionally, credit belongs where it's due—to our soldiers and diplomats, yes, but to our president as well." [116]

During a raid on a rebel held province in Syria ordered by President Trump, and conducted by US special forces on October 27, 2019, the leader of ISIS since 2013, Abu Bakr al-Baghdadi, and two of his young children, were killed when he detonated a suicide vest inside a cave.

Is Islam a Religion of Peace?

Followers of Islam are certainly passionate about their religion. There are Muslims who believe that their religion is a religion of peace and there are others who believe that they must wage war – jihad–on nonbelievers. While there are verses in the Quran that call for tolerance and peace, there are also 109 verses that call for followers to wage war with nonbelievers for the sake of Islamic rule. [117] There are also Muslims who strictly follow their beliefs in ways that can lead to the death of another family member. Such deaths are called "honor or shame killings."

> An honor killing or shame killing is the murder of a member of a family, due to the perpetrator's belief that the victim has brought shame or dishonor upon the family or has violated the principles of a community or a religion, usually for reasons such as divorcing or separating from their spouse, refusing to enter into an arranged marriage, being in a relationship that is disapproved by their family, having premarital or extramarital sex, becoming the victim of rape or sexual assault, dressing in ways which are deemed inappropriate, engaging in non-heterosexual relations or renouncing a faith. [118]

Instances include a father in West London who killed his sixteen-year-old daughter because she slept with her boyfriend. The father regarded that as a stain on the family's name, and he was desperate to restore his honor. In Texas, a Muslim immigrant was sentenced to death for killing his Christian son-in-law and another woman after his daughter converted to Christianity. He needed to "clean his honor" for his daughter's conversion. In Arizona, a

Muslim man was accused of murdering his wife, two daughters, and a man he believed to be having an extramarital affair with his wife.[119]

China and Muslims

China has been detaining Muslims in what has been referred to as "concentration camps." China says it is fighting terrorism. Muslims have been crowded into cells, subjected to daily indoctrination sessions, and some have been tortured during interrogation. China has made many aspects of religious practice and culture criminal, including teaching Islam to children and parents giving children Uighur names. In Urumqi, a state campaign has demolished neighborhoods and moved to purge their culture. Glass towers and retail strips have taken their place. Authorities have seen young migrant men, who have lost their jobs, as being instigators of violence and ripe targets for radicalization. [120]

Cyber Warfare and Nuclear or Chemical Blackmail and War

Our struggle with terrorists does not take into account other threats facing the United States and all other nations—cyber warfare and nuclear or chemical blackmail or war.

Cyber warfare refers to the use of technology to launch attacks on nations, governments, and citizens, which can cause harm comparable to conventional warfare. There are cyberattacks almost daily against government organizations and private enterprises.

Whoever wins the cyber war capability battle will have the upper hand in any future aggression. The fact is that computers and the internet are indispensable in today's world. Everybody, every business, and every government does what it can to build firewalls to protect their systems.

In the past few years, there have been many instances of computer systems being compromised, a lot of them dealing with credit cards. The businesses thought that they were safe from cyberattack because of all their firewalls. However, there are very few systems, if any, that cannot be defeated by someone intent on doing so. That can be done from anywhere in the world to any other place in the world.

In addition, the insider threat is a very real weapon in cyber warfare. Richard Snowden, who leaked millions of emails involving our government's secret activities, did it from an insider position. The extent of his damage will not be known for years, but it already has had an effect. He was a trusted employee. Every entity with internet service has trusted employees. At any time, one of them could be corrupted or bribed to take action harmful to the entity, whether business, government, or other.

What would happen if suddenly our power grids were attacked in the middle of winter throughout the northern part of the country, and electricity was shut off? Or, what about doing this in the southern part of the country in the middle of the summer? It wouldn't take long for food to spoil, for homes to get unbearably cold or hot, or for people to die. What if:

- Our public safety institutions, such as police and fire departments, were, all of a sudden without the ability to communicate?
- Our transportation systems were compromised, shutting down airplanes, buses, trains, or other public transportation systems?
- Our banking system was compromised, and people and businesses were not able to access their money and transactions could not be accomplished?
- Our government, our health systems, our telephone service, or the internet were shut down?

- Our military was cyber attacked and our defense systems and the ability of commanders to communicate with their forces were compromised.
- All of this happened at the same time?

Our world as we know it would be completely disrupted and paralyzed. If things we normally do are disrupted, people are going to get upset. They may riot, and then we face the prospect of having to use police, the National Guard, or the military to maintain order. What if this happens and whoever is responsible starts making demands on us?

What if our elections were influenced by a foreign government or entity, as Russia tried to do during the 2016 election? That led to a two-year investigation by a special prosecutor who concluded that Russia did, indeed, try to influence our election which led to a number of indictments. It is believed that Russia will continue to try to influence our elections.

China and other nations/groups could try to do the same, if they are not already doing so.

What if our enemies located nuclear weapons, like dirty bombs or chemical or biological weapons, in four of our major cities such as New York City, Washington, DC, Los Angeles, and Phoenix? Or, what if they threatened to release a chemical or biological weapon in the United States or one of our allies. The range of possible demands is endless. It could be for extortion involving anything, such as release certain criminals, pay us $100 billion, give us Alaska or Hawaii, close our military base(s) somewhere, get out of the Middle East, or quit supporting Israel. They could demand that women wear certain clothes and that their education cease and that all religious beliefs but their own be declared criminal. They could demand that the United States surrender to them or that the president, the vice president, the cabinet and the congress resign and put them in prison someplace. They could demand whatever they wanted.

Would a president run the risk of having any of these weapons used or released in the United States. What do we have that would counter this possibility?

We have a strong military with dedicated members. The Department of Homeland Security and our other security agencies have been working diligently 24/7/365 to protect the United States from these threats. On November 16, 2018, President Trump signed into law the Cybersecurity and Infrastructure Security Agency Act of 2018 which established the Cybersecurity and Infrastructure Security Agency (CISA). CISA builds the national capacity to defend against cyberattacks and works with the federal government to provide cybersecurity tools and response and assessment capabilities to safeguard the ".gov" networks. It also coordinates security and resilience efforts using trusted partnerships across the private and public sectors. [121]

But could they do anything, and, if so, would they be ordered to take military action? We have nuclear weapons and the means to deliver them. But would the order be given to use them?

What if one of our enemies actually released a deadly chemical or biological agent or weapon on our soil or someplace else in the world where it would affect the whole world.

It is our intelligence gathering entities that must locate these threats and alert the forces necessary to stop them before they occur.

There is another strong deterrent that would be given serious consideration by any country or group that would try to occupy the United States. That deterrent is the millions of American citizens who have exercised their right to bear arms. They would be a strong deterrent to any group that wanted to take over this country.

Maintaining a strong military, having strong intelligence agencies, and having a strong president committed to "peace through strength" are going to be the only things that can keep us safe.

Having leadership that believes in appeasement will leave our country exposed to whatever actions our enemies want to use against us.

China's Growing Navy

China is establishing an ocean-going navy for the first time in 600 years, which indicates its desire to have even more influence in the world.

> "The biggest challenge for U. S. national security leaders over the next 30 years is the speed and sustainability of the {Peoples' Republic of China} national effort to deploy a global navy, said retired Capt. James Fanell, who previously served as head of intelligence for the Pacific Fleet. . . In 2019, China had a 335 ship fleet, about 55 percent larger than in 2005, . . . To put it in perspective, during a recent four-year period the naval vessels that Chinese shipyards produced were roughly equivalent in tonnage to the entire U.K. Royal Navy or the Japanese Maritime-Self-Defense Force, . . . The U.S. Navy has 293 ships in its battle force, . . . When it comes to aircraft carriers, the United States is still dominant, . . . Meanwhile, China's submarine force, most of which are diesel-electric powered, could threaten U.S. carriers or other ships. The Defense Intelligence Agency has estimated that by this year Bejing's fleet would increase to 70 boats. . . The U.S. Navy currently has 69 submarines. The U.S. Navy has signed a contract for a block buy of nine Virginia-class, nuclear-powered attack submarines . . . It is also

pursuing a new class of 12 nuclear-powered ballistic missile subs, . . .[122]

China and the United States are both moving forward with building surface combatants. Unmanned systems, which could be used for a variety of missions, are the wave of the future. They are less expensive and they keep sailors away from harm. Both countries are also working on weapon systems to include new missiles and advanced weaponry. China may be developing advanced anti-ship ballistic missiles (ASBMs) which could be used to attack aircraft carriers and other navy ships of the United States and our allies. These would be a new threat, but the United States is also pursuing new weapons such as improved directed energy weapons like lasers. Both countries are working on highly maneuverable weapons that can reach speeds greater than Mach 5.

The greatest strategic challenge for the United States and our allies will occur in the waters off China and in the Western Pacific. China's growing capabilities on the seas close to China is a fundamental shift in the balance of power in that critical region.

8

IMMIGRATION

E stimates of the number of undocumented immigrants living in the United States range from 10.5 to 12 million. More than fifty percent of them have come from Mexico and another twenty one percent have come from other Central American countries.

This nation was built by immigrants and is a nation of immigrants—legal immigrants, that is. Many of the immigrants have entered the United States legally through our southern border and they have become an important part of our country. Over the past few years, there have been so many illegal immigrants coming to the United States over our southern border, which is 1,989 miles long, that it has become a major political issue, not only in the states with the influx of illegal immigrants but in the entire nation. Illegal immigrants cause major negative impacts on the infrastructure, jobs, and social structure of those cities, counties, and states where they settle. They require medical services, fire and police protection, housing, schooling, and other public services that government provides.

Secure borders help stop transmission of disease, human trafficking, terrorism, criminals, and drugs. For example, an illegal immigrant in Arizona is twice as likely to commit a crime versus a natural-born citizen. Ninety per cent of all heroin and fentanyl come across the southern border. Over 10,000 children are illegally sex trafficked across the southern border every year. There are 56,000 illegal immigrants in our federal prison system and more in our state system. They cost US taxpayers some $135 billion a year.

Open borders encourage illegal immigration and threaten American culture. They are coming in huge caravans and the over-population of illegal immigrants in our border areas is a direct result of the open border and the failure to take action to secure the border. Illegal immigrants are dying on the long trek to the border. Where they camp along the way, there are no bathroom facilities, and their camp areas are full of discarded garbage and human waste and are breeding places for illnesses. Customs and Border Patrol do not have the facilities or the manpower to care for all of the illegal immigrants. As a result, children have been separated from their parents, illegal immigrants are bringing illnesses with them, and they are dying.

Eight out of ten Americans say that the situation at the US border with Mexico is either a crisis or a serious problem that needs to be addressed.

Democrats and the liberal media are trying to blame President Trump for the problems, but the blame lies with them for their failure to act to help solve the problem.

Walls, barriers and fences are used all of the time for security. Housing developments are surrounded by walls, prisons and jails are surrounded by walls, the White House is surrounded by fences, military posts are surrounded by barriers, and swimming pools are required to have a barrier. If they did not work, they would not be there.

Former acting Immigration and Custom Enforcement (ICE) Director Tom Homan has said, according to S.A. Miller in *The Washington Times*:

"Every place a wall or barrier has been built, it has resulted in decreased illegal immigration, decreased drug smuggling. One hundred percent of the time, it has proven effective," Mr. Homan said on Fox News, where he is a contributor.

"Look at the rest of the data on the border, where arrests of MS-13 [gang] this year are up 118 percent, the seizures of guns—for God's sake—are up almost 200 percent. There's your data. Look at it. You can see why we need a wall," he said.

Mrs. Pelosi told *USA Today* that Mr. Trump was using the wall to "fear monger."

"He talked about terrorists coming in over that particular border, which wasn't so. He talked about people bringing in diseases and all the rest of that, which wasn't so," said Mrs. Pelosi, who is poised to become speaker when Democrats take control of the House next week. "He's using scare tactics that are not evidence-based, and it's wrong."

Mr. Homan said Mrs. Pelosi is "100 percent wrong."

"Allow me to educate Mrs. Pelosi," he said. "As far as crime coming across the border, ICE arrested 138,000 criminals last year. These are people who entered the country illegally and committed crimes against the people of this country."

Last year, ICE arrested illegal immigrants in more than 2,000 homicides cases, more than 11,000 weapon violations and almost 12,000 sexual assaults, Mr. Homan said.

U.S. immigration officials routinely deal with contagious diseases, including tuberculosis, measles, and chickenpox, he said.

Mr. Homan recalled the massive effort to treat an illegal immigrant man with a rare strain of tuberculosis of TB. "We had to work with CDC and Texas Department of Health to find a way to treat this gentleman, so we kept him locked up for months at great taxpayer expense. Imagine if that strain of TB were to get released into the American society," Mr. Homan said. [123]

Democrats who are now leaders in the Congress have been strong supporters of securing our borders in the past. The Illegal Immigration Reform and Immigrant Responsibility Act of 1996 was signed into law by President Clinton on September 30, 1996. At that time, the bill basically contained the promises that President Trump made. Nancy Pelosi, now Speaker of the House, and Chuck Schumer, now leader of the Democrats in the Senate, and other Democrats still in the Congress, voted for the bill and have also spoken out strongly for securing our borders in the years since. As recently as 2013, Nancy Pelosi supported a bill that required the construction of 700 miles of border fencing.

Senator Chuck Shumer and then Senators Barrack Obama and Hillary Clinton all voted for the Secure Fence Act of 2006, which passed the Congress and was signed into law by President George W. Bush. It authorized 700 miles of fencing along the United States/Mexico border. President Trump would like to put a barrier on 1,000 miles of border at a cost of $8 to $12 billion.

Bill Clinton has said that it is wrong and ultimately self-defeating to allow the abuse of our immigration laws as seen in recent years, and we must do more to stop it. Senator Diane Feinstein has said that we should enforce our borders because to have a situation where 40 percent of the babies born in California today are born of illegal immigrants creates a very real problem. Hillary Clinton has also said she voted numerous times when she was a Senator to spend money to build a barrier to try to prevent illegal immigrants from coming in and that you have to control your borders.

President Obama has said we cannot allow people to pour into the United States undetected, undocumented, unchecked, and circumventing the line of people waiting patiently, diligently, and lawfully to become immigrants.

One of Donald Trump's main campaign issues was securing our borders, and that was at least partially responsible for his election. Since his election, he has been urging the Congress to join him in legislation to secure the borders. So far the Democrats have refused to take any action to help secure the borders, arguing that a wall/barrier will not help and that there is no emergency that requires action. One of the reasons is that they do not want to give President Trump a win on this issue. They are harming the United States because of their selfish political goals.

President Trump asked the Congress for $5.7 billion to build the wall, a barrier, or a fence. Congress gave him about $1.4 billion in border wall funding, but it was far less than the president wanted. It is unbelievable that President Obama released $150 billion to Iran as a part of his nuclear deal, and the Democrats wouldn't give President Trump $5.7 billion for a wall.

President Trump identified $3.6 billion from military construction funds, $2.5 billion in Defense Department money, and $600 million from the Treasury Department's asset forfeiture fund that could be used to build a wall. The American Civil Liberties Union brought a lawsuit on behalf of the Sierra Club and Southern

Border Communities Coalition, challenging the use of the Defense Department funds. That money would be used to fund 100 miles of fencing. A trial court froze the $2.5 billion in funds, and an appeals court kept the freeze in place. On July 26, 2019, the United States Supreme Court lifted the freeze, clearing the way for the work to begin on the border wall using the Defense Department's money. The Trump administration then had an additional $6.7 billion in funds for the wall.

It has been said that "we are a nation of laws—not of men." The United States has laws that were enacted to protect our borders. When he was sworn in as president, Barack Obama swore to enforce the laws of the United States and to defend the Constitution. He did not enforce our laws and secure our southern border with Mexico. He, therefore, violated his oath of office by failing to enforce federal immigration laws. In this instance, we were a *nation of one man, not a nation of laws.*

While the federal government under the Obama administration said that immigration is a national issue and can only be regulated and enforced by the federal government, those states where illegal immigration occurs are the most immediately affected. Illegal immigrants are costing those states millions of dollars a year in services. Arizona passed a law, trying to enforce immigration laws on the southern border, but the federal government filed suit to stop Arizona from enforcing the law. The Obama administration filed suit against Maricopa County, Arizona, Sheriff Joe Arpaio for his action in enforcing immigration laws and won.

It is the height of hypocrisy for the federal government to have illegal immigration laws as the law of the land, fail to enforce them, and then take steps to stop a state from enforcing an illegal immigration law within its own borders. But, rather than hypocrisy, it is simply a calculated political decision for the Democrats' selfish goals, goals that do not coincide with what is best for the country.

The reason that the Obama administration did not enforce the law, and that the Democrats in Congress are continuing that position, was because they view illegal immigrants as future voters for their political agenda. They believe the quicker they can get them on government assistance, make them reliant on government assistance, and give them citizenship, the quicker they will get their votes. And, by allowing all of the illegal immigrants into the country, they are also counting on the votes of those already here. This is borne out by the Latino votes for Hillary Clinton in the 2016 election. She received 65 percent of the Latino vote, while Donald Trump received 29 percent. However, there is reason to believe that the Democrats may be surprised by the Latino vote in 2020 as polling displays pronounced support for President Trump. [124]

Prior to the 2012 election, Obama indicated a change of immigration policy that would permit 800,000 illegal immigrants under the age of thirty to stay in this country if they can prove they were under sixteen when they came here. These are called "dreamers" under DACA, "Deferred Action for Childhood Arrivals." President Obama accomplished this through executive order, which he conceded he did not have the authority to do, such an action needing to be accomplished by act of Congress. Again, with this action we were a *nation of one man—not a nation of laws, a*nd Obama once again violated his oath of office.

Under the executive order, "dreamers" can apply for a work permit if they are attending school, have graduated from high school, have received a GED, or are in the military or have an honorable discharge from the military or the Coast Guard. This came less than five months before the November general election. Could there be a more blatantly political action to influence an election? It was not just the 800,000 with whom Mr. Obama was trying to curry favor. It was the entire Latino community and their supporters.

President Trump signed an executive order canceling President Obama's executive order and gave Congress six months to pass a law continuing the program. President Trump spoke in favor of the "dreamers" and hoped that Congress would act, but it did not. The Democrats want to keep the issue alive in hopes that it would help them in future elections.

Kirstjen M. Nielsen was the Secretary of the US Department of Homeland Security. She sent the following letter to members of Congress, explaining why there is an emergency at the southern border. She wrote:

March 28, 2019
United States Senate Washington, DC 20510
U.S. House of Representatives Washington, DC 20515
Dear Members of Congress:

> **I am writing to you with an urgent request.** For many months now, the Department of Homeland Security (DHS) has been tracking a surge in migrant arrivals at the U.S. southern border. It is the responsibility of DHS to secure our borders, enforce our immigration laws, and provide appropriate humanitarian protections to those who need it. Indeed, Congress has explicitly directed DHS to take operational control of the southern border. But today I report to you that we are increasingly unable to uphold that responsibility given the emergency situation. We are grappling with a humanitarian and security catastrophe that is worsening by the day, and the Department has run out of capacity, despite extraordinary intra-Departmental and interagency efforts. I am especially concerned about the level of families and unaccompanied children arriving at our

borders and in federal custody. Accordingly, DHS requests immediate Congressional assistance to stabilize the situation.

The border numbers paint a picture of a dire situation. Late last year, DHS was apprehending 50,000–60,000 migrants a month. Last month, we apprehended or encountered more than 75,000, the highest in over a decade. And this month, we are on track to interdict nearly 100,000 migrants. What we are seeing is nearly unprecedented in the modern era. Unlike previous flows, these migrants are not arriving in high numbers, one-at-a-time. They are arriving in large groups. In a normal year, DHS would encounter one or two groups of over 100 migrants. Already in this fiscal year, we have encountered nearly 100 large groups comprised of 100+ migrants, nearly half of which have arrived in remote locations. Our men and women on the frontlines are simply not resourced to handle these levels, and I report to you today that we are struggling to transport and process—let alone adequately care for—this many individuals coming into our custody, especially those in hard-to-reach areas.

The volume of "vulnerable populations" is unsustainable. Our system has been able to cope with high numbers in the past, but the composition of today's flows makes them virtually unmanageable. Historically, the vast majority of aliens we encountered were single-adult males from Mexico who could be quickly removed after a short period of detention if they had no legal right to stay. Today, the majority are families and unaccompanied children, who pose a unique challenge to the system because most cannot be easily cared for, efficiently processed, or expeditiously removed, due to resource constraints and outdated laws. The result is a dangerous and growing backlog of individuals in custody that has forced us to begin releasing large numbers of aliens, most of whom will never appear for their immigration court hearings, further exacerbating "pull" factors into the United States. Unfortunately, Alternatives to Detention, such as ankle-bracelet monitoring, have proven expensive in the long run and ineffective at ensuring removals ordered by an immigration judge.

Now we face a system-wide meltdown. DHS facilities are overflowing, agents and officers are stretched too thin, and the magnitude of arriving and detained aliens has increased the risk of life-threatening incidents. At the present time, Customs and Border Protection (CBP) has more than 1,200 unaccompanied alien children (UACs) in custody, hundreds of which have been with CBP for days, an unacceptable length of stay in facilities not designed to hold children for extended periods. By law, most of these children must be transferred to the Department of Health and Human Services (HHS) for care in residential shelters. While HHS is taking steps to rapidly add thousands of shelter beds, the system is hitting peak capacity. In addition to UACs, CBP has at least 6,600 families in custody, bringing the total number of children sitting in CBP facilities to approximately 4,700. We are doing everything possible to address these numbers and reduce back-logs, but they are a symptom of a broken system.

My greatest concern is for the children, who are put at high risk by this emergency and who are arriving sicker than ever before after traveling on the treacherous trek. Our agents and officers are performing more than 60 hospital visits a day—many to ensure young people get immediate treatment—and we now are regularly seeing individuals arrive with life-threatening conditions. Moreover, as agents get pulled off the line to escort migrants to receive medical assistance, we are left with even less capacity to handle new arrivals. The humanitarian situation cannot be ignored. Reports of violence and sexual assault along the route are now pervasive, meaning that many arriving migrants require especially focused care. In some cases, girls as young as 10 years old in DHS custody require pregnancy tests so we can be sure they get essential medical support. And with increased flows, smugglers and traffickers are forcing more people into inhumane conditions along the journey and putting lives in danger. They are preying on innocent people for profit and exploiting this crisis to line their pockets by breaking our laws.

Our most urgent need is to increase throughput to avoid threats to life and property. At present, DHS border and immigration facilities are at (or over) capacity with serious over-crowding. We need additional temporary facilities as soon as possible in order to process arriving aliens, especially those entering illegally between ports of entry. Immigration and Customs Enforcement (ICE) has been urgently working to acquire additional bed space and to speed up transfers of individuals into their custody, but DHS has nonetheless been forced to temporarily release adults and families directly from Border Patrol custody. This prevents us from detaining them to ensure that they are afforded the most expeditious process under immigration law and, where appropriate, removed. Without additional assistance, we will be forced to increase the releases of the single-adult population from ICE— the only population for which we can currently effectively enforce U.S. immigration laws. As such, we are witnessing the real-time dissolution of the immigration system.

Moreover, HHS will likely need many more beds as the influx of children grows. In HHS custody, children receive accommodations appropriate for young people while they await placement with adult sponsors in the United States. However, because of the surge in arrivals, CBP has high numbers of children that have not been transferred. As noted earlier, HHS is taking steps to rapidly add thousands of shelter beds. But in the short term, HHS is still approaching its maximum capacity and will very likely require thousands of additional beds in the coming weeks and months. I must emphasize how important it is to quickly transfer children out of border locations, which are not designed for long-term stay and are especially inadequate for the care of young people. A potential overflow of children in DHS custody represents our most acute humanitarian risk.

But bed space is not the only issue. To cope with the overall volume of arriving migrants, a resource surge is needed throughout the system to ensure efficient throughput and proper care. This includes medical teams, vehicles and transportation workers, legal services, and more. We need temporary processing facilities with full humanitarian and staffing support. And we now project that we will need at least hundreds of additional personnel to support CBP and ICE in providing humanitarian and operational assistance, including conducting welfare checks, preparing meals, and accounting for personal property.

In light of the above, DHS requests immediate assistance from Congress, including emergency resources and specific authorities to cope with the escalating situation.

At this time, DHS is assessing the resources needed to make up for shortfalls and sustain critical operations. While recent appropriations provided DHS with additional humanitarian and operational funds, the Department is projecting we will exceed these resources and be unable to uphold basic mission requirements because of the severity of the flow. I will be working with the Office of Management and Budget to provide you additional details in the near future, but the situation is so dire we want to make notification to you now that we will require additional resources to reduce system backlogs to ensure immediate safety and care of individuals in our custody.

DHS also seeks authorities to address the underlying causes of this emergency and to restore order, while ensuring we can provide humanitarian assistance to those who need it. Most immediately, we need the authority to treat all arriving migrant children equally. Currently, we can reunite many unaccompanied children from Mexico with their families and return them home, when appropriate, but we are legally unable to do so for children from noncontiguous countries. The result is that hundreds of Central American children come into our custody each day, await transfer to HHS care, and, ultimately, are placed with a sponsor in the United States. This serves as another dangerous "pull" factor. DHS seeks authority to return UACs to their families and home countries in a safe and orderly manner if they have no legal right to stay. In the coming days, I will transmit proposed legislative language to Congress to fix this, along with measures to allow DHS to keep alien families in custody together through the immigration process and to allow asylum-seekers to apply for U.S. protection from within Central America, rather than take the dangerous journey north. These legislative solutions will help address the root causes of the emergency.

In the meantime, I am doing everything within my authority to prevent the situation from getting worse. This week I met with senior Mexican officials to discuss what can be done on their side of the border to help stem the historic flows. I also signed a first-ever regional compact with the countries of the Northern Triangle-El Salvador, Guatemala, and Honduras to address irregular migration, counter human smuggling and trafficking, and crack down on transnational criminal organizations that are also fueling the crisis. Operationally, we are redirecting resources and personnel from across the Department toward border security and migration management, we are putting out a call for volunteers from non-border missions, and we continue to receive support from interagency partners. We also plan to redirect field office personnel staffing ports of entry to help address the humanitarian situation. But once again, this will not be enough.

We need Congress to act immediately to address the growing emergency. Let me be clear: the journey of any migrant—especially at the hands of a smuggler or trafficker-is not a safe one. And the migrant surge has made matters worse, not only for U.S. border security but for the safety of migrants themselves. We must be able to come together on a bipartisan basis to take action. We have common cause. We all want to enforce the laws of the United States, ensure a safe and orderly migrant flow, protect our communities, reduce the flow of drugs, facilitate legal trade and travel, secure our borders, and support vulnerable populations. This is one of the most serious crises the Department of Homeland Security has ever faced, and we need your help.

Copies of this letter have been sent to the Speaker of the House; the Majority and Minority Leaders in the Senate and House; and the Chairmen and Ranking Members of the Senate Appropriations Committee, Senate Judiciary Committee, Senate Homeland Security and Governmental Affairs Committee, House Appropriations Committee, House Judiciary Committee, and House Homeland Security Committee.

Respectfully,
Kirstjen M. Nielsen Secretary. [125]

Through the middle of 2019, there were 600,000 more illegal immigrants that came to the United States compared to all of 2018.

The letter shows how dire the situation is. The only way to remedy the situation is to stop the flow of illegals into this country.

Former Homeland Security Secretary Jeh Johnson said on March 31, 2019, that America has a crisis at the southern border, and that the number of apprehensions exceed anything he encountered during his time serving under former President Barack Obama. He also supported Secretary Nielsen's number that we were on pace for 100,000 apprehensions in March 2019. This was a far greater number than anything that he saw during his three years as Secretary of Homeland Security.

Some Democrats campaigning for the nomination of the Democrat Party to run for president in the 2020 election said that they would virtually eliminate immigration by detention by Executive Order, or that they would decriminalize illegal border crossings. Senator Bernie Sanders of Vermont, one of those campaigning for the Democrat endorsement to run for president in 2020, recently announced a sweeping immigration plan that would impose a full moratorium on deportations, break up existing immigration enforcement agencies (Immigration and Customs Enforcement (ICE) and Customs and Border Patrol (CBP)), grant full welfare access to illegal immigrants, provide a "pathway to citizenship" through Congress for all illegal immigrants living in America, and set up a $14 billion federal grant program for legal defense for poor immigrants.

Secretary Johnson said that would be equivalent to having "open borders," that it would be unwise and unworkable, and that it was not supported by a majority of Americans. On a bipartisan basis, a recent and the prior Secretary of Homeland Security, made a compelling case that there is an emergency requiring immediate action.

One wonders what side Senator Sanders is on. It certainly is not immigrants who have come into this country legally. It certainly is not the taxpayers and the citizens of the United States, who have made this the greatest nation in history. Senator Sanders and the other liberal Democrats are attempting to increase the people who will vote for them at the state and federal levels, even if they came into the United States illegally. Those illegals will change the voting patterns to help the Democrats get elected.

The Democrats obviously believe that they do not have enough supporters in the United States to be successful going forward so they are importing additional voters to help them.

In response the Congress passed and the President signed a bill that contained about $4.5 billion aimed at improving conditions in overcrowded migrant detention centers to include emergency humanitarian aid to migrant children and providing funds for the Department of Homeland Security so the Customs and Border Patrol could improve conditions in border facilities, expand medical care, and provide better access to essential items like clothing, hygiene products and baby formula. The bill also contained money funding military expenses along the border, funding for Immigration and Customs Enforcement, and funding for overtime for Customs and Border Patrol employees. Until we secure our border, these kinds of expenses will continue.

President Trump then accused Mexico of doing nothing to stop the illegal immigration flow to the United States and threatened to close the southern border. He then threatened to impose tariffs on goods from Mexico. After negotiations, Mexico agreed to increase enforcement to curb irregular migration, including deploying its newly created National Guard throughout the country in addition to sending 6,000 National Guard troops to its southern border with Guatemala to stop caravans and other illegals from passing through Mexico on the way to the United States. Mexico would also take action to dismantle human-smuggling networks and work more closely with the United States to share information about immigrants. The United States said it would immediately expand the implementation of the existing "Migrant Protection Protocols" across its entire southern border, returning asylum seekers to Mexico where they may await the adjudication of their asylum claims. Mexico would authorize the entrance of all of those individuals for humanitarian reasons.

In addition, in any discussion of the problems with our southern border, it is important to note that for years the United States has provided aid to the countries of Central America, to include Mexico, Honduras, Guatemala, and El Salvador. The latter three are known as the "Northern Triangle." The aid was designed to improve the living conditions of the residents of those countries and their opportunities to find jobs so they would not need to leave their country. As an example, on December 18, 2018, the United States and Mexico issued the "United States-Mexico Declaration of Principles on Economic Development and Cooperation in Southern Mexico and Central America." It stated in part:

> The United States and Mexico today commit to
> strengthen and expand our bilateral cooperation

to foster development and increase investment in southern Mexico and in Central America to create a zone of prosperity. Both countries recognize the strong links between promoting development and economic growth in southern Mexico and the success of promoting prosperity, good governance, and security in Central America. The United States welcomes the Comprehensive Development Plan launched by the Government of Mexico in concert with the governments of El Salvador, Guatemala, and Honduras to promote these goals. The United States and Mexico will lead in working with regional and international partners to build a more prosperous and secure Central America to address the underlying causes of migration, and so that citizens of the region can build better lives for themselves and their families at home. . . The United States is committing a total of $5.8 billion in support of institutional reforms, development, and economic growth in the Northern Triangle from public and private sources. . . The United States, for its part, through the Overseas Private Investment Corporation, is focused on private and public investment in Mexico totaling 4.8 billion, to include committing $2 billion for suitable projects in southern Mexico. [126]

There are four more reasons why securing our borders is important:

(1) Sanctuary cities/states–A "sanctuary" is a place of refuge or safety, and in this context, it means providing refuge or safety to illegal immigrants. Sanctuary areas are refusing to restrain criminal activities of illegal immigrants, to include shootings, stabbings, rapes,

and human trafficking. While sanctuary jurisdictions are usurping power from the federal government, they are not protecting against domestic violence. They are allowing it and encouraging it. Some of them issue orders to local law enforcement to ignore ICE directives to remove illegal immigrants, they release criminal illegal immigrants without letting ICE know so they could incarcerate them and/or deport them, and sometimes they announce when ICE is going to conduct raids looking for criminal illegal immigrants. There have been some high-profile murders by illegal immigrants, such as the murders of Kate Steinle, Mollie Tibbets, and Deputy Ryan Thompson. These have not led to changes in sanctuary policy. There have also been instances of multiple sexual assaults where the perpetrators were released from custody, with ICE not being informed. A wheelchair-bound woman was raped in 2018, and the perpetrator served nine months. When he was released, a judge refused to report his release so ICE could detain and deport him. The predator returned to the home of the disabled woman and raped and beat her in front of her child. Each crime by an illegal immigrant is fully preventable, yet the sanctuary cities/states do nothing to change their policies. These areas are usurping the power to establish naturalization, which is unequivocally given to the federal government in Article 1 of the Constitution.

(2) Every ten years, the United States must conduct a census of those living here. The census counts citizens, legal immigrants, and illegal aliens. Democrats do not want the census to be limited to citizens of the United States. Seats in the House of Representatives are apportioned to each state, based on the state's population relative to the rest of the country. As a result, immigration has had a significant effect on the distribution of seats in the House. The apportionment of seats is a zero-sum proposition. One state's gain is another state's loss since the number of seats in the House has remained unchanged. Sanctuary states, cities, and counties, which attract and hold illegal immigrants, could be benefitted in the

number of seats in the House that they would be apportioned due to the number of illegal immigrants living there. As examples, in the 2000 apportionment, Colorado, Kentucky, Michigan, Mississippi, Ohio, Pennsylvania, and Wisconsin lost a seat to states with growth from illegal immigration.

(3) Noncitizens can, and have, voted in elections in the United States. Texas conducted a study and discovered that 95,000 non-US citizens were registered to vote in Texas. About 58,000 of them voted in Texas elections between 1996 and 2018. Should noncitizens be able to vote and influence the direction of politics in the United States? Republicans and Democrats are crying out about the attempt by Russia to influence the 2016 election. But Democrats are refusing to do anything to stop noncitizens from voting in the United States. And, with their push for voter registration, the Democrats don't care if those who register are citizens or not.

(4) Illegal immigrants also influence the Electoral College. The Electoral College was established by the United States Constitution in Article II, Section 1, Clause 2.

> The Electoral Process consists of the selection of the electors, the meeting of the electors where they vote for president and vice president, and the counting of the electoral votes by Congress. The Electoral College is a process, not a place. The Founding Fathers established it in the Constitution, in part, as a compromise between the election of the President by a vote in Congress and election of the President by a popular vote of qualified citizens.

What is the process? The Electoral College process consists of the selection of the electors, the meeting of the electors where they vote for President and Vice President, and the counting of the electoral votes by Congress. [127]

There are 438 members of the House of Representatives and 100 members of the United States Senate. As a result, there are 538 electors determined in each state by its total members of the House and the Senate. If a census results in reapportionment in the House, that affects the distribution of the electors among the states as well.

In the 2016 election, Donald J. Trump carried 2,626 counties while Hillary Clinton carried 487 counties, according to the Associated Press. President Trump received a total of 62,985,134 popular votes while Mrs. Clinton received 65,853,652 popular votes, a difference of 2,868,518 votes. The difference in Mrs. Clinton's favor came from five California counties around Los Angeles, San Francisco, and San Diego.

Democrats are arguing that President Trump did not really win the election because he did not win the popular vote. But there is no question that he won the election based on a constitutional procedure that has served this country well throughout its history. Besides, he won 84 percent of the counties, five times the number that Mrs. Clinton won. That cannot be ignored and is the reason the electoral college exists. Apparently, the Democrats will not accept an election whenever a Republican wins in accordance with the Electoral College if he/she did not win the popular vote.

The founders of this country wisely wanted all parts of the country to have influence in elections. The wishes of 84 percent of the counties in this country must be considered. Big cities alone cannot be allowed to run this country.

Our Grandparents

> From: "David LaBonte" My wife, Rosemary, wrote a wonderful letter to the editor of the OC Register which, of course, was not printed. So, I decided to "print" it myself by sending it out on the Internet. Pass it along if you feel so inclined. Written in

response to a series of letters to the editor in the Orange County Register:

Dear Editor: So many letter writers have based their arguments on how this land is made up of immigrants. Ernie Lujan for one, suggests we should tear down the Statue of Liberty because the people now in question aren't being treated the same as those who passed through Ellis Island and other ports of entry.

Maybe we should turn to our history books and point out to people like Mr. Lujan why today's American is not willing to accept this new kind of immigrant any longer. Back in 1900 when there was a rush from all areas of Europe to come to the United States, people had to get off a ship and stand in a long line in New York and be documented.

Some would even get down on their hands and knees and kiss the ground. They made a pledge to uphold the laws and support their new country in good and bad times. They made learning English a primary rule in their new American households and some even changed their names to blend in with their new home.

They had waved goodbye to their birthplace to give their children a new life and did everything in their power to help their children assimilate into one culture. Nothing was handed to them. No free lunches, no welfare, no labor laws to protect them. All they had were the skills and craftsmanship they had brought with them to trade for a future of prosperity.

Most of their children came of age when World War II broke out. My father fought alongside men whose parents had come straight over from Germany, Italy, France and Japan. None of these 1st generation Americans ever gave any thought about what country their parents had come from. They were Americans fighting Hitler, Mussolini and the Emperor of Japan. They were defending the United States of America as one people.

When we liberated France, no one in those villages were looking for the French American, the German American or the Irish American. The people of France saw only Americans. And we carried one flag that represented one country. Not one of those immigrant sons would have thought about picking up another country's flag and waving it to represent who they were. It would have been a disgrace to their parents who had sacrificed so much to be here. These immigrants truly knew what it meant to be an American. They stirred the melting pot into one red, white and blue bowl.

And here we are with a new kind of immigrant who wants the same rights and privileges. Only they want to achieve it by playing with a different set of rules, one that includes the entitlement card and a guarantee of being faithful to their mother country.

I'm sorry, that's not what being an American is all about. I believe that the immigrants who landed on Ellis Island in the early 1900's deserve better than that for all the toil, hard work and sacrifice in raising future generations to create a land that has become a beacon for those legally searching for a better life. I think they would be appalled that they are being used as an example by those waving foreign country flags.

And for that suggestion about taking down the Statue of Liberty, it happens to mean a lot to the citizens who are voting on the immigration bill. I wouldn't start talking about dismantling the United States just yet. [128]

Multiculturalism Is a Failure

By Walter E. Williams Published 4:47 p.m. CT Sept. 16, 2014

German Chancellor Angela Merkel declared that in Germany, multiculturalism has "utterly failed." Both Australia's ex-prime minister John Howard and Spain's ex-prime minister Jose Maria Aznar reached the same conclusion about their countries. British Prime Minister David Cameron has warned that multiculturalism is fostering extremist ideology and directly contributing to homegrown Islamic terrorism. U.K. Independence Party leader Nigel Farage said the United Kingdom's push for multiculturalism has not united Britons but pushed them apart. It has allowed Islam to emerge despite Britain's Judeo-Christian culture. Former British

Prime Minister Tony Blair said the roots of violent Islamism can be found "in the extremist minority that now, in every European city, preach hatred of the West and our way of life."

The bottom line is that much of the Muslim world is at war with Western civilization. There's no question that the West has the military might to thwart radical Islam's agenda. The question up for grabs is whether we have the intelligence to recognize the attack, and the will to defend ourselves from annihilation.

Multiculturalism is Islamists' foot in the door. At the heart of multiculturalism is an attack on Western and Christian values. Much of that attack has its roots on college campuses among the intellectual elite who see their mission as indoctrinating our youth. In past columns, I've documented professorial hate-America teaching, such as a UCLA economics professor telling his class, "The U.S., backed by facts, is the greediest and most selfish country in the world." A history professor told her class: "Capitalism isn't a lie on purpose. It's just a lie." She also said: "(Capitalists) are swine. . . They're bastard people."

Students sit through lectures listening to professorial rants about topics such as globalism and Western exploitation of the Middle East and Third World peoples. Some public school boards have banned songs and music containing references to Santa Claus, Jesus or other religious Christmas symbols.

The New York City school system permits displays of Jewish menorahs, the Muslim star and crescent, but not the Christian Nativity scene.

One school district banned a teacher from using excerpts from historical documents in his classroom because they contained references to God and Christianity. The historical documents in question were the Declaration of Independence and "The Rights of the Colonists," by Samuel Adams.

The U.S. is a nation of many races, ethnicities, religions and cultures. Since our inception, people from all over the world have immigrated here to become Americans. They have learned English and American history and celebrated American traditions and values.

They have become Americans while also respecting and adapting some of the traditions of the countries they left behind. By contrast, many of today's immigrants demand classes be taught—and official documents be printed—in their native language. Other immigrants demand the use of Shariah, practices that permit honor killing and female genital mutilation.

Multiculturalists argue that different cultural values are morally equivalent. That's nonsense. Western culture and values are superior. For those who'd accuse me of Eurocentrism, I'd ask: Is forcible female genital mutilation, as practiced in nearly 30 sub-Saharan African and Middle Eastern countries, a morally equivalent cultural value? Slavery is practiced in Mauritania, Mali, Niger, Chad and Sudan; is it morally equivalent? In most of the Middle East, there are numerous limits placed on women, such as prohibitions on driving.

Under Islamic law, in some countries, female adulterers face death by stoning, and thieves face the punishment of having their hand severed. In some countries, homosexuality is a crime punishable by death. Are these cultural values morally superior or inferior to Western values?

Multiculturalism has not yet done the damage in the U.S. that it has in western European countries—such as England, France and Germany—but it's on its way. By the way, one need not be a Westerner to hold Western values. Mainly, you just have to accept the supremacy of the individual above all else. [129]

How Immigration and Multiculturalism Destroyed Detroit

By Frosty Wooldridge
October 5, 2009
NewsWithViews.com

For 15 years, from the mid-1970s to 1990, I worked in Detroit, Michigan. I watched it descend into the abyss of crime, debauchery, gun play, drugs, school truancy, carjacking, gangs and human depravity. I watched entire city blocks burned out. I watched graffiti explode on buildings, cars, trucks, buses and school yards. Trash everywhere! Detroiters walked through it, tossed more into it and ignored it.

Tens of thousands and then, hundreds of thousands today exist on federal welfare, free housing and food stamps! With Aid to Dependent Children, minority women birthed eight to 10 and in one case, one woman birthed 24 kids as reported by the Detroit Free Press—all on American taxpayer dollars. A new child meant a new car payment, new TV and whatever mom wanted. I saw Lyndon Baines Johnson's "Great Society" flourish in Detroit. If you give money for doing nothing, you will get more hands out taking money for doing nothing.

Mayor Coleman Young, perhaps the most corrupt mayor in America, outside of Richard Daley in Chicago, rode Detroit down to its knees. He set the benchmark for cronyism, incompetence and arrogance... Detroit became a majority black city with 67 percent African Americans.

As a United Van Lines truck driver for my summer job from teaching math and science, I loaded hundreds of American families into my van for a new life in another city or state. Detroit plummeted from 1.8 million citizens to 912,000 today. At the same time, legal and illegal immigrants converged on the city, so much so, that Muslims number over 300,000. Mexicans number 400,000 throughout Michigan, but most work in Detroit.

As the Muslims moved in, the whites moved out. As the crimes became more violent, the whites fled. Finally, unlawful Mexicans moved in at a torrid pace. You could cut the racial tension in the air with a knife! Detroit may be one of our best examples of multiculturalism: pure dislike and total separation from America.

Today, you hear Muslim calls to worship over the city like a new American Baghdad with hundreds of Islamic mosques in Michigan, paid for by Saudi Arabia oil money. High school flunk out rates reached 76 percent last June according to NBC's Brian Williams. Classrooms resemble more foreign countries than America. English? Few speak it! The city features a 50 percent illiteracy rate and growing. Unemployment hit 28.9 percent in 2009 as the auto industry vacated the city.

In this week's Time Magazine October 4, 2009, "The Tragedy of Detroit: How a great city fell and how it can rise again," I choked on the writer's description of what happened.

"If Detroit had been savaged by a hurricane and sub-merged by a ravenous flood, we'd know a lot more about it," said Daniel Okrent. "If drought and care-lessness had spread brush fires across the city, we'd see it on the evening news every night. Earthquake, tornadoes, you name it—if natural disaster had dev-astated the city that was once the living proof of American prosperity, the rest of the country might take notice

But Detroit, once our fourth largest city, now 11th and slipping rapidly, has had no such luck. Its disaster has long been a slow unwinding that seemed to remove it from the rest of the country. Even the death rattle that in the past year emanated from its signature industry brought more attention to the auto executives than to the people of the city, who had for so long been victimized by their dreadful decision-making."

As Coleman Young's corruption brought the city to its knees, no amount of federal dollars could save the incredible payoffs, kickbacks and illegality permeating his administration. I witnessed the city's death from the seat of my 18-wheeler tractor trailer because I moved people out of every sector of decaying Detroit.

"By any quantifiable standard, the city is on life support. Detroit's treasury is $300 million short of the funds needed to provide the barest municipal services," Okrent said. "The school system, which six years ago was compelled by the teachers' union to reject a philanthropist's offer of $200 million to build 15 small, independent charter high schools, is in receivership. The murder rate is soaring, and 7 out of 10 remain unsolved. Three years after Katrina devastated New Orleans, unemployment in that city hit a peak of 11%. In Detroit, the unemployment rate is 28.9%. That's worth spelling out: twenty-eight point nine percent."

At the end of Okrent's report, and he will write a dozen more about Detroit, he said, "That's because the story of Detroit is not simply one of a great city's collapse. It's also about the erosion of the industries that helped build the country we know today. The ultimate fate of Detroit will reveal much about the character of America in the 21st century. If what was once the most prosperous manufacturing city in the nation has been brought to its knees, what does that say about our recent past? And if it can't find a way to get up, what does that say about our future?"

. . . Immigration will keep pouring more and more uneducated third world immigrants from the Middle East into Detroit—thus creating a beach-head for Islamic hegemony in America. If 50 percent illiteracy continues, we will see more homegrown terrorists spawned out of the Muslim ghettos of Detroit. Illiteracy plus Islam equals walking human bombs. You have already seen it in the Madrid, Spain, London, England and Paris, France with train bombings, subway bombings and riots. As their numbers grow, so will their power to enact their bar-baric Sharia Law that negates republican forms of government, first amendment rights and subjugates women to the lowest rungs on the human ladder. We will see more honor killings by upset husbands, fathers and brothers that demand subjugation by their daughters, sisters and wives. Muslims prefer beheadings of women to scare the hell out of any other members of their sect from straying.

Multiculturalism: what a perfect method to kill our language, culture, country and way of life. [130]

This essay had renewed interest in 2013 when Detroit filed for bankruptcy protection.

With multiculturalism, the "melting pot" will be no more. Some groups will maintain their allegiance to the country from which they came to include keeping their language as their primary (or only) language. Some could strive to retain and live by their old laws/religious teachings, to include keeping local police out of their communities. The different groups could live in ghettos or segregated areas. Some could attempt to create local terrorists to continue terrorist activities within the United States. Racial tension could increase with, as Mr. Wooldridge noted, pure dislike for one another and total separation from America.

We could end up a country of many "tribes," with many of them not owing their loyalty to the United States.

9

THE TRUMP PHENOMENON

Donald J. Trump's election to be president of the United States of America in the 2016 national election, with Mike Pence as his vice president, was a surprise to most people and most pundits. Hillary Clinton had been leading in the polls for most of the campaign. The Democrats and the national media apparently were unaware of the strong feelings that conservatives and others held about everything that had occurred during the Obama administration.

In an article entitled "US," Paul Genova provided one summary of the issues that had brought Trump supporters to the voting booths. Mr. Genova has been president and chief operating officer of Wireless Telecom Group Inc. since June 30, 2016.

> I haven't said too much about this election since the start ... but this is how I feel ... I'm noticing that a lot of people aren't graciously accepting the fact that their candidate lost. In fact you seem to be posting even more hateful things about those who voted for Trump. Some are apparently "triggered" because you are posting how "sick" you feel about the results.

How did this happen you ask? Well here is how it happened! You created "us" when you attacked our freedom of speech. You created "us" when you attacked our right to bear arms. You created "us" when you attacked our Judeo-Christian beliefs. You created "us" when you constantly referred to us as racists. You created "us" when you incessantly called us xenophobic. You created "us" when you told us to 'get on board or get out of the way.' You created "us" when you attacked our flag.

You created "us" when you took God out of our schools. You created "us" when you confused women's rights with feminism and abortion. You created "us" when you began to emasculate men. You created "us" when you decided to make our children soft.

You created "us" when you decided to vote for progressive ideals. You created "us" when you attacked our way of life. You created "us" when you decided to let our country's government get out of control.

You created "us" the silent majority! You created "us" when you began murdering innocent law enforcement officers. You created "us" when you lied and said we could keep our insurance plans and our doctors. You created "us" when you allowed our jobs to continue to leave our country.

"YOU" created "US." It really is just that simple. Pass this on if you believe this represents most of "US." I did! [131]

Dr. Henry Kissinger was the National Security Advisor and then Secretary of State under President Richard Nixon and President Gerald Ford from 1973–1977. He is still a highly respected statesman and geopolitical consultant. In an interview with John Dickerson on *CBS Face the Nation*, the following conversation occurred:

> DICKERSON: What's your feeling now about president-elect Donald Trump?

> KISSINGER: I had not thought of President Trump as a presidential candidate until he became a presidential candidate.

> And the first appearances, I thought it was a transitory phenomenon. But I give him huge credit for having analyzed an aspect of the American situation, develop a strategy (AUDIO GAP) against his leadership of his own party and prevailing.

> Now his challenge is to apply that same skill to the international situation.

> DICKERSON: You told Jeffrey Goldberg of "The Atlantic" that, with Donald Trump, it could create opportunity, but also serious dislocation.

> What's your assessment now on that?

> KISSINGER: Donald Trump is a phenomenon that foreign countries haven't seen.

So it is a shocking experience to them that he came into office, at the same time, extraordinary opportunity. And I believe he has the possibility of going down in history as a very considerable president, because every country now has two things to consider, one, their perception that the previous president or the outgoing president basically withdrew America from international politics, so that they had to make their own assessment of their necessities, and, secondly, that here is a new president who is asking a lot of unfamiliar questions.

And because of the combination of the partial vacuum and the new questions, one could imagine that something remarkable and new emerges out of it. I'm not saying it will. I'm saying it's an extraordinary opportunity.

DICKERSON: Do you have a sense of what his emerging foreign policy vision is?

KISSINGER: I think he operates by a kind of instinct that is a different form of analysis as my more academic one, that he's raised a number of issues that I think are important, very important and, if they're addressed properly, could lead to— could create results. [132]

Donald J. Trump is one of the most prepared candidates to become president of the United States, at least in our modern era. He had never been elected to a government position, but he was a successful businessman. He knew how our economy works and the importance of growth, the level of taxation and regulation, the relationship between business and government, and the importance of business principals in running the government.

As an international businessman, he traveled and did business in many countries around the world. He met international leaders and established a relationship with them. He knew the importance of the United States in world affairs and the importance of the United States' role in world affairs. He became knowledgeable of trade with different countries and with the balance of trade between them and our economy.

While never having been elected to a political position, President Trump was a savvy politician. He was savvy enough to sense that there was a need in the country that was not being fulfilled. Hence, his campaigning for and becoming president of the United States.

That he had never served in a political position was a blessing and a curse. As a blessing, President Trump is not held back by political baggage or political hesitance. As a curse, he is not restrained by political caution in some of his actions and comments. Perhaps the best example of this are his incessant tweets that enable him to keep his message out there and to keep in touch with his supporters. However, when he has been criticized by various persons, he has fought back when he did not need to. That would keep an issue open longer than necessary, and he ended up elevating a lot of those who criticized him to his level. These resulted in distractions from his accomplishments and "turning off" others who do not believe he was being "presidential."

The question for the latter group is, will their feeling toward him on this issue be extended to the ballot box, or will his accomplishments outweigh that feeling?

Why The Democrats/Liberals/Socialists Cannot Let President Trump Succeed

In the Obama administration's economy leading up to the 2016 election, not much was happening. One of the major reasons for that was uncertainty over what would happen with taxes, spending, Obamacare, and regulations after the election. There was a lot of money sitting on the sidelines, waiting for the outcome of the election.

If the Democrats had won the presidency, the money would have continued to sit on the sidelines. Who would want to invest if the tax-and-spend policies of the prior eight years were to continue?

Starting shortly after the 2016 election when President Trump was elected, many corporations announced bonuses for employees and the expansion of their business within the United States. Manufacturing jobs began to come back to the United States, something that President Obama said would never happen. He was partially correct. It would never have happened if he had remained president—another instance of the "new normal" of the high tax, spend, and regulation environment of the liberals.

President Trump is already one of the most successful presidents in United States history. One need only examine his accomplishments since January 2017 to reach that conclusion.

President Donald J. Trump Has Delivered Record Breaking Results For The American People In His First Three Years In Office Issued on: December 31, 2019

> "We are making America stronger, prouder, and greater than ever before" (President Donald J. Trump)
>
> *Promoting Economic Prosperity for All*: President Trump's pro-growth policies have led to an

economic boom that is lifting up Americans of all backgrounds.

Since President Trump's election, more than 7 million jobs have been added to the economy.

For the first time on record there are more job openings than unemployed Americans.

There are more than 7 million job openings, outnumbering job seekers by more than 1 million.

Nearly two-thirds of Americans rate now as a good time to find a quality job, empowering more Americans with rewarding careers.

This year, the unemployment rate reached its lowest level in half a century.

The unemployment rate has remained at or below 4 percent for the past 21 months.

The unemployment rate for women reached its lowest rate in 65 years under President Trump.

Under President Trump, jobless claims hit their lowest level in half a century.

The number of people claiming unemployment insurance as a share of the population is the lowest on record.

American workers of all backgrounds are thriving under President Trump.

The unemployment rates for African Americans, Hispanic Americans, Asian Americans, veterans, individuals with disabilities, and those without a high school diploma have all reached record lows under President Trump.

The booming economy is putting more money in Americans' pockets.

Wages are growing at their fastest rate in a decade, with year-over-year wage gains exceeding 3 percent for the first time since 2009.

November 2019 marked the 16th consecutive month that wages rose at an annual rate of at or over 3 percent.

Median household income surpassed $63,000 in 2018—the highest level on record.

President Trump's policies are helping forgotten Americans across the country prosper, driving down income inequality.

Wages are rising fastest for low-income workers.

Middle-class and low-income workers are enjoying faster wage growth than high-earners.

When measured as the share of income earned by the top 20 percent, income inequality fell in 2018 by the largest amount in over a decade.

Americans are being lifted out of poverty as a result of today's booming economy.

Since President Trump took office, over 2.4 million Americans have been lifted out of poverty.

Poverty rates for African Americans and Hispanic Americans have reached record lows.

Since President Trump's election, nearly 7 million Americans have been lifted off of food stamps.

Americans are coming off of the sidelines and back into the workforce.

The prime age labor force has grown by 2.1 million under President Trump.

In the third quarter of 2019, 73.7 percent of workers entering employment came from out of the labor force rather than from unemployment, the highest share since the series began in 1990.

President Trump's pro-growth policies are helping businesses of all sizes thrive like never before.

Small business optimism broke a 35-year old record in 2018 and remains historically high.

The DOW, S&P 500, and NASDAQ have all repeatedly notched record highs under President Trump.

President Trump is following through on his promise to revitalize American manufacturing, with more than a half million manufacturing jobs added since the election.

President Trump has prioritized workforce development to ensure American workers are prepared to fill high quality jobs.

The President has worked to expand apprenticeship programs, helping Americans gain hands-on training and experience with no student debt.

Since President Trump took office, over 660,000 apprentices have been hired across the country.

President Trump established the National Council for the American Worker, tasked with developing a workforce strategy for the jobs of the future.

Over 370 companies have signed the President's "Pledge to America's Workers," pledging to provide more than 14.4 million employment and training opportunities.

President Trump signed an Executive Order prioritizing Cyber Workforce Development to ensure that we have the most skilled cyber workforce of the 21st century.

President Trump signed the Tax Cuts & Jobs Act in 2017—the largest tax reform package in history.

More than 6 million American workers received wage increases, bonuses, and increased benefits thanks to the tax cuts.

$1 trillion has poured back into the country from overseas since the President's tax cuts.

President Trump is revitalizing distressed communities through Opportunity Zones, which encourage investment and growth in underserved communities.

More than 8,760 communities in all 50 States, the District of Columbia, and 5 Territories have been designated as Opportunity Zones.

The White House Opportunity and Revitalization Council has taken more than 175 actions to encourage investment and promote growth within Opportunity Zones.

The White House Opportunity and Revitalization Council is engaging all levels of government to identify best practices and assist leaders, investors, and entrepreneurs in using the Opportunity Zone incentive to revitalize low-income communities.

The President is ensuring that America is prepared to lead the world in the industries of the future, by promoting American leadership in emerging technologies like 5G and AI.

The Administration named artificial intelligence, quantum information science, and 5G, among other emerging technologies, as national research and development priorities.

President Trump launched the American AI Initiative to invest in AI research, unleash innovation, and build the American workforce of the future.

President Trump signed an Executive Order that established a new advisory committee of industry and academic leaders to advise the government on its quantum activities.

President Trump has made supporting working families a priority of his Administration.

President Trump signed legislation securing historic levels of funding for the Child Care and Development Block Grant, helping low-income families access child care.

During his Joint Address to Congress and each State of the Union Address, the President called on Congress to pass a nationwide paid family leave plan.

The President signed into law 12-weeks of paid parental leave for federal workers.

President Trump's tax reforms provided a new tax credit to incentivize businesses to offer paid family leave to their employees.

The President's historic tax reforms doubled the child tax credit, benefitting nearly 40 million American families with an average of over $2,200 dollars in 2019.

Lifting the Burden of Overregulation: President Trump's historic deregulation efforts are driving economic growth, cutting unnecessary costs, and increasing transparency.

President Trump has delivered on, and far exceeded, his promise to slash two existing regulations for every new regulation.

Since taking office, President Trump has rolled back nearly 8 regulations for every new significant one.

The Trump Administration's deregulatory efforts have slashed regulatory costs by more than $50 billion.

In the coming years, the average American household is projected to see an income gain of $3,100 per year thanks to President Trump's historic regulatory reform.

Once fully in effect, 20 major deregulatory actions undertaken by the Administration are expected to save American consumers and businesses over $220 billion per year.

President Trump signed 16 pieces of deregulatory legislation that are expected to result in a $40 billion increase in annual real incomes.

President Trump established the Governors Initiative on Regulatory Innovation.

This initiative is working to reduce outdated regulations at the State, local, and tribal levels, advance occupational licensing reform, and align Federal and State regulation.

The President signed legislation eliminating regulatory barriers that made offering retirement benefits difficult for small businesses.

The President took action to increase transparency in Federal agencies and protect Americans from administrative abuse.

This year, President Trump signed two Executive Orders to guard against secretive or unlawful interpretations of rules and prevent Americans from being hit with unfair and unexpected penalties.

President Trump has followed through on his promise to repeal the Obama-era Waters of the United States Rule, lifting a burden off American farmers.

President Trump ended the previous Administration's war on coal.

President Trump signed legislation repealing the harmful Obama-era Stream Protection Rule.

President Trump replaced the overreaching Obama-era Clean Power Plan with the Affordable Clean Energy Rule, which respects States' rights and promotes economic growth while lowering power-sector CO_2 emissions.

In 2017, the President announced the United States' withdrawal from the Paris Climate Agreement, which would have killed millions of American jobs.

The Administration has worked to undo the Obama-era fuel economy regulations by proposing the SAFE Vehicles Rule to lower the cost of new and safer cars.

President Trump helped community banks by signing legislation that rolled back costly provisions of Dodd-Frank.

President Trump established the White House Council on Reducing Regulatory Barriers to Affordable Housing Development to bring down the costs of housing across the country.

The President's deregulatory actions are removing government barriers to personal freedom and consumer choice in healthcare.

In 2017, President Trump corrected Obama Administration overreach by right-sizing Bears

Ears National Monument and Grand Staircase-Escalante National Monument.

Fighting for Fairer Trade: President Trump is negotiating better trade deals for the American people after years of our country being taken advantage of.

President Trump negotiated the U.S.-Mexico-Canada agreement (USMCA) to replace the outdated North American Free Trade Agreement (NAFTA).

USMCA includes tremendous wins for American workers, farmers, and manufacturers, generating over $68 billion in economic activity and creating 176,000 new jobs.

President Trump negotiated two tremendous deals with Japan to boost America's agricultural and digital trade with the world's third largest economy.

Thanks to President Trump's efforts, Japan will open its market to approximately $7 billion in American agricultural exports.

The President's negotiations will boost the already approximately $40 billion worth of digital trade between our two countries.

President Trump fulfilled his promise to renegotiate the United States-Korea Free Trade Agreement, providing a boost to American auto exports.

These efforts doubled the number of American autos that can be exported to South Korea using United States safety standards.

President Trump reached a historic phase one trade agreement with China that will begin rebalancing our two countries' trade relationship.

As a result of President Trump's leadership, China has agreed to structural reforms in areas of intellectual property, technology transfer, agriculture, financial services, and currency and foreign exchange.

China will be making substantial purchases of American agricultural products, marking a monumental win for American farmers.

President Trump fulfilled his promise to withdraw from the disastrous Trans-Pacific Partnership (TPP).

President Trump achieved a mutual agreement with the European Union to work together towards zero tariffs, non-tariff barriers, and subsidies on certain goods.

President Trump has worked to prepare for post-Brexit trade and made Congress aware of his intent to negotiate a free trade agreement with the United Kingdom (UK).

President Trump imposed tariffs on foreign steel and aluminum to protect our vital industries and support our national security.

President Trump imposed tariffs to protect American-made washing machines and solar products that were hurt by import surges.

The United States scored an historic victory by overhauling the Universal Postal Union (UPU), whose outdated policies were undermining American interests and workers.

President Trump has expanded markets for American farmers to export their goods worldwide, for example:

The European Union has opened up to more American beef and increased imports of American soybeans.

China lifted its ban on American poultry and opened up to American beef.

South Korea lifted its ban on American poultry and eggs and agreed to provide market access for the greatest, guaranteed volume of American rice.

The Trump Administration has authorized a total of $28 billion in aid for farmers who have been subjected to unfair trade practices.

Securing the Border: President Trump has taken historic steps to confront the crisis on our Nation's borders and protect American communities.

President Trump is following through on his promise to build a wall on our southern border.

The Administration expects to have approximately 450 miles of new border wall by the end of 2020.

The President struck new agreements with Mexico, El Salvador, Guatemala, and Honduras to help stop the flood of illegal immigration.

The President worked with Mexico to ensure they would improve their border security.

The United States is working with Mexico and others in the region to dismantle the human smuggling networks that profit from human misery and fuel the border crisis by exploiting vulnerable populations.

The Administration negotiated agreements with El Salvador, Guatemala, and Honduras to stem the surge of aliens arriving at our border.

President Trump negotiated the Migrant Protection Protocols, requiring certain migrants to wait in Mexico during their immigration proceedings instead of allowing them to disappear into our country.

Thanks to the President's swift action, border apprehensions fell by more than 70 percent from May—the peak of the crisis—to November.

The Trump Administration is stopping deadly drugs and violent criminals from flowing across our borders and into our communities.

Customs and Border Protection (CBP) seized more than 163,000 pounds of cocaine, heroin, methamphetamine, and fentanyl at the southern border in FY 2019.

The United States Coast Guard seized more than 458,000 pounds of cocaine at sea in FY 2019 and referred nearly 400 suspected drug smugglers for prosecution.

U.S. Immigration and Customs Enforcement (ICE) Homeland Security Investigations (HSI) seized over 1.4 million pounds of narcotics and made more than 12,000 narcotic-related arrests in FY 2019.

Drug Enforcement Administration (DEA) seized over 50,000 kilograms of methamphetamine and over 2,700 kilograms of fentanyl in FY 2019.

CBP apprehended 976 alien gang members in FY 2019, including 464 aliens affiliated with MS-13.

ICE HSI made over 4,000 arrests of gang members in FY 2019, including over 450 arrests of MS-13 members.

Restoring the Rule of Law: President Trump is upholding the rule of law, restoring integrity to our asylum system, and promoting immigrant self-sufficiency.

President Trump released an immigration plan to fully secure our border, modernize our laws, and promote an immigration system based on merit.

President Trump is working to combat the abuse of our asylum system that drives illegal immigration.

The Administration took action to close the Flores Settlement Agreement loophole and ensure alien families can be kept together through their proceedings.

The President released an order that makes aliens ineligible for asylum if they passed through another country in transit to our border and did not apply for asylum in that country first.

Since taking office, President Trump has stepped up enforcement to ensure there are consequences for breaking our laws.

In FY 2019, the Department of Justice prosecuted a record breaking number of immigration related crimes.

ICE Enforcement and Removal Operations (ERO) arrested 143,099 aliens in FY 2019, 86 percent of whom had criminal records.

ICE ERO removed more than 267,000 illegal aliens from the United States in FY 2019.

The Trump Administration is cracking down on sanctuary cities and increasing cooperation at the local level on immigration enforcement.

The Administration has more than doubled the number of jurisdictions participating in the 287(g) program enhancing local cooperation on immigration enforcement.

The Administration took action to protect taxpayers by ensuring that aliens wishing to enter or remain in our country are able to support themselves and not rely on public benefits.

The President issued a proclamation to ensure immigrants admitted to America do not burden our healthcare system.

The President has taken action to reduce nonimmigrant visa overstays, a problem that undermines the rule of law, impacts public safety, and strains resources needed for the border.

President Trump made our country safer by ordering the enhanced vetting of individuals attempting to come to America from countries that do not meet our security standards.

The President is taking a responsible approach to refugee admissions, prioritizing refugee resettlement in jurisdictions where both State and local governments consent to receive them.

This order is designed to ensure that refugees are placed in an environment where they will have the best opportunity to succeed in their new homes.

Creating Safer Communities: President Trump's policies are supporting our brave law enforcement officers and making America's communities safer.

Violent crime fell in 2017 and 2018, after rising during each of the two years prior to President Trump taking office.

Since 2016, the violent crime rate in America has fallen nearly 5 percent and the murder rate has decreased by over 7 percent.

President Trump signed the First Step Act into law, making our criminal justice system fairer for all while making our communities safer.

President Trump has promoted second-chance hiring to give former inmates the opportunity to live crime-free lives and find meaningful employment, all while making our communities safer.

The Department of Education is expanding an initiative that allows individuals in Federal and State prisons to receive Pell Grants to better prepare themselves for the workforce.

The Department of Justice and Bureau of Prisons launched a new "Ready to Work" Initiative to help connect employers directly with former prisoners.

The Department of Labor awarded $2.2 million to states to expand the use of fidelity bonds, which underwrite companies that hire former prisoners.

President Trump has revitalized Project Safe Neighborhoods, bringing together Federal, State, local, and tribal law enforcement officials to develop solutions to violent crime.

The President is standing up for our Nation's law enforcement officers, ensuring they have the support they need to keep our communities safe.

The President established a new commission to evaluate best practices for recruiting, training, and supporting law enforcement officers.

The Administration has made available hundreds of millions of dollars worth of surplus military equipment to local law enforcement.

President Trump has signed an Executive Order to help prevent violence against law enforcement officers.

The President also signed legislation permanently funding the 9/11 Victim Compensation Fund, aiding our Nation's brave first responders.

The President has taken action to combat the scourge of hate crimes and anti-Semitism rising in America.

President Trump signed an Executive Order making it clear that Title VI of the Civil Rights Act of 1964 applies to discrimination rooted in anti-Semitism.

The Administration launched a centralized website to educate the public about hate crimes and encourage reporting.

Since January 2017, the Civil Rights division at the DOJ has obtained 14 convictions in cases involving attacks or threats against places of worship.

The President signed the Fix NICS Act to keep guns out of the hands of dangerous criminals.

President Trump signed the STOP School Violence Act and created a Commission on School Safety to examine ways to make our schools safer.

The Trump Administration is fighting to end the egregious crime of human trafficking.

In FY 2019, ICE HSI arrested 2,197 criminals associated with human trafficking and identified 428 victims.

The President signed the Trafficking Victims Protection Reauthorization Act, which tightened criteria for whether countries are meeting standards for eliminating trafficking.

President Trump established a task force to help combat the tragedy of missing or murdered Native American women and girls.

Advancing America's Interests Abroad: President Trump is putting America first and advancing our interests across the world.

President Trump's maximum pressure campaign is countering Iran's influence and pressuring the corrupt regime to abandon its malign activities.

The President removed the United States from the horrible, one-sided Iran nuclear deal and re-imposed all sanctions that were lifted by the deal.

In response to Iran's aggression and gross human rights violations, the President authorized crippling sanctions on the regime's leadership, including the Supreme Leader.

President Trump is working to vigorously enforce all sanctions to bring Iran's oil exports to zero and deny the regime its principal source of revenue.

President Trump has held two historic summits with North Korea and earlier this year became the first President to cross the DMZ into North Korea.

The Administration has maintained tough sanctions on North Korea while negotiations have taken place.

Since taking office, President Trump has taken historic steps to support and defend our cherished ally Israel.

This year, President Trump acknowledged Israel's sovereignty over the Golan Heights and declared Israeli settlements in the West Bank are not inconsistent with international law.

The President made good on his promise to recognize Jerusalem as the true capital of Israel and move the United States Embassy there.

The President removed the United States from the United Nations (U.N.) Human Rights Council due to the group's blatant anti-Israel bias.

President Trump has successfully urged North Atlantic Treaty Organization (NATO) members to increase their defense spending and to focus on modern priorities.

NATO Allies will increase defense spending by $130 billion by the end of next year.

The Administration has worked to reform and streamline the U.N., cutting spending and making the organization more efficient.

Earlier this year, the President took action to protect our Second Amendment rights by announcing the United States will not join the misguided Arms Trade Treaty.

President Trump has promoted democracy throughout the Western Hemisphere and imposed heavy sanctions on the regimes in Venezuela, Cuba, and Nicaragua.

The President reversed the previous Administration's disastrous Cuba policy.

President Trump has enacted a new policy aimed at stopping any revenues from reaching the Cuban military or intelligence services, imposed stricter travel restrictions, and reaffirmed the focus ensuring the Cuban regime does not profit from U.S. dollars.

Earlier this year, the Trump Administration put a cap on remittances to Cuba.

President Trump is enabling Americans to file lawsuits against persons and entities that traffic in property confiscated by the Cuban regime, the first time that these kind of claims have been available for Americans under the Helms-Burton Act.

President Trump has stood with the democratically elected National Assembly and the Venezuelan people and worked to cut off the financial resources of the Maduro regime.

President Trump recognized Juan Guaido as the Interim President of Venezuela and rallied an international coalition of 58 countries to support him.

Earlier this year, President Trump blocked all property of the Venezuelan Government in the jurisdiction of the United States.

President Trump has sanctioned key sectors of the Venezuelan economy exploited by the regime, including the oil and gold sectors.

The Administration sanctioned Maduro's key financial lifelines, including the Venezuelan Central Bank, the Venezuelan Development Bank, and Petroleos de Venezuela.

The Trump Administration has secured the release of Americans unjustly imprisoned abroad, including Kevin King, Xiyue Wang, Danny Burch, and more.

The President and his Administration have worked to advance a free and open Indo-Pacific region, promoting new investments and expanding American partnerships.

The President negotiated the return from Finland of approximately 600 tribal ancestral remains and other sacred objects for the American Indian and Pueblo communities from which they came.

The Trump Administration released an economic plan to empower the Palestinian people and enhance Palestinian governance through private investment.

The President created the first-ever whole-of-government approach to women's economic empowerment through his Women's Global Development and Prosperity Initiative.

In June of 2019, the President released the U.S. Strategy on Women, Peace, and Security, which focuses on increasing women's participation to prevent and resolve conflicts.

Rebuilding Our Nation's Defense: President Trump is investing in our military and ensuring our forces are able to defend against any and all threats.

President Trump signed the National Defense Authorization Act (NDAA) for fiscal year (FY) 2020, authorizing a historic $738 billion in defense spending.

President Trump continued to invest in rebuilding our military, after signing legislation to provide for $700 billion in defense spending in FY18 and $716 billion in FY19.

President Trump signed a 3.1% pay raise for our troops, the largest increase in a decade.

The President signed legislation establishing the Space Force as a new branch of the Armed Forces, the first new branch since 1947.

The United States Space Command was relaunched in August 2019.

The President is modernizing and recapitalizing our nuclear forces and missile defenses to ensure they continue to serve as a strong deterrent.

The President upgraded our cyber defenses by elevating the Cyber Command into a major warfighting command and reducing burdensome procedural restrictions on cyber operations.

President Trump is protecting America's defense-industrial base, directing the first whole-of-government assessment of our manufacturing and defense supply chains since the 1950s.

Under the President's leadership, the United States is taking the fight to terrorists all around the globe.

ISIS' territorial caliphate has been defeated and all territory recaptured in Iraq and Syria.

The United States has brought Abu Bakr al-Baghdadi, the founder of ISIS, to justice.

The President has taken decisive military action to punish the Assad regime in Syria for the barbaric use of chemical weapons on its own people.

The President also authorized sanctions against those tied to Syria's chemical weapons program.

Honoring Our Veterans: President Trump is standing up for America's veterans by ensuring they receive the proper care and support they deserve.

President Trump signed the VA MISSION Act, revolutionizing the VA system, increasing choice, and providing quality care for our veterans.

This legislation reformed and expanded many of the existing programs to give veterans improved access to healthcare providers and offered entirely new options such as allowing veterans to get urgent care in their local communities.

The VA Mission Act put veterans at the center of their healthcare decisions, not bureaucracy.

The Trump Administration has expanded veterans' ability to access telehealth services, including through the "Anywhere to Anywhere" VA health care initiative.

President Trump has brought accountability to the VA, as promised.

President Trump signed the Veterans Affairs Accountability and Whistleblower Protection Act to ensure VA employees are held responsible for poor performance.

Over 8,000 VA employees have been relieved of their duties at the VA since the beginning of the Administration.

Veterans are seeing an improvement in quality of care under President Trump.

In the last year, the VA saw its highest patient experience ratings in history.

The Veterans of Foreign Wars found in its annual survey that more than 90 percent of respondents would recommend VA care to other veterans.

President Trump signed the Veterans Appeals Improvement and Modernization Act of 2017 to expedite the veteran appeals process.

The Administration is working to seamlessly align the VA's and DoD's electronic health records.

This new electronic health record system is on pace to launch next year in select areas.

Under President Trump, the VA launched a new tool that provides veterans with online access to average wait times and quality-of-care data.

Just as he promised, President Trump opened up a 24/7 White House VA Hotline to provide veterans access to help at all times.

President Trump has committed his Administration to addressing the horrible tragedy of veteran suicide.

President Trump signed the PREVENTS Initiative, which created a task force to develop a revolutionary roadmap to tackle the problem of veteran suicide.

President Trump signed an executive order to improve access to suicide prevention resources for veterans.

President Trump is expanding educational resources, promoting economic opportunity, and making sure our veterans have the support they need when they return home.

This year, the veteran unemployment rate reached its lowest level since 2000.

President Trump signed an executive order that paves the way for veterans to more easily join the Merchant Marine, providing quality job opportunities.

President Trump signed the Forever GI Bill, allowing veterans to use their educational benefits at any point in their lives.

President Trump expedited the process of discharging Federal student loan debt for our Nation's totally and permanently disabled veterans.

President Trump signed the HAVEN Act to ensure that veterans who've declared bankruptcy don't lose their disability payments.

President Trump signed legislation providing a pathway for Alaska Natives who served in Vietnam to receive the land allotments to which they are legally entitled.

Combating the Opioid Crisis: President Trump has made battling the opioid crisis a top priority for his Administration, and the results couldn't be clearer.

President Trump brought attention to the opioid crisis by declaring it a nationwide public health emergency.

To address the many factors fueling the drug crisis, President Trump launched an Initiative to Stop Opioid Abuse and Reduce Drug Supply and Demand.

Thanks to the President's efforts, landmark new Federal funding and resources have been dedicated to help end this crisis.

President Trump signed the SUPPORT for Patients and Communities Act, the largest and most comprehensive piece of legislation to combat the opioid crisis in history.

The Department of Health and Human Services (HHS) has awarded nearly $9 billion over 2016 to 2019 in grants to address the opioid crisis and improve access to prevention, treatment, and recovery services in partnership with State and local officials.

Nearly $1 billion in grants were recently awarded for the HEAL Initiative to support development of scientific solutions to help prevent and treat addiction.

President Trump announced a Safer Prescriber Plan that seeks to decrease the amount of opioids prescription fills by one third within three years.

From January 2017 to September 2019, the total amount of opioids prescriptions filled in America dropped by 31%.

This year, the President launched FindTreatment. gov, a newly designed website that makes it easier to find substance abuse treatment locations.

The President implemented new efforts to educate Americans about the dangers of opioid misuse.

These efforts include an ad campaign on youth opioid abuse that reached 58 percent of young adults in America.

President Trump and his Administration aggressively worked to cut off the flow of deadly drugs into our communities.

In FY 2019, ICE HSI seized 12,466 pounds of opioids including 3,688 pounds of fentanyl, an increase of 35% from FY 2018.

The Administration shut down the country's biggest Darknet distributer of drugs, seizing enough fentanyl to kill 105,000 Americans in the process.

Under President Trump, a DOJ strike force charged more than 65 defendants collectively responsible for distributing over 45 million opioid pills.

The Administration has brought kingpin designations against traffickers operating in China, India, Mexico and more who have played a role in the epidemic in America.

The Administration secured the first-ever indictments against Chinese fentanyl traffickers.

This year, President Trump convinced China to enact strict regulations to control the production and sale of all types of fentanyl.

Evidence suggests that President Trump's efforts are making a real difference across the Nation.

Preliminary data shows overdose deaths fell nationwide in 2018 for the first time in decades.

Many of the hardest hit states—including Ohio, Kentucky, and West Virginia—saw drug overdose deaths drop in 2018.

Since 2016, there has been a nearly 40 percent increase in the number of Americans receiving medication-assisted treatment.

Putting Patients First: President Trump is working hard to give Americans better quality care at a lower cost.

The Administration is delivering quality healthcare and promoting innovative treatment options for American patients.

Earlier this year, President Trump signed an order to protect and improve Medicare for our seniors, encouraging even more competition and promoting innovative benefits.

President Trump signed and implemented the Right to Try Act, which has expanded treatment options for terminally ill patients.

The President has taken action to combat childhood cancer, initiating an effort to provide $500 million over the next decade to improve pediatric cancer research.

The President signed legislation providing an additional $1 billion in Alzheimer's disease research funding.

The Administration launched a plan to end the HIV/AIDS epidemic in America in the next decade.

President Trump took action to increase the availability of organs for patients in need of transplants and provide more treatment options and improve care for patients suffering from kidney disease.

The President signed an order to modernize the influenza vaccine.

The Administration is making healthcare more affordable and transparent.

The Administration is requiring hospitals to make their prices negotiated with insurers publicly and easily available online.

The President is working to expand Association Health Plans, which would make it easier for employers to join together and offer more affordable health coverage to their employees.

President Trump extended access to short-term, limited-duration health plans, giving Americans more flexibility to choose plans that suit their needs.

The Administration expanded the use of Health Reimbursement Arrangements (HRAs). Now, HRAs allow employers to help their employees pay for the cost of insurance that they select in the individual market.

The Administration has successfully worked to reduce Medicare Advantage and Part D premiums to their lowest in years.

The Administration has improved access to health savings accounts for individuals with chronic conditions.

The President has worked to reduce the burden felt by Americans due to Obamacare and eliminated Obamacare's individual mandate penalty.

President Trump released legislative principles to end surprise medical billing and is working with Congress to give patients the control they deserve.

President Trump is following through on his pledge to combat high drug prices.

President Trump released a blueprint to reduce drug prices and expand affordability for American patients.

The Administration's efforts to lower drug prices led to the largest year-over-year decrease in drug prices ever recorded.

The President has advanced efforts to import prescription drugs from Canada in partnership with several states, including Florida and Colorado.

The President launched an initiative to stop global freeloading in the drug market, proposing a new way for Medicare to pay for certain drugs based on prices other developed nations pay.

The President signed legislation to end pharmacy gag clauses, which prevented pharmacists from letting patients know when it would be cheaper to buy drugs without their insurance.

Safeguarding Life and Religious Liberty: President Trump has made it a priority of his Administration to uphold the sanctity of life and safeguard religious liberty for all.

President Trump is unequivocally committed to protecting the sanctity of every human life.

The Administration issued a rule preventing Title X family planning funds from supporting the abortion industry.

President Trump has called on Congress to end late-term abortions.

The Trump Administration cut all funding to the U.N. population fund, due to the fund's support for coercive abortion and forced sterilization.

HHS rescinded an Obama-era guidance that prevented states from taking certain actions against abortion providers.

President Trump reinstated and expanded the Mexico City Policy in 2017, ensuring that taxpayer money is not used to fund abortion globally.

The President has taken action to end federal research using fetal tissue from abortions.

President Trump is protecting healthcare entities and individuals' conscience rights—ensuring that no medical professional is forced to participate in an abortion in violation of their beliefs.

The Administration provided relief to American employers like Little Sisters of the Poor, protecting them from being forced to provide coverage that violate their conscience.

President Trump has taken unprecedented action to support the fundamental right to religious freedom.

In 2018, President Trump signed an Executive Order establishing the White House Faith and Opportunity Initiative.

In 2017, President Trump signed an Executive Order upholding religious liberty and the right to engage in religious speech.

The Department of Justice created a Religious Liberty Task Force in 2018.

The Trump Administration continues to vigorously defend religious liberty in the courts at every opportunity.

President Trump reversed the Obama-era policy that prevented the government from providing disaster relief to religious organizations.

The Administration is preserving a space for faith-based adoption and foster care providers to continue to serve their communities consistent with their beliefs.

The Administration reduced burdensome barriers to Native Americans being able to keep spiritually and culturally significant eagle feathers found on their tribal lands.

The Administration has allowed greater flexibility for Federal employees to take time off work for religious reasons.

The Trump Administration has stood up for religious liberty around the world.

The Administration has partnered with local and faith-based organizations to provide assistance to religious minorities persecuted in Iraq.

President Trump hosted the Global Call to Protect Religious Freedom at the 2019 U.N. General Assembly, calling on global and business leaders to bring an end to religious persecution and stop crimes against people of faith.

The Administration dedicated $25 million to protect religious freedom, religious sites and relics.

The State Department has hosted two Religious Freedom Ministerials, with the 2019 Ministerial becoming the largest religious freedom event of its kind in the world.

In 2019, the Administration imposed restrictions on certain Chinese officials, internal security units, and companies for their complicity in the persecution of Uighur Muslims and other Muslim minorities in Xinjiang.

Transforming the Courts: President Trump is transforming the Federal judiciary by appointing a historic number of Federal judges who will interpret the Constitution as written.

Working with the Senate, President Trump has now had 187 judicial nominees confirmed to the Federal bench.

President Trump's remaking of the judiciary is only accelerating with 103 Federal judges confirmed in 2019, more than 2017 and 2018 combined.

The President named Justices Brett Kavanaugh and Neil Gorsuch to the Supreme Court, fulfilling his promise to appoint justices who will uphold the constitution as written.

President Trump has appointed 50 Circuit Court judges—more than any other President at this point in their Administrations.

More than a quarter of all active Circuit Court judges were appointed by President Trump.

The average age of Trump-appointed circuit judges is less than 50 years old, ensuring that these qualified jurists will continue to have an impact for decades to come.

President Trump has flipped the Second, Third, and Eleventh Circuits from Democrat-appointed majorities to Republican-appointed majorities.

Ushering in an Era of Energy Dominance: President Trump's policies are ushering in a new era of American energy dominance.

President Trump has rolled back the burdensome regulations of the past Administration and implemented policies that are unleashing American energy.

The United States is the largest oil and natural gas producer in the world.

American oil production reached its highest level in history in 2019.

The United States became a net exporter of crude oil and petroleum products in September 2019, the first time this has occurred since records began in 1973.

Natural gas production is projected to set a record high in 2019, marking the third consecutive year of record production.

President Trump is opening up more access to our country's abundant natural resources in order to promote energy independence.

Department of the Interior energy revenues soared in fiscal year FY 2019, nearly doubling since FY 2016 to $12 billion.

Applications to drill on public lands have increased by 300 percent since FY 2016, and the time it takes to complete these permits has dropped by half.

President Trump signed legislation to open up Alaska's Arctic National Wildlife Refuge to energy exploration.

President Trump is promoting energy infrastructure to ensure American energy producers can deliver their products to the market.

This year, President Trump signed two Executive Orders to streamline processes holding back the construction of new energy infrastructure, like pipelines.

In 2017, the Administration took action to approve the Dakota Access pipeline and the Keystone XL pipeline.

The Administration issued permits for the New Burgos Pipeline that will export American petroleum products to Mexico.

The Administration has streamlined Liquefied Natural Gas (LNG) terminal permitting.

In 2019, the Department of Energy granted 11 new long-term LNG export approvals.

American energy exports have reached historic highs.

LNG exports have increased by 247% since 2017, hitting record highs in 2019 and are projected to continue increasing next year.

In 2017, the United States became a net natural gas exporter for the first time in 60 years.

The United States has exported LNG to five continents and 37 countries, marking 19 additional countries from the beginning of the Trump Administration.

President Trump strengthened America's domestic energy production and supported our Nation's farmers by approving year-round E-15.

President Trump worked to ensure greater transparency and certainty in the Renewable Fuel Standard (RFS).

President Trump has promoted domestic energy production and economic growth while working to ensure Americans have access to safe drinking water and a clean environment.

The United States environmental record is one of the strongest in the world and America continues to make environmental progress in clean air and clean water.

Under President Trump's leadership, the EPA took action to protect vulnerable Americans from lead exposure by proposing changes to the Lead and Copper rule.

Under President Trump's leadership, in FY 2019 the EPA completed cleanup on the most superfund sites on the National Priority List in 18 years.

Emissions of all criteria pollutants dropped between 2016 and 2018.

Promoting Educational Opportunity: President Trump is working to ensure all Americans have access to quality education.

President Trump signed into law a modernization of our country's career and technical education system to ensure more Americans have access to high-quality vocational education.

This year, the Administration proposed Education Freedom Scholarships to expand education options for students of all economic backgrounds.

This plan will invest up to $5 billion in students through a tax credit for donations for state-based, locally-controlled scholarships.

President Trump is expanding education and training opportunities for incarcerated individuals to learn how to make a living before their release.

The President signed legislation reauthorizing the D.C. Opportunity Scholarship program.

Thanks to President Trump's historic tax reform, parents can now withdraw up to $10,000 tax-free per year from 529 education savings plans to cover K-12 tuition costs.

President Trump has made supporting Historically Black Colleges and Universities (HBCUs) a priority of his Administration.

President Trump signed the Farm Bill that included more than $100 million dollars for scholarships, research, and centers of excellence at HBCU land-grant institutions.

The Administration has enabled faith-based HBCUs to enjoy equal access to Federal support.

President Trump signed legislation providing $255 million dollars of permanent annual funding for HBCUs and other Minority Serving Institutions. [133]

While the Democrats have not done anything to help President Trump be successful, he has a remarkable list of accomplishments which show how successful Donald J. Trump as been as president.

While all of his accomplishments deserve further discussion, only three areas will be emphasized here.

Domestic policies–He has been very successful in his domestic policies. The United States economy is one of the best that has ever occurred. Briefly, here are some of the reasons: He did his job so well that 7 million jobs have been created since his election; there are 7 million job openings, and the unemployment rate reached its lowest rate in half a century; the unemployment rate for women reached its lowest rate in sixty-five years, and the unemployment rate for African Americans, Hispanic Americans, Asian Americans, veterans, individuals with disabilities, and those without high school diplomas have all reached record lows. Wages are growing, and middle class and low-income workers are enjoying faster wage growth than high-earners. Poverty rates for African Americans and Hispanic Americans have reached record lows, and 2.4 million Americans have been lifted out of poverty. Seven million Americans have been lifted off food stamps.

Robert Johnson was the founder of Black Entertainment Television and became the first African American billionaire after selling the company in 2001. Mr. Johnson supported Hillary Clinton in the 2016 election but has since had praise for President Trump. He has said that the Democrat party has moved too far to the left. President Trump's economic policies have helped minorities and others who have not previously had the opportunities that come with employment. President Trump's tax cuts clearly helped stimulate the economy, and businesspeople have more confidence in the way the economy is going. He specifically mentioned African American employment, saying "'You've never had African American unemployment this low and the spread between African Americans and whites narrowing ... A lot of people are not going to like that style,' he said, but when he says he is going to try to do something economically, you have to give him credit for taking some specific steps to do that. At the end of the day, the American people are looking for someone who can deliver economically and deliver on opportunities." [134]

Trade deals–President Trump knew that the United States had made some bad trade deals. He knew that the Trans-Pacific Partnership being negotiated was not a good deal so he did not sign it. He also knew that the North American Free Trade Agreement (NAFTA) between the United States, Mexico and Canada, was not a good deal for the United States. He renegotiated a a new trade agreement with Mexico and Canada, with much better provisions for the United States. After holding it up for about a year, the Democrats in the House of Representatives finally approved the agreement. The Senate also approved it, and it was signed into law by President Trump. Among its benefits, it will bring about 176,000 new jobs to the United States.

President Trump knew that China had been taking advantage of us for years on trade issues and that they were also stealing our intellectual property. His international business experience enabled him to confront China with the disparity in our trading relationship and bring them to the conference table to resolve the issues. He applied some tariffs on China's sales to the United States, and China retaliated. During this "trade war" there were some parts of the United States economy that were being hurt by the tariffs. President Trump was criticized by Democrats and some groups because the deal was taking to long and he was urged to quit trying to make a deal. But, he had the strength to continue to negotiate. A weaker president would have thrown in the towel. On January 15, 2020, President Trump signed a Phase 1 agreement with China. China has committed to buying an additional $200 billion of US goods over the next two years from a list of enumerated product categories, including $80 billion worth of agricultural exports. They made commitments to enforce US intellectual property rights and the agreement also spelled out how China will make it easier for the United States to sell them certain types of agricultural goods, and it makes it easier for US firms to offer financial services in China. Tariffs on $360 billion of Chines goods remained in place.

Foreign affairs–President Trump has also been very successful in his foreign affairs policies as well. Briefly, again, just a few items will be highlighted. He stopped ISIS and our military took out its leader when he authorized them to do so. Our military also took out Iran's terrorism leader when authorized to do so by President Trump. He has increased the defense budget, rebuilt our military and improved health care for veterans. He has increased the amount of money that our NATO allies are contributing to NATO and he has imposed sanctions on North Korea and Iran to halt their developing nuclear weapons.

The United States is once again respected in the world.

Impeachment and the Electoral College

The Democrats had been saying even before he was elected that they were going to remove him from office if he won the election. They knew that his campaign promises and the likely results of his policies on the economy and in foreign affairs would be anathema to them and their philosophies. They knew that his belief in a smaller government, lower taxes and regulations, a stronger foreign policy, and in other areas that have been discussed, would emphasize the difference between the policies of the Democrats and the Republicans.

The differences would be, and turned out to be, striking.

The Democrats never accepted that President Trump won the 2016 election. The Democrats hate the Electoral College, but there is a reason for its existence–the Founding Fathers of the United States wisely wanted all parts of the country to have influence in elections.

Apparently, the Democrats will not accept an election whenever a Republican wins in accordance with the Electoral College if he/she did not win the popular vote. They are refusing to accept an election result mandated by the Constitution.

The Democrats' nonstop efforts to void the 2016 election are solely based on their political differences with President Trump. Everything that they have been doing since has been designed to find something upon which they could base impeachment proceedings or use against him in the 2020 election. Their achievement of a majority in the House of Representatives in 2018 gave them an opportunity to strive for their dream.

They were going to impeach him because they did not like his vision for the United States. Not liking a president's politics is not grounds for impeachment. His removal from office should be determined by the voters in the next election.

The Democrats argued that the Constitution required that they investigate President Trump. They argued that the Constitution required it at the same time they were ignoring the Constitution and the Electoral College. But then, they have also refused to recognize other constitutional principles, such as such as freedom of speech and of the press, the right to bear arms, the freedom of religion, and the right to due process. Democrat President Obama ignored the Constitution when he refused to enforce the laws of the United States, as required by the Constitution, as evidenced by his refusal to enforce our immigration laws at the southern border.

The Democrats selectively decide which constitutional provisions they will follow and which ones they will not.

Democrats believe that their judgment in impeaching President Trump was better than the people electing him. Representative Adam Schiff, was one of the impeachment managers for the Democrats in the House of Representatives. During his statement before the Senate in the impeachment trial, he stated the following: "The president's misconduct cannot be decided at the ballot box, for we cannot be assured that the vote will be fairly won." Apparently, the Democrats believe the vote will be fairly won only in the Democrat House of Representatives.

A statement like this only makes it clearer how important the votes of the citizens of the United States are in elections. Determining who should be our president is a decision for the voters, not the politicians.

Despite the 24/7/365 efforts of the Democrats to not help pass any legislation and to harass the president, his family, members of his administration, and his supporters, they totally failed in working to not let him succeed. Their actions showed that they hate Donald Trump more than they love this country.

It also shows that the liberal media was colluding with the Democrats/liberals. They have not reported on the terrific economy or on the lifting of the regulatory burdens and on all of the other areas where Trump has been successful. They were critical of the president's actions in negotiating with China, and they have sided with the Democrats in the controversy over our southern border. They sided with the Democrats during the hearings on President Trump's nominee, Brett Kavanaugh, to join the United States Supreme Court, although he was ultimately approved by the Senate.

The liberal media was in collusion with the Democrats/liberals every step of the way. The liberal media has been responsible for the ability of the Democrats/liberals to conduct the investigations of President Trump. If the media had done at least an honest job, giving both sides of the arguments without bias, the agony of the past three plus years could have been avoided.

For a discussion of the investigation of President Trump, see Appendix C. In the same appendix, there will be a discussion of the treatment of President Trump vis-á-vis the actions of President Obama who "abused his power" in many areas on many occasions. There will also be a discussion of wrongful actions of former Vice President Joe Biden and Hillary Clinton.

The America of the Democrats If They Succeed

If the Democrats/liberals succeed, and if they are able to seize back the power of the Presidency and the Congress, they will:

- Continue their efforts to restrict the ability of conservatives to speak.
- Work to allow everyone to vote without regard to their citizenship status.
- Gerrymander voting districts to minimize the seats that Republicans could win.
- Try to eliminate the Electoral College to reduce the power of the central part of the country and to give more power to the liberal cities to further the liberal agenda.
- Ensure that the census counts illegal aliens to increase the members of Congress from the larger cities.
- Continue to harass Christians.
- Severely curtail the right to bear arms.
- Increase the number of people who receive government benefits.
- Increase taxes and regulations that will severely impact our economy.
- Use the Internal Revenue Service and other government departments to harass/punish Republicans and conservatives.
- Restrict the ability of conservative commentators and media to communicate with the people.
- Increase the use of the education system to fill students with their propaganda.
- Cut spending on defense.
- Engage, once again, in appeasement of our competitors and enemies to include nuclear deals with North Korea and Iran.

- Allow China to continue unfair trade with us and to steal our intellectual property.
- Continue to redistribute wealth.
- Impose a single-payer healthcare system with all coverages, premiums, and rules set by the federal government and without any competition.
- Bring up the "new normal" again and tell our citizens they will need to live with a lower standard of living and that our children will not have it as good as prior generations.
- Continue to pursue socialism and reduce private ownership of the economy and increase the federal government's activities in our private economy.
- Expand the use of political correctness and hate speech.
- Continue to argue that Republicans/conservatives are racists and sexists and whatever other slurs they can think of.
- Become even closer to the biased media, at least until the biased media catches on that they are being affected by them as well.
- Continue their past policies in the cities that have not worked and bring those practices to the federal government.

Totalitarianism

As evidenced by their actions, the Democrats/Liberals are trying to establish a "totalitarian" government. They are not there yet and, hopefully, they will never get there.

> Totalitarianism is a political system or a form of government that prohibits opposition parties, restricts individual opposition to the state and its claims, and exercises an extremely high degree of control over public and private life...

Totalitarian regimes are often characterized by
extensive political repression, a complete lack of
democracy, widespread personality cultism, absolute
control over the economy, restriction of speech, mass
surveillance, and widespread use of state terrorism.
Other aspects of a totalitarian regime include . . .
religious persecution or state atheism, . . . fraudulent
elections (if they take place) . . .

A totalitarian regime attempts to control virtually
all aspects of the social life, including the economy,
education, art, science, private life and morals of citizens. Some totalitarian governments may promote
an elaborate ideology: The officially proclaimed ideology penetrates into the deepest reaches of societal
structure and the totalitarian government seeks to
completely control the thoughts and actions of its
citizens. [135]

Propaganda uses lies to erode all truth and morality. "And we
learned about the critical importance of propaganda, the deliberate
misinforming of the public in order to sway opinions en masse and
achieve popular support (or at least the appearance of it.)" [136]

How are the Democrats and their media and followers
attempting to achieve totalitarian power?

- Political repression of conservatives: Harass them wherever
  they find them and instruct their followers to seek them out
  and harass them. Keep them off college campuses, use hate
  speech and political correctness, and urge their followers to
  boycott conservative media hosts and conservative business
  owners. Continue to use their liberal media to support their

liberal positions and keep news favorable to conservatives out of the news and off the airways.

- Lack of democracy: Do not pass any legislation that would help the nation if it would also help a conservative, continually argue that elections where conservatives win are not legitimate, repress free speech, do not let conservatives speak, promulgate illegal executive orders, ignore the Constitution when in their interest, fail to enforce laws they do not like, use their followers to preach bias at all levels of education, erode the moral base of the United States, let non-citizens of the United States participate in voting in our elections, establish sanctuary cities to ignore the federal government's primary power to control our borders, and ignore constitutional protections with which they disagree.
- Absolute control over the economy: The Democrats have created a big government welfare system, the recipients of which have, for the most part, so far voted in their favor. Many Democrats, and many of the candidates campaigning to be the presidential nominee of the Democrat Party in the 2020 election, have socialism as one of their major positions. This will lead to absolute control over the economy.
- Restriction of speech: See "political repression of conservatives" above.
- Widespread use of terrorism: See "political repression of conservatives" above. In addition, if the Democrats ever take control of the United States Government, they will use their power for repression and terrorism which will make it state repression and terrorism.
- Mass surveillance: Democrats are already asking their supporters to harass people who work for or support President Trump and they have released the names and addresses of people who have supported President Trump in order to find them and harass them. If they had the power of the

government behind them, there would be no limit to what they would do.

- Religious persecution or state atheism: The Democrats have succeeded to a large degree in removing Christianity from schools and public places.
- Fraudulent elections: Ignore the Electoral College when it suits them. Encourage laws, rules or practices that increase their ability to increase the number of liberal votes in elections. Voter fraud that has occurred in the past includes: impersonation fraud at the polls; false registrations using a phony name or claim residence where the registered voter does not live; duplicate voting such as registering in multiple locations or in more than one state; fraudulent use of absentee ballots by requesting absentee ballots and voting without the knowledge of the actual voter, or obtaining the absentee ballot of a voter; buying votes; illegal assistance at the polls forcing or intimidating voters, particularly the elderly, disabled, or illiterate, and those for whom English is a second language, to vote for particular candidates; ineligible voting by illegal registrations and voting by individuals who are not U.S. citizens or otherwise not eligible to vote; altering the vote count, either in the precinct or at a central location where votes are counted; and ballot petition fraud by forging signatures of registered voters on ballot petitions that must be filed for a candidate to be issued on the official ballot. [137]

The Democrats, and their biased media are spreading biased or misleading information to promote or publicize a particular cause or point of view. This just happens to be the meaning of the word *propaganda*, if you do a Google search. Another definition of propaganda is the "dissemination of information—facts, arguments, rumors, half-truths, or lies—to influence public opinion." [138]

The first play of totalitarianism is to silence the opposition because propaganda and truth cannot coexist.

Does President Trump Have A Lack Of Decorum And, If So, Is It Important?

Evan Sayet, a columnist, wrote about President Trump's lack of decorum.

> My Leftist friends (as well as many ardent #NeverTrumpers) constantly ask me if I'm not bothered by Donald Trump's lack of decorum. They ask if I don't think his tweets are "beneath the dignity of the office." Here's my answer:
>
> ... [W]hile we were playing by the rules of dignity, collegiality and propriety, the Left has been, for the past 60 years, engaged in a knife fight where the only rules are those of Saul Alinsky and the Chicago mob.
>
> I don't find anything "dignified," "collegial" or "proper" about Barack Obama's lying about what went down on the streets of Ferguson in order to ramp up racial hatreds because racial hatreds serve the Democratic Party. I don't see anything "dignified" in lying about the deaths of four Americans in Benghazi and imprisoning an innocent filmmaker to cover your tracks. I don't see anything "statesman-like" in weaponizing the IRS to be used to destroy your political opponents and any dissent. Yes, Obama was "articulate" and "polished" but in

no way was he in the least bit "dignified," "collegial" or "proper."

The Left has been engaged in a war against America since the rise of the Children of the '60s. To them, it has been an all-out war where nothing is held sacred and nothing is seen as beyond the pale. It has been a war they've fought with violence, the threat of violence, demagoguery and lies from day one— the violent take-over of the universities—till today.

The problem is that, through these years, the Left has been the only side fighting this war. While the Left has been taking a knife to anyone who stands in their way, the Right has continued to act with dignity, collegiality and propriety.

With Donald Trump, this all has come to an end. Donald Trump is America's first wartime president in the Culture War.

During wartime, things like "dignity" and "collegiality" simply aren't the most essential qualities one looks for in their warriors. Ulysses Grant was a drunk whose behavior in peacetime might well have seen him drummed out of the Army for conduct unbecoming. Had Abraham Lincoln applied the peacetime rules of propriety and booted Grant, the Democrats might well still be holding their slaves today. Lincoln rightly recognized that, "I cannot spare this man. He fights."

General George Patton was a vulgar-talking son-of-a-bitch. In peacetime, this might have seen him stripped of rank. But, had Franklin Roosevelt applied the normal rules of decorum, then Hitler and the Socialists would barely be five decades into their thousand-year Reich.

Trump is fighting. And what's particularly delicious is that, like Patton standing over the battlefield as his tanks obliterated Rommel's, he's shouting, "You magnificent bastards, I read your book!" That is just the icing on the cake, but it's wonderful to see that not only is Trump fighting, he's defeating the Left using their own tactics.

That book is Saul Alinsky's Rules for Radicals—a book so essential to the Liberals' war against America that it is and was the playbook for the entire Obama administration and the subject of Hillary Clinton's senior thesis. It is a book of such pure evil, that, just as the rest of us would dedicate our book to those we most love or those to whom we are most indebted, Alinsky dedicated his book to Lucifer.

Trump's tweets may seem rash and unconsidered but, in reality, he is doing exactly what Alinsky suggested his followers do.

First, instead of going after "the fake media"—and they are so fake that they have literally gotten every single significant story of the past 60 years not just wrong, but diametrically opposed to the truth, from the Tet Offensive to Benghazi, to what really happened on the streets of Ferguson, Missouri—Trump isolated CNN. He made it personal. Then, just as Alinsky suggests, he employs ridicule which Alinsky described as "the most powerful weapon of all."

Everyone gets that it's not just CNN—in fact, in a world where Al Sharpton and Rachel Maddow, Paul Krugman and Nicholas Kristof are people of influence and whose "reporting" is in no way significantly different than CNN's—CNN is just a piker.

Most importantly, Trump's tweets have put CNN in an untenable and unwinnable position. With Trump's ability to go around them, they cannot simply stand pat. They need to respond. This leaves them with only two choices.

They can either "go high" (as Hillary would disingenuously declare of herself and the fake news would disingenuously report as the truth) and begin to honestly and accurately report the news or they can double-down on their usual tactics and hope to defeat Trump with twice their usual hysteria and demagoguery.

The problem for CNN (et al.) with the former is that, if they were to start honestly reporting the news, that would be the end of the Democratic Party they serve. It is nothing but the incessant use of fake news (read: propaganda) that keeps the Left alive.

Imagine, for example, if CNN had honestly and accurately reported then-candidate Barack Obama's close ties to foreign terrorists (Rashid Khalidi), domestic terrorists (William Ayers), the mafia (Tony Rezko) or the true evils of his spiritual mentor, Jeremiah Wright's, church.

Imagine if they had honestly and accurately conveyed the evils of the Obama administration's weaponizing of the IRS to be used against their political opponents or his running of guns to the Mexican cartels or the truth about the murder of Ambassador Christopher Stevens and the Obama administration's cover-up.

This makes "going high" a non-starter for CNN. This leaves them no other option but to ratchet up the fake news, conjuring up the next "nothing burger" and devoting 24 hours a day to hysterical rants about how it's "worse than Nixon."

This, obviously, is what CNN has chosen to do. The problem is that, as they become more and more hysterical, they become more and more obvious. Each new effort at even faker news than before and faker "outrage" only makes that much more clear to any objective observer that Trump is and always has been right about the fake news media.

And, by causing their hysteria, Trump has forced them into numerous, highly embarrassing and discrediting mistakes. Thus, in their desperation, they have lowered their standards even further and run with articles so clearly fake that, even with the liberal (lower case "l") libel laws protecting the media, they've had to wholly retract and erase their stories repeatedly.

Their flailing at Trump has even seen them cross the line into criminality, with CNN using their vast corporate fortune to hunt down a private citizen for having made fun of them in an Internet meme. This threat to "dox"—release of personal information to encourage co-ideologists to visit violence upon him and his family—a political satirist was chilling in that it clearly wasn't meant just for him. If it were, there would have been no reason for CNN to have made their "deal" with him public.

Instead, CNN—playing by "Chicago Rules"—was sending a message to any and all: dissent will not be tolerated.

This heavy-handed and hysterical response to a joke on the Internet has backfired on CNN, giving rise to only more righteous ridicule.

So, to my friends on the Left—and the #NeverTrumpers as well—do I wish we lived in a time when our president could be "collegial" and "dignified" and "proper?" Of course I do. These aren't those times. This is war. And it's a war that the Left has been fighting without opposition for the past 50 years.

So, say anything you want about this president—I get it, he can be vulgar, he can be crude, he can be undignified at times. I don't care. I can't spare this man. He fights. [139]

The Salty Sailor and the Fireman

The following has been circulating on the internet, and it appears on many internet sites:

> The views this mother has about Donald Trump are much like many other people. Her characterization of Trump as the "Salty Sailor" or as "The Fireman" paint an excellent picture!! She has written many great books about her son and family. This is a Comment from KAREN VAUGHN, Mother of Aaron Vaughn, Navy Seal.

> Sometimes God uses the no-nonsense, salty sailor to get the job done. Appreciating what the man is doing doesn't mean we worship the salty sailor or even desire to be like the salty sailor. It doesn't even mean God admires the salty sailor. Maybe He just knows he's necessary for such a time as I believe with all my heart that God placed that salty sailor in the White House to give this nation one more chance in November 2016.

> Donald Trump is what he is—and he is still the man he was before the election—and without guilt. I very much admire what that salty sailor is accomplishing.

He's not like me. That's okay with me. I don't want to be like him. I will never behave like him. I know we've NEVER had a man like him lead our nation before. It's crazy and a little mind blowing at times. But I can't help admire the stamina and ability he has—acting with his heart rather than a calculated, PC, think tank-screened, carefully edited script. I still believe that is WHY he became our President and WHY he's been able to handle a landslide of adversity and STILL pass unprecedented amounts of good legislation for our country AND do great works for MANY other nations, including Israel.

I'm THRILLED with what he's doing for my nation, for the cause of Christ (whether intentional or unintentional, doesn't matter to me), and for the concept of rebuilding America and putting her FIRST. I will not be ashamed of my position because others don't see him through the same lens.

Should it matter to me if a fireman drops an f-bomb while he's pulling me from a burning building? Would I really care about what came out of his mouth in those moments? Heck no! I'd CARE about what he was DOING. He wasn't sent there to save my soul and I'm not looking to him for spiritual guidance. All I'm thinking in those moments is, "Thank you, GOD, for sending the fireman." AND DONALD TRUMP IS OUR FIREMAN.

I'll soon post this article again for those who still might not understand me. This man is crass. Okay. He's not careful with what he says. Okay. You feel offended that he's not a typical statesman. Okay. But he is DOING THE JOB of rebuilding the nation my son died for... the nation I feared was on a fast track to becoming a hopeless cause.

Forgive me if I'm smiling. [140]

Are the Democrats Involved in a Civil War with the Republicans?

Daniel Greenfield gave a speech to a South Carolina Tea Party Convention on January 27, 2018, entitled: "Guns Are How A Civil War Ends . . . Politics Is How It Starts."

This is a civil war.

There aren't any soldiers marching on Charleston... or Myrtle Beach. Nobody's getting shot in the streets. Except in Chicago... and Baltimore, Detroit and Washington D.C.

But that's not a civil war. It's just what happens when Democrats run a city into the ground. And then they dig a hole in the ground so they can bury it even deeper.

If you look deep enough into that great big Democrat hole, you might even see where Jimmy Hoffa is buried.

But it's not guns that make a civil war. It's politics.

Guns are how a civil war ends. Politics is how it begins.

How do civil wars happen?

Two or more sides disagree on who runs the country. And they can't settle the question through elections because they don't even agree that elections are how you decide who's in charge.

That's the basic issue here. Who decides who runs the country? When you hate each other but accept the election results, you have a country. When you stop accepting election results, you have a countdown to a civil war.

I know you're all thinking about President Trump.

He won and the establishment, the media, the democrats, rejected the results. They came up with a whole bunch of conspiracy theories to explain why he didn't really win. It was the Russians. And the FBI. And sexism, Obama, Bernie Sanders and white people.

It's easier to make a list of the things that Hillary Clinton doesn't blame for losing the election. It's going to be a short list.

A really short list. Herself.

The Mueller investigation is about removing President Trump from office and overturning the results of an election. We all know that. But it's not the first time they've done this.

The first time a Republican president was elected this century, they said he didn't really win. The Supreme Court gave him the election. There's a pattern here.

Trump didn't really win the election. Bush didn't really win the election. Every time a Republican president won an election this century, the Democrats insist he didn't really win.

Now say a third Republican president wins an election in say, 2024.

What are the odds that they'll say that he didn't really win? Right now, it looks like 100 percent.

What do sure odds of the Dems rejecting the next Republican president really mean? It means they don't accept the results of any election that they don't win.

It means they don't believe that transfers of power in this country are determined by elections.

That's a civil war.

There's no shooting. At least not unless you count the attempt to kill a bunch of Republicans at a charity baseball game practice. But the Democrats have rejected our system of government.

This isn't dissent. It's not disagreement

You can hate the other party. You can think they're the worst thing that ever happened to the country. But then you work harder to win the next election. When you consistently reject the results of elections that you don't win, what you want is a dictatorship.

Your very own dictatorship.

The only legitimate exercise of power in this country, according to the left, is its own. Whenever Republicans exercise power, it's inherently illegitimate.

The attacks on Trump show that elections don't matter to the left.

Republicans can win an election, but they have a major flaw. They're not leftists.

That's what the leftist dictatorship looks like.

The left lost Congress. They lost the White House. So what did they do? They began trying to run the country through Federal judges and bureaucrats.

Every time that a Federal judge issues an order saying that the President of the United States can't scratch his own back without his say so, that's the civil war.

Our system of government is based on the constitution, but that's not the system that runs this country.

The left's system is that any part of government that it runs gets total and unlimited power over the country.

If it's in the White House, then the president can do anything. And I mean anything. He can have his own amnesty for illegal aliens. He can fine you for not having health insurance. His power is unlimited.

He's a dictator.

But when Republicans get into the White House, suddenly the President can't do anything. He isn't even allowed to undo the illegal alien amnesty that his predecessor illegally invented.

A Democrat in the White House has "discretion" to completely decide every aspect of immigration policy. A Republican doesn't even have the "discretion" to reverse him.

That's how the game is played. That's how our country is run.

When Democrats control the Senate, then Harry Reid and his boys and girls are the sane, wise heads that keep the crazy guys in the House in check.

But when Republicans control the Senate, then it's an outmoded body inspired by racism.

When Democrats run the Supreme Court, then it has the power to decide everything in the country. But when Republicans control the Supreme Court, it's a dangerous body that no one should pay attention to.

When a Democrat is in the White House, states aren't even allowed to enforce immigration law. But when a Republican is in the White House, states can create their own immigration laws.

Under Obama, a state wasn't allowed to go to the bathroom without asking permission. But under Trump, Jerry Brown can go around saying that California is an independent republic and sign treaties with other countries.

The Constitution has something to say about that.

Whether it's Federal or State, Executive, Legislative or Judiciary, the left moves power around to run the country. If it controls an institution, then that institution is suddenly the supreme power in the land.

This is what I call a moving dictatorship.

There isn't one guy in a room somewhere issuing the orders. Instead there's a network of them. And the network moves around.

If the guys and girls in the network win elections, they can do it from the White House. If they lose the

White House, they'll do it from Congress. If they don't have either one, they'll use the Supreme Court.

If they don't have either the White House, Congress or the Supreme Court, they're screwed. Right?

Nope.

They just go on issuing them through circuit courts and the bureaucracy. State governments announce that they're independent republics. Corporations begin threatening and suing the government.

There's no consistent legal standard. Only a political one.

Under Obama, states weren't allowed to enforce immigration laws. That was the job of the Federal government. And the states weren't allowed to interfere with the job that the Feds weren't doing.

Okay.

Now Trump comes into office and starts enforcing immigration laws again. And California announces it's a sanctuary state and passes a law punishing businesses that cooperate with Federal immigration enforcement.

So what do we have here?

It's illegal for states to enforce immigration law because that's the province of the Federal government.

But it's legal for states to ban the Federal government from enforcing immigration law.

The only consistent pattern here is that the left decided to make it illegal to enforce immigration law.

It may do that sometimes under the guise of Federal power or states rights. But those are just fronts. The only consistent thing is that leftist policies are mandatory and opposing them is illegal.

Everything else is just a song and dance routine.

You can't pin it down. There's no one office or one guy. It's a network of them. It's an ideological dictatorship. Some people call it the deep state. But that doesn't even begin to capture what it is.

To understand it, you have to think about things like the Cold War and Communist infiltration.

A better term than Deep State is Shadow Government.

Parts of the Shadow Government aren't even in the government. They are wherever the left holds power. It can be in the non-profit sector and among major corporations. Power gets moved around like a New York City shell game. Where's the quarter? Nope, it's not there anymore.

The shadow government is an ideological network. These days it calls itself by a hashtag #Resistance.

Under any name, it runs the country. Most of the time we don't realize that. When things are normal, when there's a Democrat in the White House or a bunch of Democrats in Congress, it's business as usual.

Even with most Republican presidents, you didn't notice anything too out of the ordinary. Sure, the Democrats got their way most of the time. But that's how the game is usually played.

It's only when someone came on the scene who didn't play the game by the same rules, that the network exposed itself. The shadow government emerged out of hiding and came for Trump.

And that's the civil war.

This is a war over who runs the country. Do the people who vote run the country or does this network that can lose an election, but still get its agenda through, run the country?

We've been having this fight for a while. But this century things have escalated.

They escalated a whole lot after Trump's win because the network isn't pretending anymore. It sees the opportunity to delegitimize the whole idea of elections.

Now the network isn't running the country from cover. It's actually out here trying to overturn the results of an election and remove the president from office.

It's rejected the victories of two Republican presidents this century.

And if we don't stand up and confront it, and expose it for what it is, it's going to go on doing it in every election. And eventually Federal judges are going to gain enough power that they really will overturn elections.

It happens in other countries. If you think it can't happen here, you haven't been paying attention to the left.

Right now, Federal judges are declaring that President Trump isn't allowed to govern because his Tweets show he's a racist. How long until they say that a president isn't even allowed to take office because they don't like his views?

That's where we're headed.

Civil wars swing around a very basic question. The most basic question of them all. Who runs the country?

Is it me? Is it you? Is it Grandma? Or is it bunch of people who made running the government into their career?

America was founded on getting away from professional government. The British monarchy was a professional government. Like all professional governments, it was hereditary. Professional classes eventually decide to pass down their privileges to their kids.

America was different. We had a volunteer government. That's what the Founding Fathers built.

This is a civil war between volunteer governments elected by the people and professional governments elected by... well... uh... themselves.

Of the establishment, by the establishment and for the establishment.

You know, the people who always say they know better, no matter how many times they screw up, because they're the professionals. They've been in Washington D.C. politics since they were in diapers.

Freedom can only exist under a volunteer government. Because everyone is in charge. Power belongs to the people.

A professional government is going to have to stamp out freedom sooner or later. Freedom under a professional government can only be a fiction. Whenever the people disagree with the professionals, they're going to have to get put down. That's just how it is. No matter how it's disguised, a professional government is tyranny.

Ours is really well disguised, but if it walks like a duck and locks you up like a duck, it's a tyranny.

Now what's the left.

Forget all the deep answers. The left is a professional government.

Its whole idea is that everything needs to be controlled by a big central government to make society just. That means everything from your soda sizes to whether you can mow your lawn needs to be decided in Washington D.C.

Volunteer governments are unjust. Professional governments are fair. That's the credo of the left.

Its network, the one we were just discussing, it takes over professional governments because it shares their basic ideas. Professional governments, no matter who runs them, are convinced that everything should run through the professionals. And the professionals are usually lefties. If they aren't, they will be.

Just ask Mueller and establishment guys like him.

What infuriates professional government more than anything else? An amateur, someone like President Trump who didn't spend his entire adult life practicing to be president, taking over the job.

President Trump is what volunteer government is all about.

When you're a government professional, you're invested in keeping the system going. But when you're a volunteer, you can do all the things that the experts tell you can't be done. You can look at the mess we're in with fresh eyes and do the common sense things that President Trump is doing.

And common sense is the enemy of government professionals. It's why Trump is such a threat.

A Republican government professional would be bad enough. But a Republican government volunteer does that thing you're not supposed to do in government ... think differently.

Professional government is a guild. Like medieval guilds. You can't serve in if you're not a member. If you haven't been indoctrinated into its arcane rituals. If you aren't in the club.

And Trump isn't in the club. He brought in a bunch of people who aren't in the club with him.

Now we're seeing what the pros do when amateurs try to walk in on them. They spy on them, they investigate them and they send them to jail. They use the tools of power to bring them down.

That's not a free country.

It's not a free country when FBI agents who support Hillary take out an "insurance policy" against Trump winning the election. It's not a free country when Obama officials engage in massive unmasking of the opposition. It's not a free country when the media responds to the other guy winning by trying to ban the conservative media that supported him from social media. It's not a free country when all of the above collude together to overturn an election because the guy who wasn't supposed to win, won.

We're in a civil war between conservative volunteer government and leftist professional government.

The pros have made it clear that they're not going to accept election results anymore. They're just going to make us do whatever they want. They're in charge and we better do what they say.

That's the war we're in. And it's important that we understand that.

Because this isn't a shooting war yet. And I don't want to see it become one.

And before the shooting starts, civil wars are fought with arguments. To win, you have to understand what the big picture argument is. It's easy to get bogged down in arguments that don't matter or won't really change anything.

This is the argument that changes everything.

Do we have a government of the people and by the people? Or do we have a tyranny of the professionals?

The Democrats try to dress up this argument in leftist social justice babble. Those fights are worth having. But sometimes we need to pull back the curtain on what this is really about.

They've tried to rig the system. They've done it by gerrymandering, by changing the demographics of entire states through immigration, by abusing the judiciary and by a thousand different tricks.

But civil wars come down to an easy question. Who runs the country?

They've given us their answer and we need to give them our answer.

Both sides talk about taking back the country. But who are they taking it back for?

The left uses identity politics. It puts supposed representatives of entire identity groups up front. We're taking the country back for women and for black people, and so on and so forth...

But nobody elected their representatives.

Identity groups don't vote for leaders. All the black people in the country never voted to make Shaun King and Al Sharpton their representative. And women sure as hell didn't vote for Hillary Clinton.

What we have in America is a representative government. A representative government makes freedom possible because it actually represents people, instead of representing ideas.

The left's identity politics only represents ideas. Nobody gets to vote on them.

Instead the left puts out representatives from different identity politics groups, there's your gay guy, there's three women, there's a black man, as fronts for their professional government system.

When they're taking back the country, it's always for professional government. It's never for the people.

When conservatives fight to take back the country, it's for the people. It's for volunteer government the way that the Founding Fathers wanted it to be.

This is a civil war over whether the American people are going to govern themselves. Or are they going to be governed.

Are we going to have a government of the people, by the people and for the people... or are we going to have a government.

The kind of government that most countries have where a few special people decide what's best for everyone.

We tried that kind of government under the British monarchy. And we had a revolution because we didn't like it.

But that revolution was met with a counterrevolution by the left. The left wants a monarchy. It wants King Obama or Queen Oprah.

It wants to end government of the people, by the people and for the people. That's what they're fighting for. That's what we're fighting against. The stakes are as big as they're ever going to get. Do elections matter anymore?

I live in the state of Ronald Reagan. I can go visit the Ronald Reagan Library any time I want to. But today California has one party elections. There are lots of elections and propositions. There's all the theater of democracy, but none of the substance. Its political system is as free and open as the Soviet Union.

And that can be America.

The Trump years are going to decide if America survives. When his time in office is done, we're either going to be California or a free nation once again.

The civil war is out in the open now and we need to fight the good fight. And we must fight to win. [141]

Appendix A

PRESIDENT TRUMP'S ACCOMPLISHMENTS

WASHINGTON, D.C.—(Canada Free Press). Since President Donald Trump took office on January 20, 2017, he has already become the most pro-America, pro-business, pro-military, pro-law enforcement, pro-life, pro-religious liberty, and pro-Israel president in the history of the United States. About 70 federal judges, including one Justice of the U.S. Supreme Court, have been confirmed. A second Supreme Court Justice will soon be confirmed. One in seven federal Court of Appeals judges have now been nominated by President Trump and about 80 more federal judges will be confirmed by the end of this year. The impact of this one presidential accomplishment will continue his legacy for many years. Below is a partial list of a much longer list we have complied.

Here are some of President Trump's accomplishments so far:

Sanctity of Human Life

> Spoke live via satellite at the March for Life in DC, a first for any sitting U.S. president.

Mike Pence was the first VP to speak in person at the March for Life.

Cut off taxpayer funding for the U.N. Population Fund.

Signed H.J. Res. 43 into law which overturned an Obama regulation that prohibited states from defunding Planned Parenthood.

Issued guidance to stop taxpayer funding of abortion in Obama Care exchange plans.

Signed an executive order to restore the Mexico City Policy and defund International Planned Parenthood Federation, blocking $9 billion in aid from funding abortion.

Religious Liberty

Formed a new Conscience and Religious Freedom Division within the U.S. Dept. of HHS to protect religious freedom and restrict taxpayer funds from discriminating against religion.

Implemented a new policy directive within the U.S. Department of Labor's Office of Federal Contract Compliance Programs which focuses on protecting religious freedom.

Hosted the first Ministerial to Advance Religious Freedom at the U.S. Department of State.

Nominated Gov. Samuel Dale Brownback of Kansas to be Ambassador-at-Large for International Religious Freedom, Department of State.

Protected the free exercise of religion by reversing Obama-era policies with new legal guidance issued to the Department of Justice by Attorney General Jeff Sessions.

Signed an executive order on religious liberty on the National Day of Prayer.

Ordered the IRS not to enforce restrictions on political activity by churches.

Helped faith-based groups give healthcare coverage to 13.7 million Americans.

Issued a guidance protecting religious liberty within the U.S. Dept. of Agriculture ensuring that Christians who opposed same-sex "marriage" would not experience discrimination.

Took numerous actions related to homosexual, transgender, and other sex-related matters

Removed Obama web pages on LGBT issues.

Disqualified "transgender" individuals from serving in the military, thus freeing personnel from participating in LGBT training based upon their religious beliefs and conscientious objections.

Israel

Declared Jerusalem the capital of Israel and moved the U.S. embassy to Jerusalem.

Visited Jerusalem's Western Wall and prayed, a first for any sitting U.S. president.

Signed the Taylor Force Act prohibiting aid to the Palestinian Authority if it funds terrorism.

Cut $225 million from the Palestinian Authority.

Delivered the first F-35 stealth jets to Israel.

Withdrew from The United Nations Educational, Scientific and Cultural Organization (UNESCO) citing "anti-Israel bias."

Cut $300 million in aid to Pakistan.

Cut all U.S. funding for UNRWA, the U.N. agency serving Palestinian refugees-it's a politicized and pro-Palestinian organization, which perpetuates the refugee issue.

Withdrew from the anti-Israel U.N. Human Rights Council

Appointed pro-Israel Nikki Haley to serve as U.S. Ambassador at the United Nations, who has assumed a more assertive role and negotiated $285 million cut in U.N. budget.

Withdrew America from the Iran deal, imposed tough sanctions and pledged to stop Iran from obtaining nuclear weapons.

Closed the Palestinian Liberation Organization (PLO) office in Washington, D.C.

Approved a 10-year military aid package for Israel, providing $3.8 billion annually to secure Israel's defense.

Government

Stopped $230 million in rebuilding payments to Syria.

Brought back soldiers' remains from the Korean War.

Secured release of American prisoners from North Korea.

Negotiated peace talks between North and South Korea.

Signed an order calling for work requirements for welfare.

Nominated the first woman to lead the CIA.

Collected record taxes in first month under tax cuts; ran surplus in January 2018.

Proposed largest civil service change in 40 years—
"Hire the best and fire the worst."

Signed bipartisan bill to combat synthetic opioids.

Decreased federal bureaucracy by 16,000 positions
and slashed government regulations.

Economy

Decreased black and Hispanic unemployment to a
record low.

Decreased jobless claims at the lowest level
since 1969.

Black business ownership jumped 400 percent.

Increased consumer confidence to the highest level
in 18 years.

Decreased youth unemployment to 52-year low.

Increased median income to highest in history.

Increased business investments 39 percent.

Decreased food stamp use by 500,000 in one month.

Increased homebuilding permits to the highest
since 2007.

Increased oil production to 10 million barrels a day for the first time since 1970.

Increased the stock market to an all-time high.

Liberty Counsel Founder and Chairman Mat Staver said, "In one and a half years, President Donald Trump and his policies have been done more to advance life, religious liberty, the economy, deregulation, government reform, and Israel in the history of America. More pro-life and pro-religious liberty policies have been implemented in this short time than all previous presidents combined. It is no wonder certain segments of the media would rather focus on a negative narrative than these accomplishments." [142]

Appendix B

YOU COULD HAVE HEARD A PIN DROP

JFK's Secretary of State, Dean Rusk, was in France in the early 60's when Charles de Gaule decided to pull out of NATO. De Gaule said he wanted all US military out of France as soon as possible.

Rusk responded, "Does that include those who are buried here?" DeGaule did not respond.

You could have heard a pin drop.

There was a conference in France where a number of international engineers were taking part, including French and American. During a break, one of the French engineers came back into the room saying, "Have you heard the latest dumb stunt Bush has done? He has sent an aircraft carrier to Indonesia to help the tsunami victims. What does he intend to do, bomb them?"

A Boeing engineer stood up and replied quietly: "Our carriers have three hospitals on board that can treat several hundred people; they are nuclear powered and can supply emergency electrical power to shore facilities; they have three cafeterias with the capacity to feed 3,000 people three meals a day, they can produce several thousand gallons of fresh water from sea water each day, and they carry half a dozen helicopters for use in transporting victims and injured to and from their flight deck. We have eleven such ships; how many does France have?"

You could have heard a pin drop.

A US Navy Admiral was attending a naval conference that included Admirals from the US, English, Canadian, Australian, and French Navies. At a cocktail reception, he found himself standing with a large group of officers that included personnel from most of those countries.

Everyone was chatting away in English as they sipped their drinks, but a French admiral suddenly complained that, whereas Europeans learn many languages, Americans learn only English. He then asked, "Why is it that we always have to speak English in these conferences, rather than speaking French?"

Without hesitating, the American admiral replied, "Maybe it's because the Brits, Canadians, Aussies, and Americans arranged it so you wouldn't have to speak German."

You could have heard a pin drop.
And finally:

> Robert Whiting, an elderly gentleman of eighty-three, arrived in Paris by plane. At French Customs, he took a few minutes to locate his passport in his carry on.

You have been to France before, monsieur?" the customs officer asked sarcastically. Mr. Whiting admitted that he had been to France previously.

"Then you should know enough to have your passport ready."

The American said, "The last time I was here, I didn't have to show it."

"Impossible. Americans always have to show their passports upon arrival in France!"

> The American senior gave the Frenchman a long hard look. Then he quietly explained: "Well, when I came ashore at Omaha Beach on D-Day in 1944 to help liberate this country, I couldn't find a single Frenchmen to show a passport to."

You could have heard a pin drop. [143]

Appendix C

THE INVESTIGATION OF PRESIDENT TRUMP BY A SPECIAL PROSECUTOR

The FBI had been investigating whether Donald Trump or his campaign had been connected to the Russian election meddling since the summer of 2016. Beginning that year the Democrats, led by Adam Schiff (D-CA), Chairman of the Intelligence Committee of the House of Representatives, were continually telling their media and the public that they had evidence that proved President Trump and his campaign had colluded with the Russians meddling in the 2016 election. They never provided that proof but they were doing their best to convince the public that President Trump and his campaign were guilty and to keep the issue before the public.

During the 2012 and 2016 election cycles, a company called Fusion GPS was retained by the Democrats to do opposition research on a number of Republicans. In addition, Fusion was retained by a top Democrat to investigate if there was a conspiracy between candidate Trump and the Russian government prior to the 2016 election. Christopher Steele was hired by Fusion to conduct this investigation. Christopher Steele was a former British MI6 (intelligence) officer. He developed a document called the Steele Dossier that contained a number of collusion claims against candidate Trump. This was paid for by the Clinton campaign and the Democrat National Committee. Mr. Steele shared the report with the FBI.

The FBI knowingly used a dossier funded by Hillary Clinton's campaign and the Democrat National Committee—which contained uncorroborated allegations—in its investigation and in applications to the Foreign Intelligence Surveillance Act (FISA) court for warrants to monitor a Trump campaign adviser, Carter Page.

During their investigation FBI agents Peter Strzok and Lisa Page had been sharing texts containing anti-Trump messages. They called him an "idiot" and "loathsome" and openly discussed using the powers of their office—an "insurance policy"—to stop Trump if he was elected president. Even with their obvious biases, they believed that there was no connection between Russian meddling and the 2016 Trump election campaign.

Nevertheless, "FBI and Justice officials likely leaked a barrage of media stories just before and after Mueller's appointment that made the evidence of collusion look far stronger than the front-line investigators knew it to be." [144]

At the time that decisions were made to spy on the Trump campaign, Barack Obama was president of the United States. It was his administration—his Justice Department and FBI—that was in control of the world's premier investigative agencies being used in an espionage investigation against a political foe of Mr. Obama. This is extremely important because of the allegations that were made against President Trump in the Ukraine investigation.

After months of investigation, the FBI knew that the dossier was opposition research, that most of its claims were unreliable, and that they had not been able to connect Trump or his campaign to Russia's election meddling. This was confirmed by FBI agents, including Strzok, who had been the leader of the Russian probe, and Page. Strzok knew that Steele hated Trump. Strzok had texted that "there is no there there" (that there was no evidence of collusion). It was also confirmed by James Comey shortly after he was fired as FBI director.

Even though these conclusions had been reached, Robert Mueller was appointed to investigate if there was collusion between the Trump campaign and the Russians during the 2016 general election campaign. After two years and approximately $40 million, Mr. Mueller issued indictments against thirty-four people and three companies. An indictment was issued against an internet research agency, a Russian troll farm, two shell companies, and thirteen Russian nationals. Indictments were also issued against twelve Russian military intelligence officers who allegedly stole files from the Democrat National Committee and the Clinton presidential campaign. Of the thirty-four people issued indictments, twenty-five of them were working for the Russians, and all three of the companies were connected with Russia.

None of the remaining individuals were charged with working with the Russians to influence the election on behalf of Trump or the Trump campaign. Mr. Mueller concluded that neither President Trump nor anyone involved in his campaign colluded with Russia, the most critical of the inquiries that he conducted. These conclusions were known before the two-year investigation was even started.

When giving his report to the Congress, Mueller stated that he would not address matters involving the dossier because it was out of his purview. This is difficult to believe since the dossier was used by the FBI to get FISA court approval to perform surveillance on Carter Page, even though they knew that most of the claims were unreliable.

This is especially true since the Justice Department Inspector General, Michael Horowitz, issued a report that documented seventeen problems with the applications made to the FISA Court by the FBI. The presiding judge of the FISA Court, Rosemary Collyer, issued a public order, rebuking the FBI for abusing the FISA process to obtain a warrant to spy on Carter Page.

THE INVESTIGATION OF PRESIDENT TRUMP BY THE DEMOCRAT-CONTROLLED HOUSE OF REPRESENTATIVES

The Democrats had been saying that they would remove Trump as president even before he took office. They wanted to impeach him because if he was successful in implementing what he pledged during the campaign, they were afraid that the people would like what his policies did for the United States and that it would show how flawed the Democrat philosophy really is.

Having not succeeded in finding any evidence in the Mueller Report, the Democrats in the House started an "inquiry" to determine if President Trump obstructed justice. It was later changed to an "investigation." Obviously, it would not be an unbiased investigation. They were looking for things that could be used against President Trump during the 2020 general election campaign. These hearings concentrated on allegations of a "whistleblower" that President Trump had acted improperly during a telephone call with President Zelensky of the Ukraine. The "whistleblower" was not on the call. At the time they launched the "inquiry," the Democrats had not seen the leaker's complaint but had only heard reports of what it alleged. As usual, they took to the airways to argue President Trump's guilt even though they had no evidence.

In response, President Trump authorized the release of a transcript of the call, which is normally not done because such calls are confidential. During the call President Trump asked for Zelensky's help in determining the extent of the Ukraine's efforts to interfere in the 2016 election and of former Vice President Joe Biden's actions in getting a Ukraine prosecutor fired. The Democrats focused on whether Trump had applied pressure on Zelensky to get the information to see if there was a "quid pro quo," which "is Latin for "something for something."

President Trump was certainly well within his rights in asking for information regarding efforts in the Ukraine to interfere with the 2016 election. He was also well within his rights to ask about Vice President Biden's activities in the Ukraine to determine if he had violated any United States laws. Not only was it within his rights—he had an obligation to do so. Under Article II of the Constitution, duties of the president include to investigate and enforce laws. [145]

At the time, Biden had been appointed by President Obama as his point man in dealings with the Ukraine. After one trip that Biden made to the Ukraine, with his son Hunter accompanying him, Hunter was named to the board of Burisma, a large oil and gas company in the Ukraine. He had no experience for the role but was paid $53,000 per month for seventeen months. After this had occurred, a prosecutor in the Ukraine was investing Burisma and was going to question Hunter about his role. Joe Biden had been charged with delivering $1 billion in aid to the Ukraine. He was caught on tape telling the story of how he had told the Ukrainians that he would not release the $1 billion to them if the prosecutor was not fired within six hours. The prosecutor was fired. Talk about "quid pro quo" being caught on tape. [146]

Ukranian prosecutors said they tried to get this information to the US Department of Justice since the summer of 2018 because it might have been a violation of US ethics laws. One of the ethics laws that applies to government employees is 5 Code of Federal Regulations Section 2635.702:

§ 2635.702 Use of public office for private gain.

An employee shall not use his public office for his own private gain, for the endorsement of any product, service or enterprise, or for the private gain of friends, relatives, or persons with whom the employee is affiliated in a nongovernmental capacity, including nonprofit organizations of which the employee is an officer or member, and persons with whom the employee has or seeks employment or business relations. The specific prohibitions set forth in paragraphs (a) through (d) of this section apply this general standard, but are not intended to be exclusive or to limit the application of this section.

(a) Inducement or coercion of benefits. An employee shall not use or permit the use of his Government position or title or any authority associated with his public office in a manner that is intended to coerce or induce another person, including a subordinate, to provide any benefit, financial or otherwise, to himself or to friends, relatives, or persons with whom the employee is affiliated in a nongovernmental capacity.

The question is "did Joe Biden, while vice president, help his son get these opportunities in violation of 5 CFR 2635.702?"

The Democrats disregarded this obligation of the president in their investigation and argued that President Trump was seeking the information to use it against Joe Biden who was campaigning for the Democrat nomination to run for president in 2020. They also argued that President Trump made demands on Zelensky so he would get the information. President Trump denied that he had made any demands during the phone call. When the transcript was released, it was apparent that President Trump had not asked for anything or put any pressure on President Zelensky. There was no "quid pro quo."

Adam Schiff (D-CA) was still the Chairman of the Intelligence Committee conducting the impeachment inquiry. When he was initially asked if he or his staff had spoken with the leaker, he denied it. Later, he had to admit that he and his staff had met with the leaker and had helped him with his complaint.

Hearings initially were being held in secret in a basement and behind closed doors, and President Trump was not allowed to have his attorney present, to call witnesses, or to issue subpoenas. They were not giving President Trump the "right to due process of law" to which every American is entitled.

The Democrats called a number of witnesses to testify about the Trump-Zelensky telephone call. With one exception, none of those witnesses had spoken with President Trump about the call. Only one witness, Ambassador Gordon Sondland, had spoken directly with President Trump. He testified that when he asked President Trump what he wanted, President Trump responded "Nothing. Nothing, I want no quid pro quo." Republicans on the committee asked the witnesses if they knew of anything President Trump did that would justify his impeachment. They all testified that they did not know of any such action(s).

The Democrats also alleged that President Trump had with-held about $391 million from the Ukraine for its defense in order to put pressure on President Zelensky to do what he had asked. This money included funds for "lethal weapons," which the Obama Administration had never given the Ukraine. While the funds were withheld for a short period, the Ukrainians never knew about it, and it never came up in discussions before it was released to the Ukraine. It was released within the time specified when it was approved.

President Zelensky mentioned on a number of occasions that there was no "quid pro quo" and that he had never been pressured to help the United States.

The Democrats on the Intelligence Committee issued a report, and the inquiry was then turned over to the Judiciary Committee of the House. The chairman of that committee was Jerrold Nadler (D-NY). He was in the House at the time of the Clinton impeachment proceedings. At that time, he said on tape that an impeachment should not be held of any president unless there was bipartisan agreement in the Congress and unless the people of the United States overwhelmingly supported impeachment. Neither of those were happening here.

In a blatant attempt to continue their impeachment inquiry without regard for the truth, the Democrats in the House Judiciary Committee held a hearing for supposed constitutional scholars on whether the allegations against the president reached the level of impeachable offenses. The committee did not put forth any facts to support their claims. In fact, all of their suppositions were contradicted by the evidence.

The Democrats allowed four witnesses, all of them Democrats. Three witnesses were from Harvard Law School, Stanford Law School, and the University of North Carolina School of Law. All of them opined that President Trump could be impeached on the material presented. The professor from Harvard Law School said that he was a registered Democrat his whole life and that Trump could be impeached just for his comments about "fake news." The professor from Stanford Law School had appeared in an anti-Trump podcast, disparaging conservatives, and she had donated money to Barack Obama, Hillary Clinton, and Elizabeth Warren. She also had said on a tape from an American Constitution Society convention that she was walking along and saw the next building was a

Trump Hotel, so she had to walk across the street to avoid walking by the Trump Hotel. The professor from North Carolina School of Law said in a video taken shortly after the 2016 election that he was at the University of Pennsylvania Law School "yesterday, where I teach a class, and my law class is still in therapy." All of them had known biases against the president and had made up their minds long before the hearing that Trump should be impeached. By no stretch of one's imagination can these be regarded as even close to being unbiased, independent witnesses.

One witness, Jonathan Turley, is a professor from George Washington University. He was not a Trump supporter, and he did not vote for Trump. He criticized the Democrats for rushing the impeachment inquiry and asserted there was no evidence in the record to prove a claim against Trump. He said:

> One can oppose President Trump's policies or actions but still conclude that the current legal case for impeachment is not just woefully inadequate, but in some respects, dangerous, as the basis for the impeachment of an American President. I am concerned about lowering impeachment standards to fit a paucity of evidence and an abundance of anger ... If the House proceeds solely on the Ukrainian allegations, this impeachment would stand out among modern impeachment as the shortest proceeding, with the thinnest evidentiary record, and the narrowest grounds ever used to impeach a president... If we are to impeach a president for only the third time in our history, we will need to rise above this rage and genuinely engage in a civil and substantive discussion ... Impeachment needs to be based on proof, not assumptions. [147]

The Democrats did not conduct their inquiry with the safe-guards that President Clinton had in the late '90s. The inquiry was akin to a Star Chamber. Star Chambers were used in England in the fifteenth to the seventeenth centuries to oppress social and political activities through the arbitrary use and abuse of the power it wielded. [148]

Under the Rules of Impeachment, the House of Representatives is supposed to gather the facts, give a report to the Senate, and then the Senate reviews the facts and votes on whether to impeach a president.

The Democrats came up with two Articles of Impeachment. Article 1 alleged that President Trump "Abused his Power," and Article 2 alleged "Obstruction of Congress." Three of the Democrats did not vote for the Articles, one of whom switched to the Republican party, and none of the Republicans voted for the Articles.

The "Abuse of Power" allegation involved President Trump's discussions with the Ukraine regarding the 2016 election and Joe and Hunter Biden. As discussed, President Trump had the right, and the obligation, to question the Ukraine's interference in the 2016 election and Joe Biden's violation of the law in helping a family member while vice president.

For real examples of "abuse of power" by a president, see a list of President Obama's "abuses of power" a little later.

The Democrats came up with "Obstruction of Congress" because they obviously could not find an "Obstruction of Justice." The charge was based on President Trump's decision to claim Executive Privilege which would not permit his top advisors to testify or provide documents to the House. Presidents on occasion have used Executive Privilege, and if the Congress disagrees with the exercise of that right, the proper remedy is to go to court for an order that those persons comply with any subpoenas. The House decided not to do that because they were in too much of a hurry to finish their part of the impeachment process.

Should "obstruction of Congress" be an impeachable offense? If so, a president's veto of a law passed by the Congress would be obstruction of Congress. Is that really the result that we want?

Even though the House Democrats were in a hurry to finish their impeachment, their leader in the House, Nancy Pelosi, refused to send the report to the Senate. Finally, the House sent some 29,000 pages to the Senate. In negotiations with the Republican leader of the Senate, Senator Mitch McConnell, the Democrats demanded that the Senate call some witnesses. The Democrats had the obligation to hear all of the witnesses they wanted under their impeachment duties in the House of Representatives. After discussion and debate, a vote was held and the Senate declined to call any witnesses.

It is interesting that this is the same tactic that the Democrats used during the hearing in the Senate on Brett Kavanaugh's nomination to the Supreme Court. They withheld allegations that had been made against Judge Kavanaugh until late in the hearing process. They then demanded that the hearing be extended to hear an additional witness, and the Republicans acceded to their demands. Additional hearings were held, and Judge Kavanaugh's nomination was approved. That was the same tactic they used in the impeachment process. Call some witnesses but don't hear others, and then when the hearing is over, argue that you need to hear other witnesses. They wanted more than one bite at the apple. The Republicans should be aware that this will be a normal tactic to be used by the Democrats.

While the Democrats/Liberals and the media were concentrating on President Trump's relationship with the Ukraine, other Democrats were pressing the Ukraine to help them get information on President Trump. On May 4, 2018, three Democrat United States Senators, Robert Menendez, Richard Durbin, and Patrick

Leahy, sent a letter to M. Yuriy Lutsenko, general prosecutor for Ukraine. They wrote: "We are writing to express great concern about reports that your office has taken steps to impede cooperation with the investigation of the United States Special Counsel Robert Mueller . . . If these reports are true, we strongly encourage you to reverse course and halt any efforts to impede cooperation with this important investigation." Democrat Senator Chris Murphy also met with President Zelensky. He wrote in a tweet that he told President Zelensky that "it was best to ignore the requests from Trump's campaign operatives. He agreed ". . . He added in a statement that "In order to keep the United States-Ukraine relationship strong, it was much better for the president (Zelensky) to rebuff any pressure he's getting from political campaigns in the United States to conduct investigations."[149]

These were certainly threats from the Democrats. In return for the Ukraine's continuing to help with the Mueller investigation, the Democrats would support the Ukraine. This was certainly a "quid pro quo!"

So, the Democrats believed it was fine for them to threaten President Zelensky to help in their investigation, while they went after Trump when he asked for assistance in determining if any United States laws were violated.

The vote of the Senate on the impeachment of President Trump was held on Wednesday, February 5, 2020. The vote on Article 1 was fifty-two to forty-eight in favor of acquittal, and on Article 2, the vote was fifty-three to forty-seven for acquittal. Since a two-thirds vote is required for impeachment, President Trump was acquitted.

Everyone knew this would be the outcome from the beginning, but the Democrats proceeded anyway. Anything to keep Donald Trump from succeeding and from running for President again!

The Democrats kept arguing that the Constitution required that they conduct this investigation. They were doing what they could to ignore and act against other constitutional provisions and especially the Electoral College. It is interesting that they had then found a new love of the Constitution. They were using the Constitution to conduct a totally political exercise because they did not believe that President Trump was legitimately elected as president, even though he won as mandated by the Constitution.

The Democrats' hatred toward, and fear of, President Trump led them to not care what the truth was, at all times knowing that their biased media would support their efforts and not report the truth. The biased media once again showed its support of the Democrats/Liberals in inquiring into and reporting only the Democrat/Liberal side of an issue. The only collusion going on throughout all of this was between the Democrats and their media.

Other Bidens

It is important to compare what was happening now with what did not happen during the Obama administration. The Ukraine was not the only time that Joe Biden while a member of Congress, or vice president, had helped one of his relatives.

In 2009, Hunter Biden co-founded Rosemont Seneca Partners (RSP). In 2013, Hunter landed in Beijing aboard Air Force Two, accompanying his father on an official visit to China. Less than two weeks later, Rosemont Seneca Partners became a partner in a new investment company backed by the state-owned Bank of China. Hunter got a prominent role on the board in the new company, Bohai Harvest RST, and Rosemont Seneca Partners shared a stake in Bohai Harvest RST. Rosemont Seneca Partners also received a piece of a private equity fund inside the Shanghai Free-Trade Zone. Rosemont Seneca Partners, therefore, had access to deals most Western firms only dreamed of.

In 2015, a Chinese-backed real estate company acquired a controlling stake in Rosemont Realty, a sister company of Rosemont Seneca Partners, where Hunter served as an advisor. The Chinese promised $3 billion for commercial property investments in the United States. [150]

Again, Joe Biden received something for his son.

Joe Biden was also President Obama's point man with Iraq at the time. His brother, James, became executive vice president of a construction company in 2010 in Iraq. Just as Hunter with Burisma, James had virtually no experience in the construction industry. A few months after he joined the company, it received a $1.5 billion deal to build affordable homes in Iraq. The same ethics law cited earlier applies here.

The question is, did Joe Biden, while vice president, help his son and/or his brother get these opportunities in violation of 5 CFR 2635.702.

The Obama administration failed to investigate Joe Biden on these occasions.

Patrick Schweitzer has recently authored a book entitled, *Profiles in Corruption: Abuse of Power by Americas Progressive Elite*, published by HarperCollins Publishers, which records discussions of Joe Biden and other relatives, Los Angeles Mayor Eric Garcetti, and Senators Corey Booker, Elizabeth Warren, Sherrod Brown, Bernie Sanders, and Amy Klobuchar.

Hillary Clinton

Hillary Clinton is another Democrat who has been protected by the United States justice system under the Obama administration and, once again, protected by the biased media.

Mrs. Clinton set up an illegal server in her home while she was Secretary of State of the United States. That was against security rules of the State Department as classified information would have been passed through that server. At the time, her family's nonprofit, the Clinton Foundation, was under scrutiny from the FBI. In addition, at the time her emails were evidence in both a congressional investigation into the 2012 Benghazi terrorist attack and several Freedom of Information Act lawsuits from Judicial Watch, a government watchdog group.

On July 5, 2016, the FBI issued the following:

Statement by FBI Director James B. Comey on the Investigation of Secretary Hillary Clinton's Use of a Personal E-Mail System

> The investigation began as a referral from the Intelligence Community Inspector General in connection with Secretary Clinton's use of a personal e-mail server during her time as Secretary of State. The referral focused on whether classified information was transmitted on that personal system. . .
>
> I have so far used the singular term, "e-mail server," in describing the referral that began our investigation. It turns out to have been more complicated than that. Secretary Clinton used several different servers and administrators of those servers during her four years at the State Department and used numerous mobile devices to view and send e-mail on that personal domain. As new servers and equipment were employed, older servers were taken out of service, stored, and decommissioned in various ways. . .
>
> From the group of 30,000 e-mails returned to the State Department, 110 e-mails in 52 e-mail chains have been determined by the owning agency to contain classified information at the time they were sent or received. Eight of those chains contained information that was Top Secret at the time they were sent; 36 chains contained Secret information

at the time; and eight contained Confidential information, . . .

It is also likely that there are other work-related e-mails that they did not produce to State and that we did not find elsewhere, and that are now gone because they deleted all e-mails they did not return to State, and the lawyers cleaned their devices in such a way as to preclude complete forensic recovery. . .

Although we did not find clear evidence that Secretary Clinton or her colleagues intended to violate laws governing the handling of classified information, there is evidence that they were extremely careless in their handling of very sensitive, highly classified information.

For example, seven e-mail chains concern matters that were classified at the Top Secret/Special Access Program level when they were sent and received. These chains involved Secretary Clinton both sending e-mails about those matters and receiving e-mails from others about the same matters. There is evidence to support a conclusion that any reasonable person in Secretary Clinton's position, or in the position of those government employees with whom she was corresponding about these matters, should have known that an unclassified system was no place for that conversation. In addition to this highly sensitive information, we also found information that was properly classified as Secret by the U.S. Intelligence Community at the time it was discussed on e-mail . . .

None of these e-mails should have been on any kind of unclassified system, but their presence is especially concerning because all of these e-mails were housed on unclassified personal servers not even supported by full-time security staff, like those found at Departments and Agencies of the U.S. Government—or even with a commercial service like Gmail . . .

With respect to potential computer intrusion by hostile actors, we did not find direct evidence that Secretary Clinton's personal e-mail domain, in its various configurations since 2009, was successfully hacked. But, given the nature of the system and of the actors potentially involved, we assess that we would be unlikely to see such direct evidence. We do assess that hostile actors gained access to the private commercial e-mail accounts of people with whom Secretary Clinton was in regular contact from her personal account. We also assess that Secretary Clinton's use of a personal e-mail domain was both known by a large number of people and readily apparent. She also used her personal e-mail extensively while outside the United States, including sending and receiving work-related e-mails in the territory of sophisticated adversaries. Given that combination of factors, we assess it is possible that hostile actors gained access to Secretary Clinton's personal e-mail account. . . . [151]

Director Comey concluded that no charges were appropriate in this case. The statute in question is found at 18 U.S. Code 793 (f). It states:

(f) Whoever, being entrusted with or having lawful possession of control of any document, writing, code book, signal book, sketch, photomap, model, instrument, appliance, note, or information, relating to the national defense, (1) through gross negligence permits the same to be to be removed from its proper place of custody or delivered to anyone in violation of his trust, or to be lost, stolen, abstracted, or destroyed, or (2) having knowledge that the same has been illegally removed from its proper place of custody or delivered to anyone in violation of its trust, or lost, or stolen, abstracted, or destroyed, and fails to make prompt report of such loss, theft, abstraction, or destruction to his superior officer– Shall be fined under this title or imprisoned not more than 10 years, or both.

The FBI found that the 33,000 emails that Clinton produced contained items that were classified at the top secret/special access program level, and items that were classified top secret, secret, and confidential. Director Comey had also noted in his remarks that there were reportedly more than 60,000 total emails remaining on her personal system in 2014.

18 U.S. Code 793 (f) uses *"gross negligence"* as the standard to determine wrongdoing. Mr. Comey concluded that "while they did not find clear evidence that Secretary Clinton or her colleagues intended to violate laws governing the handling of classified information, there is evidence that they were *"extremely careless* in their handling of very sensitive, highly classified information."

Mr. Comey obviously did not want to use the term *"gross negligence"* in his findings and his statement because that would have indicated that Clinton was guilty of violating the statute. The trouble with that is *"extremely careless" is the same as "gross negligence."*

A synonym for "gross" is "extremely" and a synonym for "negligence" is "careless." [152]

In reality, Mr. Comey found that Clinton *was "grossly negligent"* in her actions!

Gross negligence does not require intent. Moreover, there is lots of evidence that Clinton and her colleagues had intent when they got rid of 30,000 emails in ways that would ensure they would never be found, or destroyed the appliances where the emails were originated, received, or stored. Clinton also has another problem with the missing emails.

She authorized the permanent deletion of thousands of pages of emails, which were potential evidence and federal records, claiming that they were of a personal nature like yoga classes and her daughter's wedding. Mrs. Clinton's aides installed a software program that blocked the retrieval of the documents, and her aides admitted to breaking her old Blackberries in half or of hitting them with a hammer, and the FBI could not find her thirteen mobile devices and two iPads. In addition, a program called Bleachbit that would prevent the recovery of deleted emails was installed. At the time, the 33,000 of missing emails were subject to a subpoena.

While her mishandling of the classified information remains the biggest injustice of the Clinton email scandal, the willful destruction of more than half of the 60,000 emails archived on her private, illicit server, also remains an overlooked crime for which no one has been held accountable. [153]

In addition to violating this statute, Clinton also committed obstruction of justice! No one, other than Clinton, and maybe her staff, knows what was on the other 30,000 emails that were deleted, destroyed, bleached, or otherwise disappeared, or that were on the computers, the servers, the iPads, or the Blackberrys that were smashed.

One questions: "What was on those deleted emails?" It is not possible to believe that they were all about yoga and Clinton's daughter's wedding. If 33,000 out of 60,000 emails were erased/ deleted/bleached/destroyed/hidden, and the computers/servers, iPads, and Blackberrys were smashed, while they were material to an ongoing investigation and a number of lawsuits, that certainly is obstruction of justice. Mrs. Clinton has so far not been held accountable for her actions.

So, Joe Biden and Hillary Clinton got a pass on their illegal behavior from the Obama administration. And then the Democrats in the House conducted an impeachment investigation into President Trump, continuing their efforts to nullify the 2016 election.

This clearly shows the different standards the Democrats employ when the subject is another Democrat (or two) versus a Republican.

President Obama's Abuses of Power

In addition, compare the following abuses of power committed by President Obama with the alleged wrongdoing by President Trump. In his first term, Obama's administration launched a "'We Can't Wait" initiative . . . explaining that "when Congress won't act, this president will." [154]

In his final term, Obama . . ."vowed to pursue 'audacious' executive action. . . And in his January 2014 State of the Union Address, President Obama promised to 'wherever and whenever' possible 'take steps without legislation.'" [155]

Some of those abuses are the following:

The most severe abuse of power by Obama took place when his Justice Department and FBI investigated Mr. Trump and his campaign for possible collusion with the Russians in the 2016 election, based on information that had been paid for by the Hillary Clinton campaign and the Democrat National Committee. He unleashed powerful agencies to conduct an investigation into his and the Democrats most significant political foe during an election.

The above abuse is important because, if it was legal for Obama to investigate Donald Trump and/or his campaign during an election year for wrongdoing, it was legal for President Trump to ask the Ukrainians for information about Joe Biden and his family regarding a violation of United States laws during a campaign.

Obama failed to enforce the laws securing our southern border, allowing millions of illegal immigrants into our country, to include gang members, criminals, drug smugglers, and persons with contagious illnesses.

Obama entered into a nuclear deal with Iran he knew would never pass the Congress and included releasing $150 billion to the Iranians, which has been used to pose greater danger to the United States. He did this despite the lessons to be learned from President Clinton's nuclear deal with North Korea that placed the United States in more danger and has left President Trump with the job of cleaning up that mess as well.

> In his first term ... he told immigrant activists who were pressing for unilateral action that he did not have the authority to "waive away the law Congress put in place." Fast forward a few years, and the Department of Homeland Security had located the power to confer "lawful status" on at least 4.3 million illegal aliens—a measure specifically rejected by Congress. Obama acknowledged that this was intended to "change the law." In preventing the guidance from going into effect a federal district court ... [found] that President Obama was not just rewriting the laws, he is creating them from scratch. ...
>
> Similarly, during Obama's first term, administration officials indicated they did not have the

power independently to raise the minimum wage or increase benefits for federal contract workers. Then, in February 2014 Obama signed an Executive Order 13658, which raised the minimum wage for hundreds of thousands of federal contract workers. His administration subsequently increased workplace benefits and protections for all workers at companies that held federal contracts—roughly 29 million individuals...

After he pursued climate change and cap and trade legislation failed to pass Congress, President Obama decided to pursue climate change regulation. Enter the Clean Power Plan. In order to "transform the domestic energy industry" administrators relied upon an obscure provision of the Clean Air Act of 1972—one that regulates individual power plants. Harvard Law Professor Larry Tribe, who once mentored President Obama and argued on behalf of Al Gore in Bush v. Gore, called the Clean Power Plan a "power grab" that, among other things, usurped the authority of Congress to make the law. Burning the Constitution, he writes, "should not become part of our national energy policy"...

The Obama Administration issued 560 major regulations in its first 7 years, nearly 50 percent more than the Bush administration during the same time frame, and regulations and executive orders continue to be pushed through the administration post-election. [156]

These were not the only "abuses of power" by President Obama.

In 2009, Barack Obama illegally fired Gerald Walpin, the inspector general for the Corporation for National and Community Service, without notice or providing the legally mandated explanation for the firing to Congress. Obama did this to protect Sacramento Mayor Kevin Johnson, an ally of his, whom Walpin had been investigating for misusing federal funds. Walpin had discovered a cover-up of sexual assault by minors against Johnson...

... Barack Obama and Joe Biden were both personally involved in the decision-making process to determine who got $80 billion for clean energy loans, grants, and tax credits for green energy companies in a highly politicized process that favored companies that supported the Obama-Biden campaign over those that didn't. It was no coincidence that the companies that got all the cash were donors to their campaign. In fact, DOE officials expressed concern that Obama and Biden's involvement was putting taxpayer dollars at risk. Not only did they give all this money to green energy companies that donated to their campaign, but the Obama administration also stole proprietary technology from companies that didn't get the loans to the Obama cronies who got them. This scandal was much bigger than Solyndra, but the calls for Obama's impeachment weren't there.

When Obama made a number of controversial picks for the National Labor Relations Board (NLRB), he was unable to get them through the Senate. So, in January 2012, he declared his nominees appointed to the Senate via recess appointments. Except the Senate wasn't even in recess at the time. Obama's actions were such a blatant abuse of power that experts on both sides of the aisle blasted Obama for what he did and a federal appeals court overturned the appointments . . .declaring, "Allowing the president to define the scope of he own appointments power would eviscerate the Constitution's separation of powers." The United States Supreme Court . . .unanimously agreed Obama abused his power . . .

When Title IX was written, the goal was to protect people from discrimination based on sex in education. The notion of "gender identity" or "gender expression" wasn't even a thing back in 1972 when it was passed. Nevertheless, Obama unilaterally decided that "sex" meant "gender identity" and threatened to enforce this bizarre idea. This was a huge violation of the rights and privacy of women and girls nationwide without so much as a national debate in Congress, where this issue needed to be worked out. Instead of going to Congress, Obama simply threatened educational institutions at all levels with the loss of Title IX funding if they didn't comply and allow boys to share bathrooms, locker rooms, and dorm rooms with girls, as well as allow boys to play on girls sports teams. Obama's going around this issue was a huge violation of power. Rather than attempt to have the law updated by Congress, Obama abused his power by simply reinterpreting the law on his own, knowing very well Congress wasn't going to change the law to include "gender identity. . .

... When the DREAM Act failed to pass, Obama issued an executive order creating DACA, an executive version of the DREAM Act. Obama literally bypassed Congress, changing US immigration law via executive pen to appease his pro-open-borders base.

What makes Obama's abuse of power here even worse is that he'd previously acknowledged that he didn't have the power to unilaterally create immigration law. [157]

There were a number of abuses with Obamacare:

The Labor Department announced in February 2013 that it was delaying for a year the part of the law that limits how much people have to spend on their own insurance. This may have been sensible, but changing the law requires actual legislation...

The famous pledge that "if you like your plan, you can keep it" backfired when insurers started cancelling millions of plans that didn't comply with Obamacare. So Obama called a press conference to proclaim that people could continue buying non-complying plans for another year—despite the ACA's language to the contrary. He then refused to consider a House-passed bill that would've made this action legal.

A little known part of Obamacare requires congressional staff to get insurance from health exchanges, rather than a taxpayer-funded program. Obama directed the Office of Personnel Management to interpret the law to maintain the generous benefits...

The Department of Health and Human Services granted more than 2,000 waivers to employers seeking relief from Obamacare's regulations. Nearly 20 percent of them went to gourmet restaurants and other businesses in former Speaker Nancy Pelosi's San Francisco district. Nevada, home to former Senate Majority Leader Harry Reid, got a blanket waiver, while GOP-controlled states like Indiana and Louisiana were denied...

After seeing a rise in the number of applications for tax-exempt status, the IRS in 2010 compiled a "be on the lookout" (BOLO) list to identify organizations engaged in political activities. The list included words such as "Tea Party," "Patriots," and "Israel"; subjects such as government spending, debt, or taxes; and activities such as criticizing the government, educating about the Constitution, or challenging Obamacare. The targeting continued through May 2013, with no consequences other than Lois Lerner, the chief of the tax-exempt-organizations unit, being held in contempt of Congress—and then being allowed to peacefully retire despite erased records and other cover-ups.[158]

About The Author

Leland M. Stenehjem, Jr., was born in Watford City, North Dakota. He earned a BSBA degree from the University of North Dakota, a JD degree from the University of North Dakota School of Law, and an LL.M. degree from the George Washington University National Law Center. He was a Captain in the United States Army and had the honor of serving as a White House Military Social Aide. He practiced law and had a career in banking, being President/Chairman of banks. He served as President and Chairman of the Independent Community Banks of America. He was appointed by Governor Allen Olson of North Dakota to be Commissioner of the Department of Banking and Financial Institutions and then Director of the Office of Management and Budget. He is married to Susan Stenehjem, and they have two children and three grandchildren.

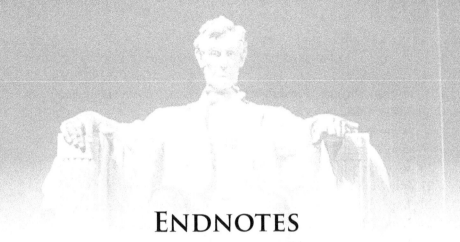

ENDNOTES

1   http://econfaculty.gmu.edu/wew/quotes/wisdom.html

2   https//econfaculty.gmu/wew/quotes/wisdom.html

3   https://www.wikipedia.org/americanrevolutionarywar

4   See https://www.tep-online/laku/usa/rights.htm

5   Brainyquote.com/ authors/ronald-reagan-quotes

6   https://www.brainyquote.com/quotes/lyn- nofziger-402554

7   https://en.wikipedia/George_Washington%27s_Farewell_Address

8   Https://founders.archives.gov/documents/Adams/99–02–3102

9   https://www1.cbn.com/cbnnews/us/2018/january/
    trump-proclaims-january-16-religious-freedom-day.

10 https://www.focusonthefamily.com/socialissues/religous-freedom/
    religious-freedom-in-danger/religious-freedom-in-danger

11 https://www.snopes.com/fact-check/school-prayer/

12 https;//en.m.wikipedia.org/ Alexis de Tocqueville

13 www.goodreads.com/author/quotes/465Alexis_de_Tocqueville

14 Alexis de Tochttps://www.inspiringquotes.us/author/7375-doug-
    las-macarthurqueville, Democracy in America, 1835

15 https://www.inspiringquotes.us/author/7375-douglas-macarthur

16 http://humanevents.com/2013/03/17dr-ben-carson-at-cpac-2013-how-
    to-destroy-america-in-four-easy-steps/

17 (www.youtube.com/claytonchristensen/onreligiousfreedom)

18 . http://humanevents.com/2013//03/17/dr-ben-carson-at-cpac-2cap-
    2013-how-to-destroy-america-in-four-easy-steps/

19 brainyquote.com/authors/ronald-reagan-quotes

20 http://econfaculty.gmu.edu/wew/quotes/wisdom.html

21 www.en.wikipedia.org/AntifA

22 www.merriamwebster.com/politicalcorrectness

23 Thefreedictionary.com/politicalcorrectness

24 www.militaryquotes.com/forum/winner-political-correctness-definition-t31925.html
25 fellowshipoftheminds.wordpress.com/2010/10/01best-definition-of-political-correctness/
26 www.merriam-webster.com/deplorable
27 http://econfaculty.gmu.edu/wew/quotes/wisdom.html
28 https://www.moodymedia.org/articles/demise-religion-freedom-america/
29 https://en.wikipedia.org/wiki/Journalism-ethics-and-standards
30 https://www.google.com/search/colluding
31 https://www.investors.com/politics/editorials/media-bias-left-study/
32 https://www.politico.com/magazine/story/ 2017/04/25// media-bubble-real-journalism-jobs-east-coast-215048
33 https://www.en.wikipedia.org/wiki/Media_bias_in_the_United_States.
34 https://www.washingtontimes.com/news/2018/apr/26/ democratic-professors-outnumber-republicans-10–1/
35 https//www.pacificresearch.org/why-are-teachers-mostly-liberal/
36 www.articles.latimes.com/2012/dec/16/entertainment/ la-et-mn-connecticut-shooting-samuel-jackson-gun-control-20121216
37 www.m.facebook.cm/story.php?story_fbid=1015622470277258&id=503147957
38 https://www.webpages.uidaho.edu/engl_258/lecture%20notes/capitalism%20etc%20defined.htm
39 www.dictionary.com/entrepeneur
40 https://business.und.edu/about/dakota-venture-group.html
41 https://www.creators.com/read/walter-williams/07/14/ spending-and-morality
42 https://www.americanthinker.com/rickmoran
43 https://www.goodreads.com/author/quotes/465Alexis_de_Tocqueville
44 https://www.econfaculty.gmu.edu/wew/quotes/wisdom.html
45 https://www.goodreads.com/author/quotes/465Alexis_de_Tocqueville
46 https://www.pbs.org/wgbh/americanexperience/features/carter-crisis/
47 https://www.washingtonpost.com/news/the-fix/wp/2014/12/12/ the-new-american-malaise/?utm_term=.3baae87cf097
48 https://.www.merriam-webster.com/dictionary/socialism
49 https://www.economics21.org/how-socialism-destroyed-venezuela
50 https://www.whitehouse.gov/briefings-statements/president-donald-j-trump-delivered-record-breaking-results-american-people-first-three-years-office/

51 http://www.thecommentator.com/article/646/
    does_socialism_work_a_classroom_experiment

52 http://www.thecommentator.com/article/646/
    does_socialism_work_a_classroom_experiment

53 http://humanevents.com/2013/03/17/
    dr-ben-carson-at-cpac-2013-how-to-destroy-america-in-four-easy-steps/

54 de Tocqueville, On Democracy in America, Saunders and Otley (1835)
    Part I, Page 291

55 https://www.heritage.org/health-care-reform/report/premiums-choic-
    es-and-government-dependence-under-the-affordable-care-act.

56 https://www.forbes.com/sites/sallypipes/2018/06/11/canadians-are-one-
    in-a -million-while-waiting-for-medical-treatment/#364d4de23e7d

57 https://www.heritage.org/health-care-reform;commentary/
    the-path-forward-health-reform-conservatives

58 https://www.npr.org/2017/10/27/560308997/
    irs-apologizes-for-aggressive-scrutiny-of-conservative-groups

59 https://www.frontpagemag.com/fpm//213333/
    big-dem-cities-big-dem-poverty-arnold-ahlert

60 http://www.newsmax.com/US/
    cities-bankruptcy-after-detroit/2013/08/06/id/519081/#ixzz4D6iy3Fgu

61 https://.www.investors.com/politics/editorials/
    how-decades-of-democratic-rule-ruined-some-of-our-finest-cities/

62 https://amac.us/
    americas-25-worst-cities-are- democrat-led-the-answer-new-leaders/

63 www.independent.org/ news/article.asp?id=11731

64 www.independent.org/news/article.asp?id=11731

65 http;//www.com/focus/f-bloggers/2986815/.posts

66 Https://www/chronicle.com/article/A-Brief-History-of-GOP/243739

67 https://richhabits.net/?s=15+poverty+habits

68 https://vantagenow.com/
    will-child-rich-poor-15-poverty-habits-parents-teach-children/

69 https://www.nytimes.com/2015/12/8/upshot/rich-children-and-poor-
    ones-are-raised-very-differently.html/

70 https://www.quora.cm/
    Teachers-What-makes-poor-children-a-challenge-to-teach/

71 https://education.penelopetrunk.com/2015/11/02/
    the-best-way-to-lift-kids-out-of-poverty-its-not-education/

72 www.unclesamsplantation.com

73 www.carolmswain.com

74 www.love4utah.com

75 www.onepoliticalplaza.com/t-23107–1.html

76 www.youtube.com/elbertleeguillory

77 https://www.americanrhetoric.com/speeches/billcosbypoundcake-speech.htm

78 https://www.snopes.com/fact-check/cos-cause/

79 https://www.dailycaller.com/2012/12/23/larry-elder-to-the-gop-s?v=y-iPXyHG3actop-talking-to-blacks-like-they-are-children/. For further reading on Larry Elder see: https://www.youtube.com/watch?v=y-iPXyHG3ac); This is why Black Men are Failing, and (https:///www.youtube.com/watch?v=piwaBO6U43U; Black Lives Matter, Racism a Conservative

80 http:/townhall.com/columnists/walterewilliams/2012/05/23/should_black_people_tolerate_this/print

81 http://online.wsj.com/news/articles/SB100014240527487048813045760 94221050061598.

82 https://en.wikipedia.org/wiki/Jussie_Smollet_alleged_assault

83 https://en.wikipedia.org/wiki/Wilfred_Reilly.

84 https://www.spiked-online.com/2019/07/12/the-demand-for-bigots-exceeds-the-supply/

85 https://www.theburningplatform.com/2017/09/30/im-mad-as-hell-and-im-not-taking-it-anymore/

86 https://www.wikipedia.org/racial-segregation

87 https://archives.gov/exhibits/featured-documents/emancipation-procla-mation/ transcript.html

88 https://answers.yahoo.com/question/index;_ylt=Awr9DtujwXde LIEAZjFXNyoA;_ylu= X3oDMTEyaWw0NTdy BGNvbG8D Z3ExBHBvcwMyBHZ0aWQDQjk1NjBfMQRzZWMDc3I-?qid=20140804081019AAc8WMz: For further reading see David A. Nichols, "Ike Liked Civil Rights," New York Times, 9/12/2007. https://www.nytimes.com/2007/09/12/opinion/12nichols.html

89 https://blog.blackbloggersconnect.com/2011/10/17/from-nothing-to-something-young-black-men-supporting-positive-change/

90 https/www.montanapioneer.com/the-party-of-lincolns-record-on-racial-justice/

91 https://en.m.wikipedia.org/wikiJim-Crow-laws

92 https://www.army.mil/article/181896/meet_sgt_ william_carney_ the_ first_african_american_medal_of_honor_recipient

93 The History Learning Site

94 http://econfaculty.gmu.edu/wew/quotes/wisdom.html

95 https://Wikipedia.org/Appeasement.

96 https://en.wikiquote.org/wiki/Thirteen_Days_(film)

97 http://econfaculty.gmu.edu/wew/quotes/wisdom.html

98 https://en.wikipedia.org/wiki/ First_inauguration_of_Franklin_D._Roosevelt

99 https://www.nytimes.com/2009/09/24/us/politics/24prexy.text.html

100 https://www.theatlantic.com/international/archive/2016/04/ obamas-worst-mistake-libya/478461/

101 https//www.www.washingtonpostexaminer.com/ alan-dershowitz-the-jerusalem-conflict-is-all-barack-obamas-fault

102 https://www/heritage.org/report/the-clinton-nuclear-deal-pyongyang-road-map-progress-or-dead-end-street

103 https://www.Nbcnews.com/id/15210254/ns/politics/ mccain-criticizes-bill-clinton-north-korea/

104 http://transcripts.cnn.com/TRANSCRIPTS/1311/24/sotu.01.html

105 https://www.truthorfiction.com/powell-empires/

106 https://www.cnsnews.com/news/article/terence-p-jeffrey/ obama-was-first-president-spend-more-welfare-defense

107 https://spectator.org/59687_jimmy-carters-legacy-war/

108 https://en.wikipedia.org/wiki/Assymetric_warfare

109 https://dictionary.com/caliphate

110 https://en.wikipedia.org/wiki/Peshmerga

111 https://www.thefiscaltimes. com/2015/06/04Fog-War-US-Has-Armed-ISIS

112 https://cru.senate.gov/?p=news&id=2987: The terrorist Osama bin Laden was killed by Navy Seals on May 2, 2011 in Abbottabad, Pakistan

113 https://www.wilsoncenter.org/article/ timeline-the-rise-and-fall-the-islamic-state

114 http://humanevents.com/2012/09/25/ no-surprise-america-under-attack-again-in-the-mideast/

115 https//wilsoncenter.org/article/trump-administration-isis-al-queda

116 https://www.foxnews.com/politics/ny-times-columnist-praises-trump-for-winning-against-isis-hits-media-for-not-giving-credit

117 https://www.thereligionofpeace.com/pages/quran/violence.aspx

118 https://www.wikipedia.org/honor-killing

119 https://www.thereligionofpeace.com/pages/quran/violence.aspx

120 https://www.wsj/articles/after-mass-detentions-china-razes-muslim-communities-to-build-a-loyal-city-11553133870; https:www.reuters.com/article/us-usa-china-concentrationcamps/china-putting-minority-muslims-in-concentration-camps-us-says-idUSKCN1S925K

121 http://www.dhs.gov

122 https://www.nationaldefensemagazine.org/articles/2020/3/9/eagle-vs-dragon-how-the-us-and-chinese-navies-stack-up

123 https://www.washingtontimes.com/news/2018/ dec/26/tom-homan-former-ice-chief-rips-Nancy-pelosi-doubt/

124 https://www.realclearpolitics.com/articles/2019/12/16/trump_may_win_elusive_latino_support_for_the_gop_141963.html

125 http://www.dhs.gov

126 https://sv.usembassy.gov/united-states-mexico-declaration-of-principles-on-economic-development-and-cooperation-in-southern-mexico-and-central-america

127 https://www.archives.gov/electoral-college/about

128 https://www.freerepublic.com/focus/f-news/2504963/posts

129 https://www.creators.com/read/walter-williams/09/14/multiculturalism-is-a-failure

130 http://www.newswithviews.com/Wooldridge/frosty506.htm

131 https://www.850wftl.com/us-paul-genova/

132 https://www.cbsnews.com/news-face-the-nation-transcript-conway-kissinger-donilon/

133 https://www.whitehouse.gov/briefings-statements/president-donald-j-trump-delivered-record-breaking-results-american-people-first-three-years-office/ For more of President Trump's accomplishments, see Appendix B.

134 https//www.legalinsurrection.com/2019/07/bet-founder-robert-johnson-democratic-party-has-moved-too-far-to-the-left/

135 https://en.wikipedia.org/wiki/Totalitarianism

136 https://www.openculture.com/2017/hannah-arendt-explains-how-propaganda-uses-lies-to-erode-all-truth-morality.html

137 https://www.org/voterfraud

138 https://www.britannica.com/propaganda

139 https://townhall.com/columnists/evansayet/2017/07/13/he-fights-n2354580

140 https://huntforliberty.com/salty-sailor-the-fireman/

141 https://www.zerohedge.com/news/2018–01–27/
daniel-greenfield-guns-are-how-civil-war-ends-politics-how-it-starts

142 https://canadafreepress.com/article/trumps-accomplishments

143 www.Ihatethemedia.com/you-could-have-heard-a-pin-drop

144 https://thehill.com/hilltv/rising/406881-lisa-page-bombshell-fbi-could-
nt-prove-trump-russia-collusion-before-mueller

145 https://www.scholastic.com/browse/article.jsp?ud=4684/thepresidentsjob

146 https/www.youtube.com/
bidenmadeukrainefiretopprosecutorinvestigatingsonsfirm

147 https://www.foxnews.com/politics/legal-scholars-in-hearing-over-wheth-
er-trump-commited-impeachable-offense

148 https://en.wikipedia.org/ wiki/Star Chamber.

149 www.bostonherald.com/2019/09/25/
democrats-pressed-to-cooperate-with-mueller-investigation/

150 https://nypost.com/2019/10/10/6-facts-about-hunter-bidens-business-
dealings-in-china/

151 https://www.fbi.gov/news/pressrel//press-releases/statement-by-director-
james-b-comey-on-the-investigation-of-hillary-clinton2019s-use-of-a-
personal-email-system

152 https://www.collinsdictionary.com/us/dictionary/english-thesaurus/gross
and https://www.thesaurus.com/ browse/ carelessness.

153 https://tennesseestar.com/2019/06/20/
commentary-why-wasnt-everyone-looking-for-hillarys-missing-emails/

154 https://www.cato.org/publications/commentary/
top-10-ways-obama-violated-constitution-during-presidency;

155 https://thehill.com/blogs/pundits-blog/the-administration/311608-
obamas-curtain-call-a-look-back-on-a-legacy-of.

156 . https://thehill.com/blogs/pundits-blog/the-administration/311608-
obamas-curtain-call-a-look-back-on-a-legacy-of.

157 https://pjmedia.com/trending/
five-times-obama-abused-his-power-and-democrats-didnt-care/

158 https://www.cato.org/publications/commentary/top-10-ways-obama-vi-
olated-constitution-during-presidency. For further reading see:
https://www.govinfo.gov/content/pkg/CHRG-112hhrg75846/
html/CHRG-112hhrg75846.htm; https://www.frc.org/ file/
download-pdf-president-obamas-administration-abuse-of-
power-and-troubled-ethics; https://www.askheritage.org/

how-is-president-obama-abusing-presidential-power/;https://www. usa-today.com/story/opinion/2018/02/02/nunes-memo-exposes-abuse-power/1088772001/;https://www.washingtontimes.com/news/2019/dec/9/obama-administrations-abuse-of-power-literally-wor/